Peace Train
to Beijing
and Beyond

For you, Barbara
Newfound friend and sister
on the journey

Love,
Beth

BETH GLICK-RIEMAN

Peace Train to Beijing and Beyond

The Hope and Promise of the UN Fourth World Conference on Women

Northstone

Editors: Michael Schwartzentruber, Dianne Greenslade
Cover and interior design: Margaret Kyle
Consulting art director: Robert MacDonald
Cover photos: Beth Glick-Rieman
Photo of woman in rice paddy: © Wolf Kutnahorsky, Berkeley Studio

We acknowledge the financial support of the Government of Canada through the
Book Publishing Industry Development Program for our publishing activities.

Northstone Publishing Inc. is an employee-owned company, committed to
caring for the environment and all creation. Northstone recycles, reuses and composts,
and encourages readers to do the same. Resources are printed on recycled paper and more
environmentally friendly groundwood papers (newsprint), whenever possible.
The trees used are replaced through donations to the Scoutrees For Canada Program.
Ten percent of all profit is donated to charitable organizations.

Canadian Cataloguing in Publication Data
Glick-Rieman, Beth, 1922–
Peace train to Beijing and Beyond
Includes bibligraphical references.
ISBN 1-896836-15-1
1. Glick-Rieman, Beth, 1922– Journeys–China. 2. World
Conference on Women (4th: 1995: Peking, China) 3.
Women's rights–Congresses. 4. Women–Social conditions–
Congresses. 5. China–Description and travel. 6. Former
Soviet republics–Description and travel. I. Title
HQ1106.G54 1998   305.42   C98-910017-0

Published by Northstone Publishing Inc.
Kelowna, British Columbia, Canada

Printing
9 8 7 6 5 4 3 2 1

Printed in Canada by
Transcontinental Printing Ltd., Louiseville, Quebec

For the women and girls of the world who need care,
for those who do care,
for the men and boys of the world who join us,
and especially for
Jill, Marta, Eric and the Grand-ones.

Contents

Thanks

To Anne, who cooked up the idea of sponsors, and those like her who went with me vicariously through their generous contributions which made the trip possible: Dwight and Emily, Elaine, Sylvia and Keim, Barbara and Wendell, Cathy and Curt, Danny, Ed and Gina, Tom and Gail, Johnnie and Jerry, Judy and Bob, Wayne and Barbara, Marti and Carl, Ted and Jane, Mickie and Ralph, Ruth and Allyn, Barbara and Bill, Ruth and Bob, Loren and Claire, Anne and Bob, Ann and John, Suzanne, Carol, Carl and Emily, Ken, Bess, Ellen and Charlie, Judith, Lydia, Ruth W., Donna, Virginia, Jim and Joyce, and Julie.

To Tom Hurst of On Earth Peace Assembly, and David Radcliff, Church of the Brethren Peace Consultant, for financial help.

To Cynthia, for hours and countless hours transcribing tapes of interviews.

To Ken, Julie, Gay, Lois and the Storymaker writers for reading and critiquing the unfolding chapters.

To my children, who believe I have something worthwhile to say and told me to hurry up and write the book because they want to read it.

To Margaret Kyle, who missed hearing my scream of delight when I saw the book cover she had designed just the way I wanted it.

Especially to Mike Schwartzentruber, my Northstone editor, who refused me at first, told me why, and gave me a second chance. This book is a better book than it could ever have been without Mike's encouragement and skilled, insightful editing.

Most of all, I give thanks to the Spirit of Life that has strengthened me in the hard times of my own journey, motivated me to keep growing and expanding my world, created in me an unstoppable hope, and urged me to create, out of the chaos of my life in the 20th century, my singular contribution to the present age.

Preface

This book is a snapshot of the grand canyon of women's and girls' lives on the brink of the 21st century, a gross oversimplification of an experience that could be called "the break in my cosmic egg." It is a fragment of my actual experience of seven weeks on a train with 240 people from 42 countries, visiting cities in transition and conflict, culminating in China in a gathering of 1,000 NGOs (Non-Governmental Organizations) and 189 nation states gathered to give serious attention to the injustice and inequities endured by the women and girl children of the world.

For me to describe what happened on this journey is like using an anthill to paint a picture of the Ural Mountains of Asia, or a sidewalk to acquaint the reader with The Great Wall. The immensity of what happened inside and outside the Peace Train and in the United Nations Conferences in China is vastly beyond the understanding of any one person who took the trip. So I speak only for myself, for one small woman among the many. The women portrayed in this book are bursting with life, a pointer aimed at millions of other lives who stand in the shadows.

The story is true in the sense that it is my perception of what happened, and of what that means for the world's women and girls.

The book is not "for women only," nor is it in any way meant to exclude men. Its focus *is* women, however; its intent, to empower. I believe that for every woman who looks honestly at her situation and gains respect, rights, responsibilities and freedom, there is a man, a girl or boy child, or a family whose lives will have more dignity and purpose, more grace and joy, as a result of her courage to see and to act.

The book is not mine alone. It belongs to all those who have made it possible: my parents and grandparents, whose respect for human life and the Creation rooted itself in my soul; my brothers and sisters, who honor me as one of them; my children who believe that mothers have something important to say; and my grandchildren who think I am wonderful. It belongs to all the women whose lives are revealed in its pages.

And now it belongs to you. Transform these words into meaning and challenge for your life, as they are for mine.

1

The Trip Before the Train

The old pond –
A frog leaps in,
And a splash.[1]

Self-empowerment is the most deeply political work there is,
and the most difficult.[2]

In 1915, in protest against the unrest between nations and the beginnings of World War I, a group of women in Sweden created an organization called Women's International League for Peace and Freedom (WILPF) and crossed Europe on a train, pleading for an end to all wars, challenging the nations to be a world at peace.

Almost a century later, in November, 1994, I got news that WILPF was sponsoring a second Peace Train. It would make its way on a brand-new route from Helsinki, Finland, to Beijing, China, crossing nine countries on the way, visiting women's groups and government officials in eight cities, culminating at the United Nations Fourth World Conference on Women. Instantly, I knew that I was to be on that Train, that somehow it was an integral part of my life journey, a "mission" I needed to undertake. But it would cost a lot of money, money that I did not have, as much as $4–5,000. It turned out to be nearly $6,000.

I argued with myself about it and confided to a friend that I had decided to give it up. Her response startled me: "Beth, write and ask your friends to sponsor you by making a contribution. I'd like to send you a check. Since I can't go in person, a little bit of me would be there with you."

The idea shocked me at first, then intrigued me. I had never asked anyone for money for a cause of my own. I hated what seemed to me to be the indignity of it. For three months I vacillated back and forth, toward and against writing such a letter. The resistance in me was so strong that it surprised me. Finally, I knew that I could postpone my decision no longer. I swallowed my pride and invited 43 relatives and friends, and several organizations, to help me make this trip possible.

Once the letter was written and sent, I thought the hard part was over, but I was mistaken. When the first check arrived in the mail, I broke into tears. All in all, 35 people responded, some of whom had not even received my letter, but had heard about my need from others. As the days went by, I was almost overwhelmed by the generosity and well-wishes that were showered on me. These people believed in me, cheered me on, trusted that I knew what was right for me to do. One giving friend who distrusted the feminist movement wrote: "I can hardly believe that you are connected with that women's conference in Beijing. I don't believe at all in what those women are doing, but I believe in you and I want you to go and see for yourself what is going on, so I'm glad to send you this check." Over and over again, I found it harder to receive the financial support and good wishes of these sponsors than it had been to ask for it. As my "cloud of witnesses" grew in number, I felt tender, vulnerable and very supported. One by one each giver was tucked away in my spirit-place to take the journey with me.

The pendulum swept both ways, however. A millionaire brother wrote: "I cannot contribute to your playing halfway around the world. Nor do I think that we should be going over there telling those people how they should live their lives. If you needed housing or were hungry, I would be glad to help you out, but not for this." I was in pain over that one. I had tears, some sleepless nights, and did a lot of soul searching. I had always thought of that brother as very generous. I knew well that he would never let me as a widow suffer from lack of food and a roof over my head. The pain was that he had misunderstood me, that he did not know what my life is really about. He could not see that in my lone journey as "widow," I need food of a different sort, to stay alive and involved, and to undertake the task to which I had set myself – writing this book as an outcome of the adventure. I learned and appreciated how staunchly he lives by his values, how strong he is in his beliefs, and for sure, that he really does care for me.

Some folks made contributions and asked for something in return, a kind of "What will I get out of it?" attitude. I told them this journey is not a sightseeing trip with shopping as the focus; rather, it is to become a creation – a picture of a network of women around the earth, a horde of Holy Termites, women eating away at world structures of dominance and submission, injustice and horror, women making a difference for the sake of the human family and our Mother Earth.

In fact, it occurred to me that I might be making this trip in the name of Peggy, my 19-year-old daughter, who died as a result of the carelessness of a driver and of a doctor who devalued young women and was not gentle with the resources of the earth. It was way back in 1972 that that driver's car plowed into hers as she was going to get paper to make posters announcing a peace march. In the hospital where she had lain in a hall unattended for over six hours, I had protested her lack of proper medical care. That male doctor's response haunts me still: "She has her whole life ahead of her. I am busy with folks who do not have long to live." She died four days later.

At one point in my struggle to decide whether or not to go on the Peace Train, I sat among the pictures of my loved, healthy, privileged children and grandchildren. Peggy's picture pointed me to the countless numbers of people whose lives are circumscribed or shortened by the same violence and carelessness that took hers. They are the family I need to care for now. I knew with a deep knowing that it was because of them that I was taking this trip. I knew I wanted these weeks of time to be engaged with the world's women in order to find ways to make the rest of my life a testimony to peace and justice. There was a kind of "divine imperative" about this trip.

As I began to make plans, anxieties tugged at me. The application made it clear that it would not be an easy trip, that we would encounter difficulties, would have to handle our own luggage, would often be without bathing facilities, would be housed in "second-rate" hotels. It warned that this was not a sightseeing or shopping trip, that we could expect to be tired and possibly ill. The questions piled in on me: Could I physically manage the stresses of the trip? Would I get sick? Was I too old in my 70s to be going so far from home? Could I get everything done that needed to be done to get ready? Was it right – or wrong – to leave my son who was struggling with a major illness? Was I right to be so far away from my daughters and their families? Always a clear answer came: "It *is* right for you to go on this trip. When the Peace Train pulls out of the Helsinki station, you must be on it."

As I began to prepare in earnest, the struggle in the homeplace intensified. Since our final destination was Beijing, China, the NGO Forum and the United Nations Conference on Women, I had telephoned Meng, my Chinese niece whose parents live in Beijing. I told her I would like to meet them during my stay there, and asked if they could give me any help in finding overnight accommodations. She would call them and talk about it. It was the middle of March. I was to leave home for Helsinki on August 1.

I had known that the situation with the NGO Forum was sensitive: in January, there was some question as to whether or not the Forum would even be held, since the Chinese government had moved this branch of the United Nations Conference an hour and a half distant from the main event. The stated reason was that the Workers' Stadium "was deemed unsuitable because of structural problems." Official sources, however, had called this an excuse, declaring that city and Communist Party leaders were fearful that women's groups might stage embarrassing protests in Tienanmen Square or other central locations.

When Meng called me back, she was clear, "Dad and Mom said they would gladly entertain you and show you the sights of China if you would just come as a tourist, but it would not be good for them to have connections with anyone involved in the Women's Forum or the UN Conference. The Chinese people will be watched closely during this time, and any connections might have dangerous repercussions later. My father has already come under suspicion because he is not a member of the Communist Party. It is unfortunate that the conferences are being presented there in such a negative way." It was my first taste of repression, and I felt frustrated, angry for my loss and theirs.

A couple of weeks later, I got my second dose of what it means *not to be free in your own country*. Two months before I was to leave for Helsinki, I had mailed to the Chinese embassy in Los Angeles my passport and the documents needed to get a Chinese visa. I had made the mistake of not certifying the letter, not requiring a signature of receipt. Several weeks went by. I heard nothing from them, and lots about the problems women everywhere were having trying to get Chinese visas. I got uneasy. Every day for a while, I called the embassy, always getting a machine message to call at the time I was calling. Finally, ten days to flight time, I drove the four-hour trip to appear in person at the visa window.

My white hair and skin quickly defined me as the only Caucasian in a line that proceeded slowly toward the man behind the glass. After an hour's wait, my turn came. Before I could open my mouth to ask if my documents had arrived, the dark almond eyes narrowed, he pointed to the far side of the room and scowled, "No time for you! Stand over there!"

"But! All I want to know is…" He interrupted me fiercely.

"I said 'no time for you'." Pointing. "Over there."

Assuming that he had some reason for making me wait, I did as I was told. Another hour went by while I stewed inside, feeling frustrated and helpless. I took a trip to the women's room, came back and stood alone at "my place," wondering what to do, embarrassed, uneasy. Finally, I decided to try again. I went to the back of the line, waited another hour and got to the window. He took one look at me and repeated, "I said no time for you. Stand over there." Lunch time had come and gone. I was hungry and I was furious.

"Who is your manager?" I asked without moving. "I want to speak to someone about the fact that you are refusing to wait on me."

His knitted brow told me I had gained no brownie points for that one. "I'm the one. You speak only with me." The pointed finger again. "Stand over there." I decided to go next door to the General Consul Building and find someone to whom to protest what was happening. Churning inside, with every discomforting eye fixed on me, I walked past the full line of waiters and out the door to the street. Next door, I stepped inside a six-foot-square foyer to face squarely into a camera held by a Chinese woman behind a bulletproof screen. At the same instant, I noticed a doorknob inviting me to go straight ahead. I was turning it naively when a tall man in uniform (there aren't many tall Chinese men) towered over me. He had appeared from nowhere, something I learned in China these officials do with amazing ease. His voice was stern. "What do you want?"

"I am being refused service by the man at the visa agency. I want to speak about it with his supervisor."

"Do you have an appointment?"

"This is crazy," I thought. "Of course I don't. I did not know until now that I would be refused service this way."

"There is no one here you can speak with. I'll give you a phone number you can call." It was final. I groaned inwardly, found a phone booth, called and got a machine. It was 1:30. I went back to a full waiting room, got in the rear of the line, waited another hour to the window, got the same message and said, near tears, "Sir, I have waited here for hours. Now I need to know if you intend to help me or not?"

"When close the office. Stand over there."

I turned to the couple next in line and realized I was speaking so everybody in the room could hear.

"I got here at 9:30 this morning, have waited my turn in this line three times and he (pointing toward the window) will not wait on me." A look of embarrassed sympathy overtook their faces.

The young man of the couple behind me spoke to the agent. "She was here before we were. Please wait on her."

The agent motioned the couple sternly to the window. "I decide!" With an apologetic look, the young man stepped to the window in front of me, motioning the woman to follow. The agent gave them his full attention, completely erasing my presence in the process.

It was not the last mixture of emotions I would experience in my dealings with the Chinese. I felt respected and touched by the young man's actions, and I was in a rage at the "unbending authority" of these representatives of the Chinese government. One more time I took my place at the far side of the room. During the two-and-a-half-hour wait that followed, the kindness of the Chinese people and their paralyzed silence in the face of "authority" was etched forever on my brain.

At 4:30, the office empty except for me, the agent locked the outer door and disappeared into the inner sanctum behind the windows. My throat was dry and scratchy; my head ached; I was on the verge of tears. I shuffled about uneasily, afraid of what would happen next and determined to get information about my documents. A long ten minutes later, the agent reappeared and asked bluntly, "What do you want?" ("May I help you" does not seem to be translatable into the Chinese language.)

"I am here to pick up my passport and other documents and to get a visa."

"Documents not received. No visa until August 5."

"But I sent them weeks ago. And I leave for my trip on August 1. Surely the documents must be here."

"I say documents not here!" He was angry. "I prove." He disappeared. Another ten minutes and out he came with a fat ledger. He opened it, pointed to names and addresses written in Chinese and said, "Not here, see?" I realized with a jolt what it is like to be illiterate. I couldn't read a word of it.

"But what do I do now?" I heard myself pleading. He shrugged his shoulders.

"Sorry!"

"No, that won't do!" The desperation and anger in my voice were palpable. "I must have my passport and the visa by next week. What can I do about it?"

That awful shrug again. "Sorry!" He walked to the door, unlocked it and motioned me through.

It was not the last time that brick wall shrivelled my insides. It happened often later in China. In the car, I let the tears roll, got hold of myself, started through the traffic jams toward home, and decided I would just have to take another trip to L.A. tomorrow to get a new passport.

At home I told my story to a friend who was visiting from Scotland and knew a lot about getting visas. "You were naive, Beth," he said. "If you had flashed a $50 bill, your passport would have appeared as if by magic. I've been treated the same way by US officials."

The next day, more time, more traffic, more lines, more waiting at the Federal Building. And then, instructions regarding my new passport: "You may pick it up on Tuesday. It is good for only one year since you lost the other one."

I protested: "I did not lose the other one. The Chinese embassy did."

"In any case, it is good for only one year. In the event you find your old passport, you may get an extension for the full 10 years. Also, you need to know that it is illegal to hold two passports." Her smile was friendly.

"I doubt that is likely to happen." Inside me, a voice: "At least this woman speaks my language." I relaxed.

An all-day trip and a hundred greenbacks later, my application was in the works. I got home to a machine message from Mr. Wong of the Chinese embassy: "Your passport and documents arrived today. You come back, pick them up." It was Friday. I called to tell the phone machine I would pick them up on Tuesday.

Tuesday, six days to flighttime. An air of defiant triumph surged through me as I left the Federal Building with my new passport in my hot little hand. "I *will* be on that Peace Train, I *will*, with or without visa!" I announced to myself. Not about to trust what might happen at the Chinese visa agency, I had kept to myself the fact that the old one had been "found."

I made my way across town, reluctant to go through this, and determined to follow it through. The same man was behind the window. When he saw me in the line, he pointed toward me and indicated a different window. Before I had time to protest, a different man appeared, holding in his hands the seven required documents I had submitted, including my passport.

"You go away three hours. You come back. I give you visa."

"Three hours?" I groaned. But I was getting near home base. Did I hear him rightly – that I would get the visa? I went away, came back in three hours and there he was behind the glass, holding the passport with the visa and an air of personal triumph.

"I called China. Got special permission for you." He was pleased with himself.

I squelched the urge to grab the visa out of his hand. He handed it over; I thanked him, walked away, wondering, "Who is crazy here – me or the Chinese?"

At home, I encountered a new dilemma: "Which passport should I take?" The old one had been reported lost and might get me into trouble on the trip. The new one had a whole different number. I tucked them both into my wallet. When the plane roared off the runway six days later, I was on it bound for Helsinki – illegal.

Settling into my seat, with hours of flying time ahead, I took a deep breath, felt a strange mixture of exhaustion and exhilaration. "Beijing," I said to myself, "get ready. Here I come." I reached for the trusty Pearlcorder dictating machine that was to become my constant companion. We had not yet even reached cruising altitude.

7:15 a.m., August 1, 1995. Aboard Delta flight #409 from San Diego to Kennedy, I feel thankful. The engines growl; we rise through the heavy cloud cover into sunlight high above the desert floor, into infinity. The actual journey has begun. Misty fog hugs the valleys below; mountaintops peek out above it all, adding a sense of mystery to the far journey into a world I have never known before.

Leaving behind son Eric's illness and big decisions about buying a house; leaving behind daughters Jill and Marta and their dear ones; leaving behind all my friends.

I put them all on my heart shelf to return to them a different person with an expanded understanding of the world. This journey is a kind of rehearsal of my death for them all, and for me a test to see if I can truly live by my dreams.

At cruising altitude, I realized that mixed emotions were busy inside me, nagging uneasiness, excitement churning with the engines. I was as bumpy on the inside as the plane was on the outside as we touched down in Phoenix, moved steadily eastward out over New Mexico, Texas, Oklahoma, Missouri, Illinois, Indiana, Ohio, Pennsylvania and on into New York's Kennedy airport. An hour later, I had mailed some letters, made some good-bye calls and for the moment felt as if I had left the home front behind me, both geographically and emotionally. It was in the darkness of early evening when the mighty engines of Delta's 1011-500 purred on the runway in readiness to thunder into the skies over the Atlantic. As we roared into the air, the voice of the pilot from the cockpit clinched my separation from home and country.

"Ladies and gentlemen, welcome aboard Delta's Flight 42 to Helsinki, Finland. We have about seven and a half hours of traveling time ahead of us. You can trace our progress on the monitor. The last weather report from there is 70 degrees Fahrenheit, a nice summer day. Turn your clocks forward seven hours. This plane carries 140,000 gallons of fuel and we will need only 120,000 to get there; so sit back and relax and enjoy the flight."

"I'm really on the way; I'll soon be ten hours from California!" I said to myself as the message was repeated in Finnish. A little red flag of anxiety fluttered in my insides: "Are you going to be able to live with seven weeks of foreign languages? Will it be too much for you?" Instantly, I countered that thought with another: "What an incredible privilege it is to be on this journey!"

My seatmate was a good-looking, clean shaven man in his middle 40s, I judged. His blonde hair was cut short and his eyes were a startling blue. I liked him immediately. He was jolly, talkative and excited to be making this trip to bring back "home" his 18-month-old daughter and his Finnish wife who was pregnant again and had been "away" visiting her parents for several weeks. "Interesting use of words," I thought. He was a professor of chemical engineering in a college in Oregon and knew a lot about Finland. He talked up a storm when he realized I was enjoying the conversation.

"Finland," he said, "is a country full of golden wheat fields, deep forests of evergreen and birch, and lakes and more lakes. There are 5 million people living there and there are 5 million cottages on lakes. There must be that many saunas or steam baths, too. The bathers in the sauna sit on wooden benches. To get steam, they pour water over red-hot stones. Then they beat themselves gently with small switches made of birch leaves. This beating increases the cleansing effect of sweating caused by the heat and steam. After that, they cool off rapidly in a cold shower. In the winter, they will sometimes roll in the snow. The result is that they feel completely relaxed, both physically and mentally. The people of Finland are friendly and the air is cleaner than in the United States."

Much later, in the midst of his travelogue, I fell asleep. Then, awake, I became intrigued with the monitor. On the screen was a picture of the world as we were crossing it – Greenland's "icy mountains," which I sang about as a child in Sunday school; Belgium; France; England and Scotland to the south of us; the Atlantic 37,000 feet below; the Norwegian Sea; the plane heading toward the Barents Sea and the Scandinavian countries. Stockholm. Amsterdam. Copenhagen. St. Petersburg to the east. Moscow, farther out east. Berlin. Warsaw to the south of the spot marking Helsinki. On out and over, and then the screen said, "One hour and 45 minutes to our destination."

The cabin was becoming restless, a baby crying, children moving about, aisles full of coming and going to the bathroom. A sallow-faced man across the aisle slept with his mouth hanging open. A fat woman looked as if she were between worlds, her head thrown back on her pillow, her hands clasped across her ample stomach. A tall Finn with thin hair suddenly shouted in Finnish across a couple of aisles at a woman with rumpled auburn hair and a sour face.

It was still dark when dinner was served – baked salmon on a bed of noodles with delicious peapods to go with it. As we ate, the very short night was over; darkness began to fade. The skies became pearly gray and the rising sun lit up strings of continually shifting clouds. Wispy mists floated in and cast a veil over the whole scene, adding a pink glow to the delicate blues and whites. A wide and glorious day had come to welcome us to Finland. As the pinks deepened and the day became full of summer sunshine warming the earth, I felt the thrill of adventure, thankful that I was healthy, that my "cloud of witnesses" had made this trip possible and were traveling with me in spirit.

An hour later, the big bird dived down through the cobalt sky to a safe landing, and over the PA system in two languages came the tired voices: "Ladies and gentlemen, welcome to Helsinki."

2

Five Days in Finland

This is my song, O God of all the nations,
A song of peace for lands afar and mine.
This is my home, the country where my heart is;
Here are my hopes, my dreams, my holy shrine;
But other hearts in other lands are beating
With hopes and dreams the same as mine.

My country's skies are bluer than the ocean
And sunlight gleams on clover leaf and pine.
But other lands have sunlight, too, and clover
And skies are oftimes blue as mine.
Oh hear my song, O God of all the nations
A song of peace, for their land, and mine.[1]

On the Finnair bus, I glanced around at the mixture of brunettes and blondes, the fair-skinned, tall Finns, and the broad, open faces of the Swedes. "M-m-m," I thought, "Here I am, thousands of miles from home and these people don't seem so 'foreign'."

We drove through the middle of a very modern downtown, the air so clean it put San Diego to shame, the streets full of milling people. As a child, I had thought naively that Finland was a never-never land, so far away nobody could live there, and here I was in Helsinki, a city as busy, prosperous and alive as any I had ever known.

At Hotel Helsinki, I learned that my roommate would be Susu, a woman from Minnesota who had not yet arrived. I set myself to the task of unpacking on one side of the small room. When she blew in a half hour later, heavy-set and noticeable in a flowing purple skirt and blouse with large circular splotches of white and pink, she filled the room. Her luggage had not come and her frustrations and anxieties expressed themselves in a hurried sense of self-importance and a judgmental air of disdain. She gave me a fleeting glance and burst out, "The Chinese act like babies!"

"I'm Beth. Tell me about yourself," I responded.

"I'm Susu Fredericks. I named myself. I'm a witch, a friend of Starhawk. I used to be a minister of papers but I couldn't take the hospital calls, the death of children and doing marriages. I don't want to get married, don't want to have anything to do with men, so why should I marry other people? I've had skin cancer on my neck. When they told me that, I knew that I had been hanged to death as a witch in a former life." Her luggage arrived and she busied herself with unpacking, done with self-revelation for the moment. Conversation closed.

Our room was compact and dark, space enough for one desk, twin beds with an aisle in between. The bathroom was like a playhouse, heated towel racks and a little hose gadget to spray away the leftover debris after using the spotless modern sink. The shower beat mine at home hands down, a fine spray with lots of force. The hotel was not "second-rate," as we had been told to expect; rather, it had the feel of Old World elegance. When I rode the teeny elevator down and pulled the metal lattice gate open by hand, it creaked like bones in old age. The formal lobby was framed in beautiful, dark wood.

I joined a group of women who were talking in American English about my first priority, getting a visa for Turkey. Black-haired Midge of Minnesota seemed to be the organizer of the group. "Let's get one of those 8-passenger buses," she said, "and go straight to the Turkish embassy."

I spoke up. "We're supposed to go to the conference center first. It says so in the instructions." Neither she nor any of the others gave any indication they had heard me. I felt a little tremor of withdrawal and said no more. Feeling uneasy about being completely on my own to find my way to Unitas Centre, I went with them. At the embassy we were told to go back to the conference center.

"Why didn't I insist?" I chided myself. We got another bus and took the long trip out into the beautiful countryside, through pine, spruce and fir forests, green fields and outcroppings of gray granite streaked with pink. Signs along the way looked familiar: Toyota, Nissan, Michelin Tires. "The corporate power structure is alive and well in Finland," I thought to myself. Then, a sign I had never seen on the highways in the US: "Be wise. Use condoms. Be safe with Trojans." Whew! There it was, right out in the open, not under the counter as it was in the US until the AIDS epidemic woke us all up with a start!

When we arrived at the center, the pace quickened. A session of the WILPF Congress was going on in the meeting hall. Women were milling everywhere getting registered, taking care of last minute details for getting visas. A woman coming out of the makeshift registration office said to anybody who happened to be listening, "You're going to need an additional $180 US to pay for food along the way, so if you need to change money, you'll save time if you go and do that now. It has to be in US dollars."

"But I'm paid in full," came a woman's voice out of nowhere.

"Well, you may think so, but I have news for you. This is a new assessment."

An electric shock ran down my spine and the long queue. I had already felt a nagging fear that I would run out of money before it was time to leave Beijing, and I was angry that they would pull this trick on us without warning. The women muttered uneasily. Some left the line. At the desk I asked the travel agent for information and protested, "It's not fair for us to have to come up with that much more money when we didn't know it beforehand and thought we were paid in full. It's a terrible hardship."

She was as cool as I was hot. "We did not know originally that we would have to pay for meals at the different stops. What's more, our time will be limited, and you may not have enough time to find food on the street. It'll be a lot cheaper, too."

I was frustrated, angry, feeling as if there were no other choice. Small comfort knowing that others were in as much of a bind as I was.

That edict was not the last wedge to be driven through the middle of the group, separating us from one another, but it was a penetrating one. It effectively changed the community into "haves and have nots," a fact that colored our interactions for the entire journey on the Train. As it turned out, it was a misrepresentation, too, however unintended. It was not true that it was less expensive. I could have eaten for much less money everywhere we stopped. Nor was it difficult to find food on the streets. Over and over I wished I had not taken the travel agent's word as law.

The way it separated us into two groups hit me personally at every stopover, and I got more and more irritated and uncomfortable with it. Barbara of Canada, straight blonde hair touching her neck, her clothing plain and simple, was one of my compartment mates on the train and my roommate in the hotels. She had no choice. That extra $180 was out of the question for her. I managed to find it, so I was "in" and she was "out." At our stopovers, she went to the streets to find food while I sat in privileged places eating sumptuous meals. I felt embarrassed; she fumed about it: "They act as if all North American women are wealthy. I hate it! Having enough money is a struggle for me, too."

Time after time, we had to go our separate ways when I wished we could be together. One time in particular made me churn inside. It was in St. Petersburg, Russia. A remarkably luxuriant buffet had been prepared in the high banquet hall and we were all together. Hostesses, not knowing the situation, were inviting those still standing to take a seat at the table. Barbara and others were in a quandary, embarassed not to accept their invitation and embarrassed to do so. I hated the whole situation, wished I had stayed with the "have-nots" where I belonged. I hated the inequities, the injustice of it all. I hated the loss of whole community it created everywhere we went. I hated the fact that I had to say I could not help Anna, who had come to me in hopes that she could borrow the money. No doubt about it, the economic injustices that create barriers to peacemaking in the world were already well set even before we boarded the Train.

At the desk, feeling helpless, I parted with my $180 and headed back to the hotel for the luxury of stretching out in a bed, disappointed, dead tired, and on jet lag. I slept the afternoon away and awoke to realize that it was near time to go to a reception at Town Hall honoring the women of WILPF and the Peace Train.

Susu was busily dressing. I wore my black Indonesian batik skirt spattered with red and gold designs. Susu gave me the once over.
"Is that the most dressed up you have along?" she asked. "This may be high class, political."

It took me aback for a moment. My first thought was that I would stick out like a sore thumb and ought to change. My second thought was that I was under no obligation to please anybody but myself. So I said, "I do have a long skirt, but this is what I'm wearing."

In the high-ceilinged hall with its gilded white columns, I nibbled on berries, quiche, Brie cheese and Ritz crackers. Suddenly I looked up into the face of a very pretty, young and tall blonde American woman at my elbow. She looked distressed. I introduced myself. She said her name was Amelia.

"That woman over there just insulted me." There was anger in her voice. I followed her eyes and found Susu.

"That's my roommate."

"She told me to forget my vegetarian scruples and eat whatever I'm offered in a foreign country. She acted as if her values are superior to mine, as if her judgment is good and mine isn't. She made me mad."

I told her what Susu had said to me and added, "I think I need to confront her. She won't make any friends that way." I knew from firsthand experience that an attitude of superiority often masks a shaky self-image.

The next morning, Susu gave me a perfect opening. "I'm not good at inter- and intrapersonal stuff," she said.

"That's true," I agreed with her. "I knew it because of your comment last night about what I was wearing to the reception."

"What did I say?"

I told her and added, "It implied that you felt you had a superior understanding of the situation. I didn't like that."

She was genuinely sorry, asked me to accept her apology, and I did. "I think that kind of insensitivity hurts you as much as others," I added. "It distances people from you." I didn't mention Amelia.

"A lot like racism," she said, "hurting the racist, too."

"A lot like that," I responded.

We ate together at the breakfast buffet. Seven kinds of bread, pickled fish, cold cuts of ham and salami, cheeses, sweet rolls, cucumbers, red peppers, pickles, berries, gruel, cottage cheese, lettuce and tea and coffee. This was surely not the fare of a Third World country!

No meetings of Peace Train participants were announced, so I slept the morning away and awoke wondering what was going on in the WILPF meetings at Unitas Centre. Armed with a trusty street map, I braved the metro and bus and found myself in a session that seemed all too familiar; all about finances, budget and the nitty-grittys of keeping an organization going.

I decided to do some journaling about my frustrations and write cards to my sponsors back home, so I left the session, wandered about the center awhile, and found a free table in the dining hall facing tall pines and white birches on the banks of the Gulf of Finland, brilliant blue in the afternoon sunshine. Nearby an auburn-haired American woman had her nose in a book; a black-haired Palestinian concentrated on her writing; an African woman gave another woman a bit of her "sweet." Several women walked by speaking German. From the kitchen came the sounds of Finnish talk. Two Spanish-speaking women punctuated their conversation with urgent gestures. A woman with badly twisted legs walked by on crutches. A little group of women was drinking in every word being spoken by a Sudanese woman draped in a flowing blue scarf. Smokers on the patio lollygagged above a bank of yellow daisies swaying in the wind. The air seemed charged with possibilities. I felt a surge of excitement and gratitude. With this wonderful diversity, I would have all kinds of new understandings of others' worlds when I returned. I felt the thrill of being a part of an historic event building bridges across many chasms. I hoped this trip would really help to make peace with justice a reality in the world to which we were going.

Then I found myself thinking and writing about Susu and what was happening to me as her roommate.

One of the things that has been hard for me is that she really is a takeover kind of person and has spread her stuff all over the room, at times asking, for example when I want to use the desk, if I want her to move her things away. She really acts as though she is the only one in the room, at times has even moved my stuff around. That kind of controlling gets to me. It will be interesting to see how many women on the Train are the kind of people who need to either be taking care of other people, or at least taking care of other people's property. When we were about to go the reception, she told me not to forget my glasses. As if I ever could, as nearsighted as I am! I know she means to be helpful, but it's been a little hard to deal with. And there will undoubtedly be more of it as time goes on.

My cards all finished for the moment, I walked the hall reading the international clothesline started by WILPF people in California. Signs like: "Birth, rape, oral sex, sodomy, the gifts Daddy had for me. In the dark, Mom said she didn't see the mark he left on me." Another, "60 to 80% of women in prison have been physically or sexually abused as children." And, "Ray, your son raped me. You put the shame on me. I'll carry that for the rest of my life." Another, a picture of a child, painted red, with the word "Innocent" on it. Then, "A man beats a woman every 15 seconds. A woman is raped every 6 minutes. 35% of all homicides are committed by the woman's husband or lover." A green, sleeveless shirt signed "Maureen" said, "I deserve inner peace." And they went on and on and on.

Farther down the hall, the banners of other WILPF groups lined the walls. One that caught my eye had a circle of women in the middle, surrounded by trucks, tents, campfires, pliers, doves and a wigwam. It said "Greenham Common." I was suddenly back at Greenham sitting with those women at the campfire years ago, listening to their stories about protesting nuclear testing and the US military presence in England.

The Peace Train meeting that evening was all visa talk. A lot of the women had done almost nothing about getting visas and WILPF staff people were working hard on it. My only missing one was Turkey, so I was bored, itching to get connected with the women who would be in my rail car on the trip. I wished somebody would get us together so we could learn to know one another here. The trouble was, the main focus of the leaders was the 80th anniversary celebration of WILPF. Apparently they had not delegated responsibility for building the Peace Train community to those of us who volunteered and had the time, willingness and know-how to get it done. That really bothered me.

At least I was getting to know a few of the women. I took a walk through the market square in the evening with tall Mary and Amelia and black-haired sister Genevieve of the USA. Lynette of Australia joined us, her dark eyes smiling, her manner friendly. We talked as if we were old friends. Mary was outgoing and proud to have daughter Amelia along. I thought of my Jill and Marta and wished they could have been there. Genevieve was shorter, fair of face, somewhat reticent. As we walked, Mary referred back to "the woman who put us all on edge" and added the comment, "Certainly there will be a process whereby these kinds of things can be brought out in the open and people given different roommates. I'm sure they will deal with these issues very quickly."

"Well, if it's a peace train," I said, "we must first of all make peace among ourselves."

"And it's got to start within each soul," Mary said. What we did not know then was that there would not be such a process nor would "they" deal with such issues at all, with the exception of one community meeting that I found out later was focused on racism. It was a great loss to us all that peace within the community was not given the care and attention that it needed before we boarded the Train, where there was no place large enough for us all to meet.

Lynette laughed at me as I talked into the dictaphone. "What's that for?" she asked. I told her I would be writing a book about this experience when I got back home, so she'd better be careful what she said! She chuckled. "Be sure to say that everywhere I look there are massive, solid-looking yellow-brick buildings with beautiful archways and carved facades."

We passed the World Trade Center and Lynette commented, "The guide on our tour this morning said the early influence in Helsinki was by Russian architects. Then in the 1960s, the Finnish architects took over and the newer buildings were designed by local people." Her "Aus-trallian" accent made me want to hear more.

She went on. "You'll notice that all the street signs are written in two languages. The tour guide said that is from the time when Finland was owned by the Swedes. Now that they have gained their independence, they have the Finnish language on top and the Swedish language underneath. Still, about 8 percent of the population are Swedish and by law they must use the two languages. They have Finnish speaking schools and Swedish speaking schools; they have Swedish high schools and a Finnish university."

The next day, since there were still no announcements of meetings for Peace Train people, I took the bus tour. It was fun to see the city through the eyes of a native guide. At one point, she gave a quaint commentary on the women of Finland:

Something you might like to know about the Finnish women of today. At the moment, all the Finnish housewives are busy picking blueberries and raspberries and making jam and putting the berries into the freezer and, what is very typical in Finland, we make this steamed juice out of cranberries and black currants. It's very popular. When you have a cold in winter, then you always drink black currant juice. This summer has been quite dry. It hasn't rained a lot, so a lot of blueberries have dried out, but still on the islands in the archipelago there are a lot of berries.

People who go to work here have a summer holiday of four weeks and most of the Finns, at least every third family, has a summer house, so we go to the lake. There are 3,000 miles of waterways, lakes, streams and canals.

Several things stick out in my mind about Helsinki. The monument to Sibelius, their most famous composer, gave me goose bumps. Since childhood I had loved the tone poem, *Finlandia*, which he had composed. Our guide spoke with pride:

Jean Sibelius composed seven symphonies, actually, there were eight, but he was very critical when he grew old and he destroyed it. In 1967, ten years after his death, this monument was built here. A Finnish sculptor worked with this monument for seven years. During that time she had to learn how to weld because it is welded in stainless steel. At that time nobody understood it. They said she was too modern and "Where is Sibelius? You can't see him anywhere." "Where's his face?" Of course, he didn't write any music for the organ and it looks like an organ, so she had to compromise and make his face on the side of the monument.

The monument *did* look like a great pipe organ. Soldering lines ran down the edges of pipes carved with holes in different shapes and sizes. As the sun hit it, it gave off a glow as of pink-gray molten metal, strikingly beautiful. Off to the side, there was this gray metal likeness of Sibelius which looked grotesque to me, very added on.

We were given 15 minutes to take pictures. I wanted to stay longer, to extend that feeling of sacred awe, the sense of being spiritually connected with this great musician. At one point I pulled away from the others and sang *Finlandia* to myself. I did not know it then, but that tune would become a kind of theme song for me during the trip. I often heard myself singing it as I stood at the windows of the Train, drinking in the beauty, seeing the people of country after country.

We would be building, temples still undone
O'er crumbling walls their crosses scarcely lift.
Waiting till love can raise the broken stone
And hearts creative bridge the human rift.
We would be building, now to each of us
Reveal the life that God would have on earth.[2]

I was quieted in my soul as we left that place.

The harbor was another place of wonder for me. A Statue of Peace done by a Finnish sculptor stood guard. The guide told us about two big cruise ships that were in port ready to sail for Stockholm, and added, "The yellow buildings are a sea fortress which was built against the Russians by the Swedes in the middle of the 8th century."

What caught my eye most were the huge icebreakers. I had never seen such pieces of machinery, had never even thought what it would be like to have water in a sea frozen so deep that it had to be broken up to let cruise ships and cargo vessels go about their daily runs during the winter. I was amused by the guide's comment.

Our harbor is normally icebound four to eight weeks in the winter. Of course there is no ice here in the summer, so it's very popular to take a tour on the icebreakers. The President brings guests to do this exotic thing.

When we came to Senate Square at the very center of Helsinki, we got a history lesson.

Helsinki was founded in 1550 by a Swedish king, Gustav Vasa. It was quite a small town, under Swedish rule for many years. When Finland was taken over by Russia in 1812, the Russian emperor declared Helsinki the capital because it was nearer St. Petersburg. At that time Helsinki had about 5,000 inhabitants. Most of these parts were just hills and wooden houses. Now there are 500,000 inhabitants, 800,000 if you consider the adjoining suburbs. Finland became an independent country in the early 1900s. Usually big demonstrations start here in Senate Square; there'll be a big one here tomorrow against Hiroshima. All these buildings are in the neoclassic style. They used to say that Helsinki was St. Petersburg in miniature.

The next day, when I went back to the square alone, I saw what she meant about demonstrations. A long line of protestors halfway across the square carried signs in Swedish, Finnish, English: Stop the War in Bosnia. Lots of them were young people and children, mostly dark-haired, and a few old-sters, most probably in their 30s and 40s. Police cars, splotchy black and white with POLIS written on the side, led the parade when they started out of the square toward the street. One sign in English said, "Let the Bosnians be alive." It felt good to see these people saying no to war, and saying it with official protection. Church bells tolled in deep tones as the march moved on in front of me. Several hundred people held aloft orange, red, and white signs. One said, *"Golit a Bosnu."* I guessed that meant "Free Bosnia."

Back on the tour, I began to realize what a prominent part churches play in Helsinki. The Lutheran church dominated Senate Square. It was built of beige marble with white Corinthian columns and rounded, aquamarine on-ion domes. The guide told us that almost 90 percent of the people are Lutheran. She called attention to the 12 apostles stationed in stately array on the roof. They were made of zinc, and had been on top of the church for 150 years. Some people were afraid they would fall down because they were so rusty, so the city decided to see if the statues could be repaired. There had been a big celebration the previous week, brass band included, when they took the first one down. The guide added, almost apologetically, "Perhaps not very religious, but it was a big event to see if they could get down the apostles." Finland had belonged to Russia for more than 100 years so I was surprised to learn that only about 1 percent of the hymns were of the Ortho-dox religion. Russia's influence seemed far greater than that.

From there we went to visit the famous so-called rock church. It is called "The Church of the Temple" and is also Lutheran. The guide told us it is used by the international church on Sundays.

It was built in 1969. The architects were two brothers, very young at that time, and they didn't want to build a traditional church on the hill. This church is totally different from the other churches. Inside you will see the extraordinary ceiling. It is not very high and the acoustics are very good. There are lots of concerts here.

On the outside wall someone wrote "Biafra" in red paint and there was some disagreement among the people whether to spend large sums of money to wash it off or to send that money to the starving children in Biafra. They decided to wash it off, and I'm glad they did, because if they had sent the money away, we wouldn't have this wonderful looking church. We are not building any churches now and I suppose if we were, somebody would be writing Bosnia or Yugoslavia on the walls.

Never mind the children who starved.

Inside the church, I marveled at the huge, solid granite boulders laid one upon another to form the inner walls. Some of these had been carved out to form the altar. It was like being in a kiva – round, solid, part of the earth. Boulders reached up eight or nine feet to the glass ceiling where wooden beams revealed yet another layer of granite blocks on the outside. Someone was playing the organ. I sat quietly a few minutes, and it pulled me into a wondrous sense of awe. The way the architects had used nature to combine the human and the divine stirred in me a sense of deep reverence.

Our visit to the Russian Orthodox church was a sharp contrast. It was built in 1868 by a Russian architect, dark red brick trimmed with a dull, washed-out green. The ornateness inside was breathtaking. Gold arches silhouetted all kinds of men – saints and bishops no doubt, scattered among scores of icons. A choir was singing and on the altars were burning candles. The dome was blue tile, with dark red, three-paned windows edged in black, and at the apex, gold stars twinkled in blue crystal. A wreath of fake flowers was draped around the Christ on the cross with nails in his hands, a stole covering his half-naked body. I shuddered. The real Christ cannot be celebrated with fake flowers. Nor is suffering and abuse the focal point of our inspiration, but rather the Easter triumph over it. Three tiers of candles lit by electric bulbs formed the central chandelier. I was surprised to see folding chairs; I had understood that the people stood for worship. Two crowns sat on a little stool in the center toward the main altar. (The guide told us that the chairs and crowns were there for an upcoming wedding.) Ornate gates separated the inner sanctum from the people – one more reminder that the hierarchy of the church is adamant about separating people from clergy, as if to keep the people under control and the power in the hands of "God's anointed." Dualistic thinking there.

I was still thinking about that outside the church when the guide's comments interrupted my thoughts.

Only the priests are allowed behind those gates. The empty coffin draped with a gold-fringed white cloth is a symbol of Christ's grave. At Easter, these coffins are draped in black to represent the empty tomb.

I thought her theology was a little off on that one.

Uspenski [the name of the cathedral], from the slavic word, uspenia, *means when Holy Mary died and went to sleep. The Finnish people like to refer to it as Greek Orthodox, although it was built by the Russians for their soldiers during the time Finland was a grand duchy of Russia.*

Outside again, the market square seemed to me to be like a city within a city. Everything imaginable was being sold from booths that stood side by side and back to back across a wide expanse of cobblestone. Red and yellow flowers circled a fountain near a female sculpture. The guide obviously enjoyed talking about the sculpture.

At the time this sculpture was placed here, they thought it was very indecent because the lady was naked. The sculptor was poor and tried to get a loan from the bank but he didn't get it, so he turned her back to the bank. This lady is always crowned every first of May, a students' festival actually. Different faculties of the university, the

School of Economics and so on, they put a white student's cap on this lady the night before and that's when the May Festival starts.

That old-looking yellow brick building with bas-reliefs of workers carved on the front is the Finnish School of Economics. The girls in these schools study harder than the boys. There are fewer girls at the technical schools and on the faculties than boys.

Children go to school and to day care. The mothers are working the whole day. There are possibilities to have the child stay at the school for some hours until the mother comes home. There are also family day cares where someone takes care of several children and they can stay after school. I think at the moment the unemployment rate with women is higher than with men. We have about 18 and a half percent unemployment with men, at least 19 percent for women.

You can have one year of maternity leave, and also the father gets father's leave for six to 12 days. And after this one year, you can stay at home until your child is three years old and the employer cannot give you notice during this time. The law has changed a little bit, so if the company is having difficulty and is changing, notice can be given, but earlier it was almost impossible. And the employer is obliged to take the person back after two or three years to the same kind of job. Of course, it's very hard if you stay on maternity leave for two or three years, because your work might have changed quite a lot. You are not paid during this time. But for 154 days, even if you are not working, you get an allowance which depends on your salary, but a minimum of 80 marks per day.

When you have a baby, you get a baby package from the government that has everything for a newborn baby, diapers and blankets and everything, and it is worth about 2,000 marks. You can take the money if you like, but it is only 500 marks. Most mothers take the package. It is so handy that it is also sold abroad. When Finnish mothers are having their babies abroad, they order this package.

The next day was the big 80th birthday celebration of WILPF. It began in the upstairs banquet hall at Unitas Centre, wide picture windows opening to the blue gulf waters through white birches and black pines. It was an enormous spread: fish salad, goulash with mushrooms and beef over rice, a corn and carrot dish, strawberry cream cake for dessert.

Over half the women who might have been at the banquet were not, and I was sure that the cost of the meal was what kept them away. Shyama, born in Scotland and living in Western Australia since 1967, was standing beside me, her piercing blue eyes and ruddy complexion as intense as her involvement in "the politics of pollution." She echoed my thought, talking to me in "Aus-trallian English" with a Scottish brogue. "I think it's against the principles of WILPF to have this elegant meal and to separate the meal from the program. It should have been simpler and therefore available to everyone, rather than just for the privileged few."

In the auditorium an hour later, there were speeches of appreciation for the women who had been carrying the load, especially Edythe, President, and Barbara, Executive Director of International WILPF in Geneva. Greetings were read, spoken or sung from Germany, the USA, Palestine, Sri Lanka and many other countries. Banners prepared for use on the Peace Train were unfurled across the stage. Two men and six or seven women brought greetings from the Palestine section. Seven Japanese women dressed in wide-belted, colorful kimonos presented a check from their organization to the chair, who spoke in Swedish English in response: "It is a lot of money that you have raised for us and we are thankful to you."

One of the Japanese women spoke in English: "We held a contest throughout all the high schools asking them to send in songs on the theme of all the world as friends. And one of our most famous women poets was the judge and the girl child that got first prize was only 18 years old. I will repeat the first three lines of the song: 'Dear brother, I weep and mourn for you. Did our mother bear you to let you become a soldier? Did our father raise you for ten years to let you kill and be killed?' So now this is a song that someone translated into English. We will sing the song in Japanese. Here are the words: 'The world living together in true love is our hope and our desire. So let us sing; let us join hands, singing the song of friends and peace. Let us never cease our link one to the other, so the world must all be joined, too, as friends. Oh sun of love, burn bright and clear. The world and we are one big family'."

One of the singers got the giggles and soon everybody in the room was laughing and clapping.

Peace Train participants from Vermont held up a postcard map they had created, picturing the cities on the journey. These were being sold to make money for WILPF. A very old woman dressed in a long, elegant robe was seated centerstage and a Scandinavian woman announced, "We are going to present for you a few songs that were written for the 80 year anniversary celebration. We have had no time or capacity to get them translated into English, so I will tell you in short what they are saying. The first song celebrates the League women's marches; the first one to Paris, the second from Moscow to Minsk, and the third one from New York to Washington. The second song celebrates the great peace journey when peacekeepers from all parts of the world visited the UN government to present issues of peace, disarmament and development. The third song is a congratulation song to the 80-year-old WILPF ladies represented by this old lady here." Their singing was lusty, with no giggles.

A toy engine (black with red wheels, and with doves of peace painted on the sides), which held a bouquet of roses, was brought on stage, accompanied by a woman playing guitar. She taught us *The Peace Train Song.*

It's our birthday there (here) in Helsinki.
Women go, women go, women go, go, go.
The international "FREEDOM WOMEN"
want to go to celebrate.
(have come here to celebrate)

"WILPF" is the greatest organization.
Women go, women go, women go, go, go.
We fight for freedom in the whole world,
for human rights and against torture.

We'd like to tell you about our journey.
Women go, women go, women go, go, go.
We're off to Petersburg, Kiev, and Bucharest,
Sofia, Istanbul, Urumchi to Beijing.

Do you know the women? They wear black clothes.
Women go, women go, women go, go, go.
They have the power, we seek together
for a peaceful, wonderful world.

The nuclear plants and all the weapons.
Women help, women help, women help, help, help.
We are afraid of threatening danger.
We want to find the peace again.

(Spoken loudly):
"Women, help, women help, women help!"[3]

A dozen women from Australia invited everyone to join them in singing their "unofficial national anthem," *Waltzing Matilda.* The leader pitched it too low, stopped us, laughed and said, "Let's start over and do it right." We did start over, louder. They sang the verses and we laughed and clapped and shouted and made the rafters ring on the chorus. I wondered how many of us knew that we were singing about defying laws and those who defend them.

Down came a jumbuck to drink at the billabong
Up jumped the swagman and grabbed him with glee,
And he sang as he stowed that jumbuck in his tuckerbag
You'll come a-waltzing Matilda with me.
Up rode the squatter, mounted on his thoroughbred,
Down came the troopers, one, two, three…

Up jumped the swagman, sprang into the billabong.
You'll never catch me alive, said he.
And his ghost may be heard as you pass by that billabong
You'll come a-waltzing Matilda with me![4]

The meeting was still going strong when Lynette and I took the last bus back to the hotel. We got a taste of "real life" in Helsinki on that ride. As we got on the Metro, so did a dozen 17- to19-year-olds, loud and obviously "under the influence." It was quite a scene. They immediately pulled from their brown bags bottles of beer and a bottle of Vodka and passed them around from person to person. When the Vodka came to one young woman, she took a piece of gum out of her mouth, threw it on the floor right where people would step on it, upended the bottle and took a big swig. A minute or two later, she and her young man were on the floor of the aisle, licking each other, hugging and touching in sexually provocative places. Another couple snuggled together on one seat of the car kissing, getting wilder and noisier and more feverish the farther we went.

"Well, well," Lynette said in my ear. "Some of the youth of Finland are just like some of the youth anywhere else, careless about property, raucous, full of energy and into heavy drinking." I was relieved to get to a quiet room and to bed.

Our last day in Finland dawned fair, and for the first time I felt rested, as if it really were morning rather than the middle of the night. I awoke feeling anxious, pulled toward home and Eric's illness far away. The words to a song he had written flashed through my mind, so I "bit down hard and swallowed tenderness," and one more time in my mind's eye, put him on my heart shelf. I invoked the Spirit of healing to be with him and gave myself to my own journey.

At the center, I learned that I would be on the Red Wagon, number 14, that there would be 36 women on that coach, nine compartments of four women each, from Italy, New Zealand, Holland, Sweden, Australia, Switzerland, Egypt, Germany, Britain, Philippines, Denmark, Netherlands, Taiwan, Canada, and a lot from the USA. I tried to get the "Reds" to meet, but only two others came: Elise from Holland and Eva from Sweden. We had a good time together.

Later at the plenary session, a young Japanese woman sat beside me. I smiled at her and said, "Hello, I'm Beth."

"Hayashi," she smiled back.

"Hayashi?"

"Michiko."

"Michiko," I repeated after her. She laughed at my attempt to say it.

"Michiko. Do you know the Japanese Empress?"

"Michiko? Oh, are you the assistant Empress?" She laughed again.

"Oh, no, no, no, no. But she is very beautiful and she can speak English and Japanese very easily."

"Oh. And is the name you're called by 'Michiko'? When your friends talk to you, would they say 'Michiko'?"

"No, Hayashi. My name is Hayashi."

"And the Empress's name is 'Michiko', the same as yours?" She was pleased that I was interested. One tiny little bridge spanned the distance between the USA and Japan.

On stage, the focus was on the different countries we would visit on our way to Beijing: Russia, Ukraine, Rumania, Bulgaria, Turkey, Kazakhstan, and Urumqi, capital of Xinjiang, the northwestern region of China. We were told that a woman from each country would be on the Train with us, briefing us about what is happening in her country. One by one, these women were introduced and each one gave a short talk. Letitia of Russia, blonde and ruddy-faced, spoke through an interpreter. "When you are coming to St. Petersburg, you will see that it is the most beautiful city in the world." A slight twitter went through the audience and she was obviously embarrassed. I thought the embarrassment should have been ours.

Black-haired, dark-eyed Zinaida of Ukraine smiled broadly and said, "Dear sisters, dear friends. I am so happy to come here and address such a big and important forum. I have never been so happy as now, because I can speak not only for myself but for all women and children and other people of my country. I see everything from their eyes and from their gratitude and their wishes to be helpful and that is certainly to be so exciting. I am involved in International Association of Ukraine. Our Association was founded in October, 1990. It is an independent NGO organized for women's and children's rights in the former Soviet Union. The Association is giving attention to equal education, women's rights and feminist issues. In the workshops, there will be attention to these. In June, 1993, the president of our organization addressed the Parliament, and the vice-president of the Human Rights Commission took part in the Second World Conference on Women's Rights. Ukrainian women are in very critical situation now. On the tenth of this month the Parliament will meet with the women of NGOs. There are 48 NGO organizations. Thank you very much for your attention."

Elena Petrovici of Rumania, fair-skinned, dark-haired and serious, spoke in English difficult to understand. A lot of what she said escaped me. Then I heard, "I will speak now about the situation in my country. Women in employment is 44 percent of the general employment. Unemployment compensation is the same percent for men and for women – at 65 percent of the last wages. Thank you very much. Excuse me my English."

Ayse may have been in her late 30s. She had dark, somber eyes and light brown hair that wisped around her golden tan face. She spoke fluent English. "I want to say hello to all my sisters on the Peace Train. I am coming from a country where the prime minister is a woman. I think we should have a very good time in my country, because she is in favor of women and a constitution that includes women and women's issues. I hope that the result of this will be that the United Nations will be exposed to women from all the different countries.

"In Istanbul, I am happy to say I am very excited and that you on the Peace Train are very welcome. We have a very young women's liberation movement, about 15 years old and in the workshops we will like to give you an idea about the history, the artists, and the Women's Federation.

"Our country is now approaching two important questions: one is the Fundamental Islamic woman, which is very important, what it means for women. We would like to discuss that and give you an idea about that. We have a different nation living within the boundaries of our country and there's a war going on, so we would like to give you some idea and some information about our Kurdish problem. Also, we would like to share our experiences of peace in our country. That's all for now."

Nestai Ismailova of Kazakhstan, with dark hair and the round face of many Middle East women, spoke in halting English of a country about which I knew almost nothing. "Dear sisters, I bring you greetings from our section of WILPF. Also, I want to thank you for the cordiality of the Finnish people. I want to express on behalf of my Kazakh people in Almaty and on the part of my country and especially of myself the appreciation of the generosity of WILPF, an organization that has such a large, long experience. Kazakh people are friendly."

At that point, Barbara Lochbiler, whose strength as executive director of WILPF belied her fragile peaches-and-cream looks, brought the reality of the Train trip into sharp focus: "I would also now, at the beginning of the Train, like to thank everybody who made this process possible. First of all, I would like to thank the officers of WILPF who got slowly used to the idea and also the energy and trust and money they put into it and the experience to make it happen. And I would like to thank each one of you who worked together in the planning of the tour that what we planned together will be implemented and will help us to progress as we go on. Our theme is "Crossing Borders." One of the borders we are crossing is language. Samira has been with us from the beginning and she is going to speak French; try to listen."

Samira had a smile that warmed the heart. Her long, flowing dark hair ringed a friendly face. Her French was fluent and beautiful, and I did not understand a word of it. So much for college French. Thank goodness for translators.

Barbara spoke again: "Now I will give the floor to the organizers, the travel agents from Germany. This is Esther. She will be with us on the train. She knows everything about Russia and all the countries and China, and she won't have a language problem."

Esther was tall with very dark hair and an intriguing accent. "Hello, everybody. I am quite impressed by the number and by the atmosphere here, so I'm nervous." A chuckling murmur of empathy went through the group. "I want to introduce myself. My name is Esther. I'm from Switzerland, but I have lived abroad for almost ten years by now. The first time I came to Beijing was in 1981. At that time, at the age of 20, I was going to learn a language for one year, that's all, but it turned out to be four years altogether, so I spent four years in China. When I came home in 1985, I started to work as a tour guide with a Chinese company in Tibet and Mongolia. I have made several trips from Moscow to Beijing, but I've never been in such a large group and I'm very happy to be here."

Two other tour guides were introduced, one a man. His first comment elicited nervous and uncertain murmurs: "Now we are crossing another border with a man speaking." Some of the women were uneasy about men being on the Train.

"We'll do our best," he went on, "to make this a good trip, crossing into eight countries on a train that has never run before in the history of the railroad!" Everybody clapped.

"You are taking part in a real sensation and my feeling is that it really is great and it will be so good that you will not want to leave the train in Beijing." More applause.

"You will find that your time will be short on the Train. Have no fear of that. I have just traveled on the Trans-Siberian train two times and I had a great summer, and I know what I'm talking about. Thank you. I will be with you until Kiev or Bucharest, I don't know yet, and then I am booked again into Alma Ata. I'll be there waiting for you if you need me. Thank you very much."

As Barbara spoke again, I could almost hear the rumble of the Train on the tracks: "So now we look forward to visiting the cities, the countries. And you have not been knowing each other, but we have a tight program and we try to communicate so that you can know who is who on the Train. And we are thinking of who will organize communication on the Train. We will go now into the program.

"We have a special program for young women, The Rolling School, whoever is young is invited to attend, and we have several marvelous women who are the conveners of this school: Ida Harslof and Regina. Now we have a very difficult system of communication on the Train, the loudspeakers; it is only one way, but to get the connection and suggestions back to the steering committee, we suggest that each wagon nominate two spokespersons for each wagon. To get that process going, we have appointed two temporary persons and perhaps all these spokespersons could stand up and introduce themselves so you know who is who and which color car or wagon you are in."

All over the room women stood up and gave their names. That was all. I felt frustrated that there was no attempt to get us together, to learn to know our particular spokeswomen or others on our coach.

Barbara closed the session: "I hope we have a wonderful time together and a very fine gathering in Beijing also. And now it's up to you, the participants, if this will be a real peace train. The first train we will take is not the special Peace Train, but a regularly scheduled one. This train leaves the station tomorrow morning at 6:30 for St. Petersburg. Be there."

3

The Train on the Tracks

Chug, chug, chug. Puff, puff, puff...
I think I can, I think I can...
I thought I could, I thought I could.[1]

There is nothing more difficult to take in hand,
more perilous to conduct, or more uncertain in its success,
than to take the lead in the introduction of a new order of things.[2]

As dawn overtook the darkness on August 7, 1995, the railway station in Helsinki was as full of milling Peace Train women as the air was pregnant with excitement, expectation, determination, hope, and the dream of a world without war.

It was a colorful crowd, a woman from Peru in native dress, black skirt and red top embroidered in gold patterns, an upturned, wide-brimmed hat to match; a Sudanese woman with a delicate blue shawl draped over her black hair; women in pants like me, or very American western dress with red coats and blue and white skirts; a nun in long blue habit; a Japanese woman in bright flowered kimono; a Guatemalan woman with dark skirt and white embroidered blouse; an Indian woman in flowing white sari; a German woman in a flowered, two-piece pantsuit. It was striking to see on this journey women of every part of the world and every skin color: Central and South America, Europe, Asia, Australia, New Zealand, North America, Japan, Philippines, India, Africa; black, white, and many shades of brown.

Banners waved everywhere. People clapped, shouted, stirred about, clicked cameras. I stood there, tingling, between two tracks of trains, one marked "St. Petersburg," on which I had already put my luggage, glad that it was not any heavier than it was. I flicked on my tape recorder.

"Are you documenting this trip?" I asked one photographer.

She saw my dictaphone and responded, "Yes, and you, what are you doing?"

"I'm writing a book about this journey. What is your name?"

"Isabelle, from Geneva, Switzerland."

"Your country is beautiful."

"Say in your book that I just saw that the train is made in Switzerland. The engine is Swiss made."

"Then we can ride safely, right?" She laughed and moved on.

Several women were singing heartily to the accompaniment of a robust guitar. I joined them, "Oh when the saints, oh when the saints…" The Netherlands women, waving a flag in their colors of blue and white, wore a sign like mine: Stop French Testing Now. The banner read, "Cheen walpens naarvrede." Other beautifully decorated banners broadcast our mission as WILPF peacemakers. I was thrilled to be in this wonderful gathering of women and to know I'd be with them for three whole weeks!

"All aboard!" came the call.

Inside at the windows, we looked out on another sea of women just as colorful, waving, singing, wishing us well, the women of WILPF who would not be on the Train. We moved out smoothly, as if we were not moving at all, leaving them all behind. Our mood became subdued. We were actually on our way.

In minutes we passed by an inlet of the Gulf of Finland, boats at dock, serene, shadowed from the brilliant gleam of the early morning sun, into woodlands of the ubiquitous white birch and dark oak. Above us, cloud banks in pink and gray seemed to stand still, and the soft, gentle pulsing of the train in swift movement matched my rapid heartbeat.

There were no compartments on this train, no assigned seats. Beside me, Isabelle, loaded down with professional looking camera equipment, was speaking French with another Swiss woman. When she noticed I was listening, she said, "There are four languages spoken in Switzerland in the mountains in the central part: French, Italian, German, and there's an old, old language that only old people speak now, Romansch." I tried to imagine what it would be like to have different languages spoken from one state to another in the USA.

The Train moved through meadowlike fields of chartreuse and golden grain alternating with deep woodlands, and here and there a body of water. Some of the fields had bales of hay waiting to be put into dark red barns twice the size of the white frame houses. Beds of lavender flowers, tall like blue gentian, lined the railway tracks. We passed a granite quarry, a lumberyard, a ski lift, a gorgeous lake where a man in a red, wooden, flat-bottomed boat fished in the bright morning sunshine. A dove of peace sat in the upstairs window of a brownish orange house. "I could almost be in the Shenandoah Valley of Virginia," I thought to myself. "There is such a sense of peace and tranquillity about this countryside."

We began to see small, individual homes, a contrast to the apartment high-rises of Helsinki. Into and out of Riihimäki, a stop in Lahti, and in Kouvola, uniformed Russian soldiers recorded our passports by looking at them, looking at us, making a checkmark and moving on. I wondered, "Have we now crossed into Russia?" I nibbled at peapods, ate a couple of Majestic biscuits and thought, "There's a kind of luxurious elegance about just sitting here, letting someone else take care of all the travel arrangements, having food prepared for me, and being with people who share common values."

Three dark-haired women were attaching strange little boards to the windows, boards connected to cords of all kinds. I guessed they were recording, maybe making a video of the trip. They were a colorful trio, one dressed in a green top with khaki pants; another in an army-type jacket with black sleeves and flowered pants; the third with black jeans and a Levi's® shirt. All kinds of clothing on this Train.

An announcement came over the PA system, first in Russian, then English, then Swedish, then French: "Please remain seated until the formalities are over." The train screeched to a halt in a town called Vainikkala. A ruddy, heavy-set man stood at the window in the station as we came to a stop along-side log-shaped window boxes full of white daisies, red and pink geraniums, red lilies and tall purple-blue flowers I couldn't name. The frame of the door looked like mottled granite. In front of him, some of our women strolled on the platform.

An hour later, we moved out into a rugged wilderness area, forests as dense as dark night. Homes here and there looked very poor – run-down shacks with small gardens of cabbages, potatoes and always flowers blooming in wild array. A hard life, a struggle for survival, an appreciation for beauty, all mimicked by a sky dark and heavy with rain. The train windows streaked and steamed. Women sang song after song to the strumming guitar: "If you miss the train I'm on, you will know that I am gone; you can hear the whistle blow a hundred miles…" Then a Holly Near tune to which we made up words as we sang: "We are the Peace Train women, and we are singing, singing for our lives. We are anti-nuclear people; we are women of all colors; we are women of many nations; we are strong, determined women, and we are singing, singing for our lives…"[3]

We came to a halt beside a sign that said, "Vyborg," and someone shouted, "Welcome to Russia!" The customs official said in a jolly voice, "You are now in an old Russian town." I felt a tug in my solar plexus; my heart beat a little faster and I turned my watch ahead one hour. Officials in navy blue vests and pants and light blue shortsleeved shirts took our passports. Two officers in dark gray uniforms with stripes on their shoulders, red bands and insignia on their caps, were framed in a doorway between humongous columns decorated in white plaster with leaf designs.

As we pulled out of the station, I wondered where our passports were. An hour or so later, when the train came to a sudden, jerky stop between two woodlands, in what looked like the middle of nowhere, I found out. We were at a tiny little station. Lavender crown vetch and yellow daisies stretched in wild array from the tracks toward the woods. We pulled aside for another train to pass and a voice we learned to know well came over the PA system: "This is Esther speaking. We are stopped here because they have just discovered that our passports were left behind in Vyborg. It would never happen in Finland, but this is Russia. We will have these delays, so swing with it. They have sent someone back to get them." The whole car came alive with murmurings. Some women moved out onto the platform to find food or to wait. Esther was right; one thing was sure about this Peace Train: pre-announced schedules changed!

Forty-five minutes later, the Train began to move, and it seemed no time at all until a husky, male voice announced: "Ladies and gentlemen, welcome to St. Petersburg!"

Buses were waiting to take us to Moskva Hotel, which, as Josephine of London said, "had a look of jaded, ancient glory." We had begun 24 hours of absorbing all we could of this remarkable city and its people.

The next day those same buses ploughed through a circle of gnarled traffic into a seething mob of travelers, all pushing to get to their trains at the elaborately blue and white tiled Moskva Station. There, our own specially-made-up, Russian-staffed Peace Train of 15 coaches was waiting, on which we'd travel until we reached the Chinese border.

On the Peace Train, each coach or wagon had been given a color: red, white, purple, gray, pink, blue, green, orange, and yellow. Each one of us had been assigned our own special compartment and compartment mates. Each person's bed had a number. My wagon was number 14, the Red car; compartment1, bed 1. The cars looked almost new. Brown-grained formica walls. A red, wool runner on the floor. Gold curtains. Red seats. And on the tiny table between beds, a gold cloth with a purple spray of artificial flowers in a small white plastic stand.

My compartment mates were Barbara Anderson of British Columbia, Mary Ann Mattoon, and Patricia Hawley, both of Minnesota. Barbara was in her early 30s maybe, on the Train to produce a video; Patricia was probably in her 50s, a Lutheran pastor on the Train for R & R; Mary Ann might have been in her early 60s, a psychotherapist back home, on the Train to help the cause of peace along; and I at 72 good years, was a consultant, minister, writer, on the Train to put my body on the line for justice, because there absolutely can be no peace without it.

We had been told to limit our luggage, to pack in a couple small suitcases rather than one large one. When Pat brought hers in, it almost filled up the space between the beds! I was wondering how we'd manage, when we discovered storage space under the beds and above the top bunks. I stored my stuff under my bunk, which gave me some frustration as the days went by. Someone always seemed to be sitting there when I wanted to get into my suitcase and I didn't like to uproot people and interrupt conversations that were going on from one bed to the other. When everybody's stuff was "stored," a couple of us could move around the snug little six by six room, if everyone else got out of the way. That turned out not to be a problem since all four of us were considerate and easy with each other.

There were no showers or baths, only at each end of the coach a triangular "bathroom" the size of a postage stamp, with a commode and a sink whose faucets needed two hands and an engineer to operate. Someone posted a funny little poem in protest of the fact that the 36 women in our wagon had the same facilities as the adjoining car with 18 women. Money does talk; they paid more. Having grown up in the 30s with no bathroom, an outhouse, and 11 brothers and sisters, I did not consider that to be a major drawback. I was glad for a flush toilet and running water, doubly glad for the sterile, hot water samovar that gave us safe drinking water at all times.

A Russian "hostess" rode on each car and regularly vacuumed the halls, furnished us with clean linens, and was available to help in any emergency. Letitia took care of the Red wagon. In spite of the language barrier, as the days went by, we developed a warm feeling of camaraderie and taught each other a few words of Russian and English. I was impressed by her desire to learn: on the wall of her own little private compartment, she had posted a list of English words she was practicing. On her tiny desk, a study guide of English phrases lay open. She taught me that "Good morning" is *Dobre Udo* and "Goodnight" is *Dobre Noche*. "Thank you" is *Spaciba*. I never could say the word for "fork" correctly and the Cyrillic alphabet was a mystery!

Three coaches of the Train were marked Pectopah, where we would dine in style and enjoy bantering with blonde, ruddy-faced Viktor and the other friendly and hard-working cooks and waiters. One day I asked Viktor for a fork and he asked: "Fok? What mean?" I drew a fork in the air and away he went to get it. He held it tantalizingly over my head and said the word for fork in Russian, then laughed when I tried to repeat it. It was wonderful to be with the Russian people in this way. I said a little thank-you prayer that the iron curtain had been ripped to shreds and the walls between our nations had crumbled.

This Train was ours, specially made up just for us, a place we would come to think of as home. Two coaches had been emptied and were available for group meetings. When the Train was on the tracks, those empty coaches came alive with activities and events. At any one time they might be a university classroom, a sewing club, an arts and crafts center, a poetry writing class, a playground, a health club or gymnasium, a singing or dance studio, a meditation point, a journal writing area, a drama department, an interview place, a sign-making shop, a photographic viewpoint, the Rolling School, a party hall, and always, a cultural encounter.

The women on the Train were self-starters, activists on justice issues ranging across the board, including alternative economics, racism, traffic in women, violence against women, the plight of refugees, lesbian concerns, nuclear testing, violence against girls, environmental problems, legislation for change, human rights and on and on. They clamored for time and space to give workshops or to have meetings of the people on their car.

Each "program" coach had ten chairs. Everybody else sat on the thin radiator edges, the floor or stood up during the presentations. One time I had been lucky enough to get a chair. I was making notes and concentrating hard, then decided to get up and stretch a minute. As I was standing, out of the corner of my eye I saw a man's hand reach out to my right. Without realizing what was happening, I sat down and went all the way to the floor. I scrambled up and gave him a hard look. He immediately relinquished the seat. I made a note of it in my journal. The next thing I knew, a woman who was sitting beside me handed me a note that said, "I am reading your note on the chair incident for which I apologize. Jack did not touch the chair. It was my mistake. – Teresa."

I turned on her and snapped, "I saw him pull the chair away. And have you been reading my journal? Journals are private, you know. Besides, do you think you have to cover for him? Let him speak for himself!"

I was surprised at the intensity of my response, and I've wondered since if I was mistaken. It certainly didn't build any friendship between us. Later, as I thought it over, wondering at my flash of anger, I realized she had pressed two hot buttons of mine. The first has to do with the sacred privacy of journals; the second, my relationships with men. I've spent my whole life trying to get free of covering for men, taking care of them, putting their needs, their work, their interests first, and it always gets to me when I think other women are caught in the same web. One thing I know about myself: I have a short fuse and an automatic reaction whenever I sense injustice toward me or anyone else. Someone had said that several men were on the Train because their wives would not come without them. I wondered cynically if it was the other way around: they wouldn't stay at home without their wives to take care of them, or they wouldn't "let" their wives come unless they came along. In any case, I felt mean and ugly about my certainty and short-temperedness, and regretted my response.

Briefings by the women from the various countries were especially informative and valuable. Every country we visited was in transition or conflict or both. Poverty, violence, literacy, health, citizenship, the impact of war, burdensome military budgets, the struggle for survival, and traffic in women and girls were the concerns all of them held in common.

Most of the countries we visited bordered the Balkan region. This area had been ravished in the early 1940s by World War II, and before there was time to heal from these atrocities, Tito had brought six republics together in what he called "unity and brotherhood" to form the nation of Yugoslavia. All six (Serbia, Croatia, Slovenia, Bosnia-Herzegovina, Macedonia and Montenegro) had their own ethnic majorities, and all were a mix. While Tito lived (1945-1980), Yugoslavia had incurred a terrible debt by borrowing heavily from multinational banks in order to develop into an industrial power. Defense was one of its biggest industries. US companies who traded with the new "nation" enjoyed huge profits from the arms trade and the development of weapons.

When Tito died, loan payments were demanded by the banks, and the economy declined. Political uncertainty and economic insecurity created distrust and divisiveness among the various ethnic and religious groups and separatism was seen as the solution. Power was held in the hands of a few who used the countries for their own personal gain. Ownership of resources once held in common became competitive and several republics declared independence. Massive violence broke out in 1991, and three years of brutal war had left the whole region reeling. Thousands of women had been raped as trophies of "victory." Six million land mines had been planted throughout the region and continued to add to the casualties. We could feel the tremors as the Train rolled along the borders of this war-torn area and came close to the fighting.

A late 50s, vocal and confident ruddy-faced Mary Rusinow of Pittsburgh, Pennsylvania, was a Peace Train rider. She had lived in Croatia for six years and in Zagreb from 1972 to 1978. At first, I was turned off by her as she became the self-appointed authority on the region, but I soon began to realize that she knew a lot from firsthand experience and I looked forward to hearing her interpretation of the situation. She had a shortwave radio and reported developments daily over the PA system. Later, she included "newscasts" from Zaire, Chechnya, Peru, Guyana, all areas of boiling conflict. She brought the outside world into the protected haven of the Train, keeping us aware of what this trip was all about.

Blue-eyed, blonde Natasha spoke of the effects of the similar breakup of the Soviet Union. With the coming of the so-called "free market economy," the situation of women in Russia worsened miserably. "There are more things to buy," she said, "and less money to buy them. There are more people who are homeless. There are more people who are hungry. The help and support we had come to expect from our government has been withdrawn and women in particular are hurt by this. The gap between the rich and the poor has gotten bigger."

Dark-eyed and intense, Zina spoke of what we could expect in Kiev, Ukraine, the area of the Chernobyl disaster. "At the beginning," she said, "there were the mass evacuations, 4000 people dead, fires out of control, tens of thousands of casualties. As if that was not bad enough, now we are dealing with the fallout of disease and malnourishment from poisoned lands. The foods the farmers grow are full of radiation. It is a kind of genocide, two and three-year-olds without teeth, 11- and 12-year-olds with 70 percent of their teeth extracted or diseased, a phenomenal rise in thyroid cancer, women afraid to become pregnant for fear of birth defects." Her pain for her people was palpable. I had trouble sleeping that night.

Gentle Elena told us that 70 percent of the people of Rumania live below the poverty line, with little or no hope of changing that reality. I was reminded of Kaplan's comment about Romania in *Balkan Ghosts*: "Romania was always alone, always surrounded by enemies who wanted pieces of her."[4]

Nikolina of Bulgaria spoke through an interpreter: "Bulgaria is the crossroads of Eastern Europe. Organized crime is a big problem here. In the last five years, it has increased by four times. Women are frequently the object of these crimes. There is exploitation. There is sexual violence."

Ayse's round face and solemn eyes bore the marks of suffering. "In my native Turkey," she said, "I have been arrested and jailed twice for the crime of being a feminist. We have very great problems with fundamentalist Islam and the war with the Kurds."

Nestai of Kazakhstan echoed Natasha's comments about the "free-market economy" and how the burden of that rests on the shoulders of poor women. "They are the ones hurt most by the fact that the state no longer pays for many things they had come to expect. Before the breakup of the Soviet Union," she added, "Kazakhstan was the testing ground for nuclear missiles. Now we are working hard to make it a nuclear-free zone."

The Train was not all serious study and listening to the pain and struggles that burden the shoulders and hearts of women in every part of the world. It was also a place of play and relaxation. There were wonderful parties. One day an invitation was whispered above the clackety-clack of the wheels on the tracks: "It's Joan's birthday. Come tonight to celebrate in car 14." Joan Reynolds from Brattleboro, Vermont, was a wiry, active, feisty 50- or 60-some-year-old who had vitality coming out her ears. I knew she was in the same compartment with Mary, Amelia, and Genevieve, and they were great party makers, so I didn't want to miss it.

More women than could get into that compartment were stacked on top of each other that night, and the hall was full of others clamoring to get in. We sang or spoke birthday greetings in 12 languages! There were candies, boob balloons, a smoking Russian soldier toy, champagne, wine, and of course, cake. We made merry way past midnight. I'm sure Joan will never forget that birthday!

After the cooks were finished with meals and preparations for the next day, drinking and partying started in the dining cars and lasted into the wee hours of morning. The Iron Curtain was no longer iron, but permeable and crumbled. The Russian staff joined in the frivolity, and friendships were made that will last for lifetimes.

One very special party highlighted the differences between East and West. Tayba Sharif, an Islamic woman of Egypt, was married while we were on the Train. With a shining face one morning, she announced that her father faraway in Sudan had signed the nuptial agreement with her fiancé. She had left as a single woman and would return as a married woman. She invited all of us to come that night to her bride's nuptial party. This was an event "for women only"; men were not even to walk through the car. I was sitting with her at dinner that day.

"I'm so happy for you, Tayba. Is it hard for you not to be there with them for the signing of the agreement?"

"Oh, no," she said. "I would not be at the signing of the contract even if I were at home. That is done only by the groom and the bride's father. It upset me awhile ago when one of the USA women told me that she was so sorry for me that men shut me out of that important time. I told her that I did not like it that she felt sorry for me. This is a very happy day for me. I want everyone to be glad for me because my father has agreed to let me marry the man I want to marry. It has been hard for him. For a long time he has refused."

"It's so different from our customs, Tayba. I guess she just didn't understand at all how it is for you."

"The wedding is different from the marriage," she said. "That will be in October when I get back. That is the time when everyone will be together to celebrate the marriage. I invite you to come."

"Oh, how I'd love to be able to do that, and I can't because I don't have the money. I'll remember, though, and be with you in spirit. I'm so glad for your happiness and I wish you blessings that will last your whole life through."

That night a couple hundred women piled into a railway car that was big enough for 50, jammed in tightly, almost on top of one another, close around Tayba whose black face shone with joy and young love. A thin, flowing veil covered her hair like a halo. She led us through a ritual of painting hands with henna and talked about its significance as a symbol of loyalty among women, long life, and support for the marriage. Then there was music, and singing and dancing, yes, in that crowded space. We were women together on one woman's journey that touched deep chords in me. I felt a kind of mystical connection among us, a connection permeating the lines of language, culture and customs. Tayba will always have a special spot in my heart; she's a sister to me, no matter how great the distances between us. Egypt is no longer some faraway and unknown place; it is where Tayba lives as a refugee from Sudan.

Our time on the Train had its share of tensions and troubles, an inevitable reality when people from widely diverse cultures, races, religions and personalities live in close quarters and share common resources. It became apparent quickly that "there are too many USA women on this Train. They take over and act like they own it." And, "USA women are loud and complaining and I get tired of that." And, "USA women are not sensitive to the women in the cities we are visiting. They talk too much and listen too little." I hated the stereotyping, but thought the criticisms had some validity, and it made me sad. While I thankfully claim the USA as my homeland, I am not always proud to be a US citizen. The very fact that out of the 232 women on the Train, 113 were from the USA, demonstrated how privileged we are and how easy it is to think of ourselves as normative.

A situation on the Red wagon brought this home to me forcefully. As Barbara told us in Finland, two spokespersons had been designated for each car. These two would meet with the leaders and take messages back and forth between "headquarters" and the participants. Annelisa of Italy and Megan of New Zealand were to represent the Reds. Speaking English was a major task for Annelisa; she was not always easy to understand. Megan was young, shy, and soft-spoken. Neither one had taken the initiative to build community among the 36 of us, and it may well be that they did not see that as a part of their assignment.

One day early on, a meeting of the Reds was called, and it turned out that it was called by Melodie of Tallahassee, Florida. Melodie was a jolly, energetic, pleasant woman whose black eyes radiated warmth, whose black skin shone. She led us in singing *This Little Light of Mine*, giving our names around the circle, doing some get-acquainted stuff in twos, introducing our partners, and then admonishing us jovially to be kind and loving to one another. I felt good about our finally having the chance to know one another a bit, and I appreciated her skill in bringing us together. But I was uneasy about what Annelisa and Megan felt about it. To my knowledge, Melodie had taken the leadership without it being a group decision. What made me most uncomfortable was that Annelisa had made notes on what she wanted to tell us and when she tried over and over to make her report, Melodie cut her off by interrupting. Annelisa never did get to tell us what she had written, and Megan didn't even try to get into the conversation. At another time, Megan tried to speak above Donna of Minnesota and finally gave up. I felt frustrated and embarrassed about this. "This is what the women mean by US takeovers," I thought, and I asked Donna, "Are you now the spokesperson? I don't understand what is going on here."

"We're doing it together," she responded angrily, and went right on dominating the meeting. I went to Annelisa and Megan to ask them how they felt about it. "I don't like what is happening to you. It feels like a US takeover."

"It's all right," Annelisa said. "I know my English is bad."

"It's okay," Megan said. "My voice is soft and I've never done this before."

It felt unresolved to me; I wanted to bring about some peace on the Red car. A couple days went by and I decided to do what I thought I could do: lead the group in a time of reconciliation and re-connection. I asked Annelisa and Megan about it and they agreed to have me call and lead a meeting. I planned it carefully: moments of centering, silence and passing a loaf of bread around the circle which we would all eat together; sharing times when we felt really connected to others in the Red car or on the whole Peace Train; then, in trios, raising questions and making suggestions about how we could deepen our community; sharing those suggestions in the total group and closing with the song, "From you I receive; to you I give; Together we share and by this we live."[5]

It was a good meeting with lots of good suggestions: slow down the language; move across age lines; when you disagree, don't make judgments on others as to their being right or wrong; form small interest groups; US women be sure not to dominate; always say something nice before you say something negative.

As we left the session, Melodie tapped me on the shoulder. "You led it well," she said, "It's what I do. But why wasn't I told I was going to be replaced as facilitator?" I was shocked.

"I wasn't replacing you. I thought we needed such a meeting, and I asked to lead it. You had said that we would have rotating leadership."

"But that should be a group decision."

"You're right. I felt that should have happened when you took over the leadership, too. I'm sorry I didn't speak with you about it. I assumed that anyone on the Train is free to take leadership as they choose."

I was glad she confronted me and let me know her feelings, appreciative that she was straight and clear. I felt good about our conversation, but it felt unfinished. A couple days went by and gentle Molly approached me: "Beth, I really liked what you did for us. Will you please hold another meeting like that?"

I was in a quandary: I didn't want to be thought of as a "US takeover person" myself. I didn't want to offend Melodie again. So I said, "I will do that if it can first be decided by the whole group, Molly. Will you call a meeting and bring it up?" She never did, so I asked Annelisa, Megan and Melodie if the four of us could talk about it together, and included Beth Petersen who had agreed to take Annelisa's place. That didn't happen, either, and at one point, Beth said in irritation, "Do whatever you want, Beth. It makes no difference to me." Her cutting off the dialogue left me feeling disempowered. I didn't try again.

Even now, I feel sad about the way it all happened. I pondered it in my journal.

Once again I learn that the best of intentions can result in misunderstandings. The human element is always there and I just can't know ahead of time the effect my actions will have on others, particularly in a complex social system, all these people living together under stress and a hierarchical mode of leadership. One thing is clear to me. We can't build friendship and a sense of community and oneness unless we stay engaged with each other until each one feels important, accepted, and an integral part of the whole.

I awoke one morning to great layers of mauve clouds riding high above vast, uninhabited plains, the sun casting a radiant glow over it all and heightening the deepening blue of the skies. Dusty trees and a few apartment buildings appeared on the horizon as we moved along. We stopped at a platform where a forlorn canine mongrel sat as if having never had the attention he needed as "man's best friend." A mustached, thin man in dirty jeans and an orange vest over a blue worker shirt, leaned against a blue cement archway which led to a courtyard behind a low, white wall. He clamped a cigarette between his teeth and sent smoke rings circling into the air.

Inside the Train, about half of the women were ailing with fevers, sprained or broken ankles, toothache, diarrhea, flu and asthma. Mary Ann puffed her ventilator; Barbara blew her nose with increasing frequency; and Pat alternated coughing and tending to her sprained ankle. Next door, Gisela looked miserable with a debilitating fever. Dozens had colds and stomach aches.

Two doctors were available for help when it was needed. One time, Mary Ann scalded herself as she was pouring boiling, sterile water from one container to another and Dr. Brigitte was quick to respond. Another time, Brigitte stayed with me as we rushed frantically through the streets of Istanbul to replace eyedrops I had lost, a medication that was essential to my recovery from cataract surgery that I had had three weeks before I left home. I wondered when my time would come. It would have been so easy to have an accident as we moved about in lurching train cars going at high speeds, stepped over the roar and clang of twisting connectors between cars, or on and off the Train, negotiating outlandishly high steps. I diligently resisted eating the fresh vegetables that looked so innocent and good. I lived on Echinacea and Vitamin C with garlic pills to help my cause along. Thankfully, I stayed well and free of accidents.

Station platforms were turned into farmers' markets. One day Grieke of the Netherlands and I were at the Train windows taking in one such scene. Her graying hair was windblown and her eyes sparkled. "Now that's what you call recycling." She pointed toward the platform. I followed her finger and there were two baby buggies parked among the melons, pota-toes, tomatoes and cabbages, all stacked in neat piles, the buggies loaded down with garden produce. "Ingenuity, thy name is woman," I said.

Our cooks replenished supplies at these stops, stacking the 100-pound sacks on top of each other between cars. Women on the Train often bar-gained at the open doors for fresh-baked breads and melons. Gray-haired Bertha's eyes smiled at the delight of children catching the candy she tossed from the high Train door, when suddenly, the mood changed. One father spoiled the fun by pulling a child roughly away. No peace in that action!

On August 26, Esther's now well-known voice came over the PA system: "Esther speaking. We will reach the Chinese border at 4:00 p.m. There we will say good-bye to this Russian train and the rest of the journey will be on a Chinese train. Our Train will be on one side of the platform; the Chinese train on the other. Passports will be checked. The forms that were given out you will need when you leave China. Write NO in every space. Stay on the Russian train until notified to move over."

We collected a "purse" as a thank-you to our Russian staff and said good-bye with warmth and appreciation. Once more, I put my watch ahead an hour.

There was a change in the air when we boarded the immaculate Chinese train decorated in blue with lace curtains alongside green dust ruffles. On the beds, brightly colored comforters were covered with pure white covers. The floors in the compartments and halls were carpeted with clean, bright green carpets. The Chinese attendants and waitresses were austere and for-mal in their chic chartreuse pant or skirt outfits, small white scarves on their heads and white gloves on their hands. Security officers wandered through the train incessantly, about every 15 minutes. Unlike the Russian train, there was an air of control that almost forbade interaction of any sort.

It was 11:15 that night when the first shift had a tasty 4-course dinner of roast beef and gravy, peapods, cabbage, steamed dumplings, soup, tea and coffee. The second, very tired shift was served at 1:00 a.m. Tables in the three dining cars were spread with white linen tablecloths covered with plastic. We saw so much plastic and styrofoam during those three days that it made me a little sick. I fell in love with those Chinese *cha sui bao,* steamed dumplings. Yummy! The Chinese know how to make dumplings like Mama's!

At first, the attendants were openly distraught at our persistence in opening the hall curtains so that we could see the countryside. We opened them; they closed them. Finally, they gave up and even became guardedly friendly as the days went by.

By now we knew that there would be no stop in Urumchi, and indeed that our only stops for the three days and nights' travel into Beijing would be "rest stops" of about 20 minutes in places the Chinese government had chosen. At one of these places, someone inelegantly and accurately commented, "I feel just like a dog that has been let out to pee."

The platforms were surreal, completely cleared of people. It was as if someone had cut the throats of millions of Chinese or whisked them off to Siberia. A notable exception were the guards covering every door the full length of the train, and at times, in watchtowers with guns at ready. Was the government acting out of the age-old notion that men needed to protect "the weaker sex"? Was it courtesy being given "visiting dignitaries"? Or, was it outright control of this strange creature, the Peace Train? Who knows? In any case, to be perceived as a "dangerous" woman was a strange, incomprehensible feeling to me, and the presence of so many officers cast a mood of suspicion, if not outright distrust.

Inside the train, however, we went right on with our activities; we held or attended workshops; we read books on China; we danced; we sewed; we wrote and read poetry; we worshiped; we exercised; we slept; we partied; we sang.

And we built ourselves into a community of women whose goal was to make peace in this war-weary world.

4

Making Peace
in a War-Weary World

Prepare war, stir up the mighty men.
Let all the men of war draw near, let them come up.
Beat your plowshares into swords,
your pruning hooks into spears;
let the weak say, "I am a warrior."[1]

Come, let us go up to the mountain of God that we may
be taught the ways of love. Beat your swords into plowshares,
and your spears into pruning hooks; nation shall not lift up
sword against nation, neither shall they learn war any more.[2]

Those two ancient prophets, Joel and Isaiah, were as far apart in their views of
resolving conflict as the Peace Train people and the military men of nations.

From the time those words were written, between the tenth and second centuries before Christ, to the present day, our world has functioned

out of the assumption of the prophet Joel – that war is the way to peace. "Fight it out to the finish," seems to be the motto. Shed blood to avenge the shedding of blood, that's Joel's admonition, and the nations of the world have behaved that way. The classic example of that attitude is one report during the war in Vietnam: "We have destroyed the village in order to save it."[3]

Wars come out of a win/lose, enemy/friend, in/out, us/them, power-over mentality, and our whole social structure is based on it. In such a world, making peace, learning the ways of love, as the prophet Isaiah says, means turning that assumption upside down. It means learning a different way of being nations and peoples together in an unjust and radically diverse world. It means talking across and through differences of opinion with both parties' interests in mind. It means believing that there is a "security" other than military might, indeed, that military might is no security at all. It means addressing injustice without shows of physical strength. It means being able to "live and let live," rather than imposing my way of life on another culture or people.

Making peace is not easy, for it requires changes in attitudes and behavior, and change always meets with resistance. People who have power do not easily relinquish it. Justice is not achieved without struggle. The Peace Train was no exception. It was a journey for peace, but it could not be called a "peaceful journey."

Jesus said it 2,000 years ago: "One's foes will be those of one's own household."[4] A look at the Peace Train, not to mention all the "civil" wars around the earth right now, show how startingly prophetic he was.

An announcer on TV just said that "One cause for hope right now is that at no place in the world are two nations in gun wars with each other. The wars going on are internal to nations, between tribes, religions and cultures." That is a cause for hope? After traveling in the war-torn Balkan region, where Serbs, Croats and Bosnians live so intermingled as to be like "a household," I believe that at the root of every war there is racial hatred, coupled with God-talk that claims supremacy, blessing self-proclaimed "truth" as worthy of defense at whatever price.

Kaplan speaks of this in *Balkan Ghosts*: "In Serbian legend, the Nemanjic kingdom sacrificed itself to the Turkish hordes in order to gain a new kingdom in heaven; meanwhile, here on earth, as Mother Tatiana, a Serbian nun in Tito's time, said bitterly, 'The greatness of Italy and the other nations of Europe was constructed over our bones. I am a good Christian, but I'll not turn the other cheek if some Albanian plucks out the eyes of a fellow Serb, or rapes a little girl, or castrates a twelve-year-old Serbian boy.'"[5] Christian, Jewish, and Muslim animosities are as rife today as then.

"Winning" wars is like doing something that is detrimental to everyone, with the twisted satisfaction of doing it with more bravado and brutality than anyone else. "Making peace," on the other hand, is doing something that is beneficial to everyone, with the genuine satisfaction of knowing you've done your bit, whether or not it makes a dent in the superstructures that seem to have all the power.

Clementina of Peru, dressed in her snug, colorful native dress, wore the aura of pitifulness that is often evident among suffering and oppressed people. "They say that the schedule is full," she sounded helpless. "There's no time left for me or Marta to talk about the situation of our indigenous people. And I just found out that a man has been given time to give a workshop on 'The Life of a Once Married Gay Man,' to talk about how he's been oppressed because he's gay." Her voice took on an edge of anger. "It's just how white men have taken over the lands of indigenous people in my country." She was close to tears.

I agreed with her, and said so. "Here we are on this Peace Train, supposedly acting out peacemaking, and instead we're doing the very things that make for war, refusing access to people who have no voice, letting males in power take over. It's what happens everywhere on the face of the earth. I'll see if my voice can make a difference, Clementina. I really want to hear your story and know what's going on with your people."

What I learned from these two women about what's happening to the indigenous peoples in their countries resonated with my own experience. In the US, our Native Americans have been treated the same way – shut out of decision making and shunted off onto reservations in the most barren lands of the country. The Garra Revolt of 1851[6] was started by a Kupa Indian in protest of a government policy of taxation without representation, which he named as "tyranny." He was hung for his courageous action.

A park ranger in Anza-Borrego State Park in California said, in a presentation he made recently, "We treated the Mexicans no better. To end the Mexican War, we signed the Treaty of Guadalupe at Hidalgo in 1848, when we took from Mexico nearly half of its territory – what is now California, Nevada, Utah, most of New Mexico and Arizona and part of Colorado and Wyoming. That treaty is still in effect. It guarantees unlimited and free border crossing privileges. Do we honor it? Just the opposite! Border officers probably have never even heard of it, and the cost of patrolling the border today reaches into the millions. What's more, we American citizens have just been told that the number of patrolling officers will be increased to 10,000 as soon as possible." I found that revolting. Robert Frost said it succinctly: "Something there is that doesn't love a wall."[7]

I am convinced that we can't "make peace" in the world and continue to "teach war" and aggression. In Joseph Heller's funny and awful *Catch-22* masterpiece on the tragedies and insanity of war, he paints a picture of boot camp and war games as brutalizing men to become better brutes than the enemy on whatever "playing field" there is.[8] Then they're sent home to wives and families with all the tenderness drained out of them and they're supposed to be good husbands and citizens and never be violent again.

We were talking about Lynette's younger years, her dark eyes intense as she spoke about her firsthand experience of that. Now happily married, with teenage daughters, she told me her husband, their father, is not the man she first dated with serious intentions. Unlike millions of women in every country, she was smart enough to escape being one of those unlucky wives whose husbands have been trained to be hard enough to kill. I asked her how that happened, how she got into peace and justice work.

"Probably the Vietnam War was the turning point for me. It was before I met my husband, and I was going with a young man who joined the army and got sent to Vietnam. I could soon see the changes that war was having on him as an individual."

"What kind of changes?"

"There was just a whole mental change, a mind-set change. He had never been self-centered, but he came back thinking he was pretty invincible; he was drinking more alcohol than he had ever drunk in his life; I think there had been some dabbling in drugs. He had been through some terrible experiences. I saw what it did to him. I saw what it did to my cousins. I saw how my brothers' friendships changed, and I couldn't accept what it was doing to the young men. So I stopped going with him and got into the protests against Vietnam. In 1969, we started calling for a moratorium. It was certainly the Vietnam War that brought me into the peace movement. How did you get into peace work, Beth?"

"I was born into a family and church that has peace as its central commitment," I said, "so I got it with my mother's milk. That was in the state of Virginia. Even now, that state is a strange mixture of peace-loving people and military activities. I love the state and hate the military mind set of a lot of the people. Virginia Military Academy is located in the Shenandoah Valley there. It's the last bastion of all-male training in the United States. Officials just announced on TV that if they *must* abide by a court order to do so, they will accept women. Then the spokesman added, 'There will be no "concessions" or changes in the program. The women will be put under the same rigorous training as the men.'

"Sure," I thought. "What he means is 'let's make these women cold and tough enough to be as brutal as their male counterparts.' It's that kind of continuing attitude that peace people want to change. It's why I joined this Peace Train. I want to be spending my time and energy changing warring attitudes, letting the world know that some people hate violence and injustice."

From the beginning it was evident on the Train that our motives as peacemakers were mixed. Some of us were passionately dedicated to using political analysis and corrective behavior to address the issues of injustice and violence that get in the way of peace. Some found the Train to be a place where we could tell our stories and give leadership in workshops. Some were a part of the system, and behaved out of the patriarchal model of dominance and submission, "power-over" instead of "power-with." Some were along for the ride and just wanted a time of R & R. Some wanted to see the sights and bring back treasures from the East.

At times, I felt excluded and afraid to be who I really was and, from the comments of others, I was not alone in that. At other times, I felt helpless to change what was going on and withdrew into my compartment. Some of us confronted what was going on – or was not going on – and resigned ourselves, perhaps too quickly, to what we thought we could not change. Some knew nothing about the grassroots termites called NGOs, and did not even realize that they are crucial to the tasks of correcting the injustice that blocks the coming of peace. Some put their own agendas above the well-being of the community, drawing attention to themselves to the detriment of others, much as "national interest" is used as an excuse for waging wars which seem to wipe out our efforts toward peace on a global level.

There were also real peacemakers on the Train, those who, when they saw conflicts building between themselves and others, or between groups and individual interests, took the risks of engaging the other and encouraging dialogue around differences, helping each to find the points of commonality that lead to a win-win situation for both parties. That is what peacemaking really is. Black-haired, American Molly was soft-spoken and clear, able to see both sides of any conflict, tender in her confrontation, gentle in encouraging respect for all points of view. Some who sincerely wanted to be peacemakers shot themselves in the foot with their unilateral decision making and deliberate or unwitting exclusion of others, much like the 50 nation states right now who are killing off their own people in civil war.

I thought that blonde, blue-eyed Ida of Sweden was one of those. She had cut me to the quick by excluding me from participation in the Rolling School because my white hair screamed that I was well past her idea of "young." She was adamant about keeping intact the boundary lines between "old" and "young." I was adamant about making available to both young and old the wisdom of the other. She was in power as "the leader," and I was not. I gave in, and it took me days of licking my wounds before I could go to her and talk about it.

When I did, I protested, "This is not the way to build a sense of community. Your excluding me hurts because it has built a wall between me and the young women. It's all the more troubling because in Finland we had stimulating conversations and real rapport with each other. Now, I feel exposed, like an outcast, and all because of my age, over which I have no control."

Ida defended her decision. "We are trying to develop leadership among the young women," she said. "They are not able to speak up when older women take over the conversation. It is important for them to be together just as a peer group."

I was angry at her insinuation. I hate being stereotyped as an old, insensitive, self-centered woman.

"Ida," I said with an edge in my voice, "I did nothing but listen when I attended that first session. I did not say a word. I do understand that there are times when groups need to establish and keep boundaries clear in order to have the benefits of support from their peers. There was never any announcement that The Rolling School was for that purpose. The description said it was to brief and debrief our experiences in the various countries, and I was eager to be a part of a group with that as the agenda. I wanted to test my own perceptions of what was happening over against those of the young women. Besides, when I was with those young women in Finland, they certainly did not appear intimidated. We engaged in very challenging conversations with lots of give and take, and they were quite articulate. Anyway, who made the decision that older women could not be included?"

"I did." There was finality in her tone. I was silent. Then she softened, "Now, if you would like to be a part of it at another time, you could come to Greece this summer." I knew that she was holding out the olive branch, wanting to make peace. The truth was that she got in her own way by assumptions that shocked me. First, that my taking a summer course would take the place of the Train experience; second, that I could make a trip to Greece just by wanting to do so. I was glad she was willing to talk about it; but sad to leave the conversation feeling resentful and helpless, not the least bit peaceful.

I had felt so good about my relationship with young Indian Sonimi in Helsinki that I went to her and asked if she would intercede for me with Ida and the group. She said simply, "No, I won't. That's the way it is, Beth." More feelings of being unacceptable and exposed. I tried to relate to the young women individually, but I was to feel more and more alienation from them as the Train moved along, a loss greater than I can explain. It is clear to me that all kinds of behavior can be allowed if we "go by the rules" made by someone in authority, but it does not bring peace either in the heart or in the outer community. I still grieve that loss.

We had it all on the Peace Train. On the inside, with its representation of 42 nations, it was a microcosm of the 189 nations of the world that we would meet in Beijing. Together we learned firsthand what we already knew at the head level, that making peace with justice is no easy task. Struggle is inevitable and, in fact, it cannot be done without courage and skill, sensitivity and openness to those with whom we differ and whose agendas are not our own. Nor can it be done without pain. Peacemakers are as affected by their own actions as others are. We must be big enough to forgive the hurts, respect the rights, persons, bodies and homes of others and commit ourselves to "talk it through," whether that be in the privacy of our homes or in the halls of our nations.

Peace, as I use the word here, is the absence of war, and it is much more than that. It is the presence of genuine community where the well-being of all persons and the planet is the modus operandi, where persons are valued in their own right and no one feels excluded. However sincere our attempts, as a total community, we did not achieve this on the Train. Our hearts were in the right place, and great good came out of the journey, in spite of the fact that we fumbled in much the same way we see the men fumbling at the negotiating tables in high places.

Looking back, it is easy to see that some of the essentials to genuine peacemaking were lacking from the beginning. Months before I was to leave for Helsinki, I was excited to receive the questionnaire asking me to tell what contributions I would like to make to the life of the Train. I returned it eagerly, wanting to give some of the gifts I believe I have. It was never followed up, and I was disappointed and frustrated. If others' responses were given attention, I did not hear of it. Even the scheduling of workshops to be presented during the ride was done by the people at "the top" after the Train was on the tracks.

Understandably, in Helsinki, precedence was given to the business of celebrating WILPF's 80 great years of working for peace and to keeping the organization alive as an international movement. There was also the monumental task of handling the logistics involved for dozens who needed visas for nine countries and information about how the whole thing was going to work. Not to mention handling the details of meeting these peoples' needs for food and lodging for 22 days on 17 rail "wagons" spread engine-to-caboose in one long line. Seven overnight stopovers on the way were a logistical challenge in themselves. It was even more complicated, given the fact that our entrance into some of the countries was through a "collective" visa, and individual Chinese visas were hard to come by. The planners were remarkably efficient in dealing with all these details.

As an ordained minister of The Church of the Brethren, (a name that is long overdue to be changed) I thought it was like a lot of weddings I've performed, where so much attention is given to preparing for the ceremony that there's no time left to prepare for how to live together for a lifetime. I understood the need for the first and felt frustrated that the more important part was subsumed under the lesser. We did not take enough time to hear each others' pains, joys, struggles, needs and hopes, and to hear them openly, without judgment or put-downs. I wondered often during that week in Helsinki, when there was so much "free time" for Train participants, if the people in charge did not see community building as a high priority, or did not know how to harness the gifts of women who had the skills to achieve it, given all the obstacles and pressures. What was clear, in the words of the Good Book, was "this we ought to have done and not to have left the other undone."[9]

Communication was complicated and difficult from the beginning. We did not have a language common to us all. Those who did not have English as a first language were at a tremendous disadvantage. Those of us who spoke only English found it hard to understand both the words and the implications of what others were saying when they spoke English. As someone said, "You never heard English spoken in so many ways in your whole life." At the beginning, a lot of faulty and conflicting "information" whirled around among the staff. I had trouble figuring out what was accurate, and who was responsible for what.

Once on the Russian train, a PA system made it possible for us to receive messages straight from "the horse's mouth," meaning Barbara, Executive Director of WILPF, and Esther, the travel agent in charge. Barbara's fair face was ringed with black hair and gave the impression that a smile was always ready to break through. She was the contact person with the women of the various countries and usually knew what the arrangements were. Even she, however, had incomplete knowledge of situations that developed as we traveled. All of us came to "alert" when Esther and Barbara's voices came over the air. We knew we needed to hear whatever they said. Representatives from each car diligently met and brought back information from "headquarters."

A lot of peacemaking and community building happened in informal settings. New friendships were made, within and across national lines. Liaisons were created; webs of support and encouragement were woven.

One such web that gave me hope was created back in Helsinki when I was with eight young women. Two of them, Anna of the US, fair and blonde in contrast with brown-skinned Josephine of London, were waiting for the others to go out to dinner and invited me to join them. We sat on a bench in the Square, and I asked Josephine to talk about her home, family and work. Her dark eyes smiled and she spoke with passion.

"I have 14- and 16-year-old daughters. I got started early at 17. I'm really concerned about the plight of black women in the EU [European Union] and that's at the heart of my work. It's so important to me. I get discouraged because the changes come so slowly."

"I think I know something of how you feel," I said. "I often think of Moses. He never got to the Promised Land; he only got to see over into it. But he seemed to think the wilderness journey was well worth the effort, in spite of the 'murmurings' and displeasures of the people he was leading."

"That's good!" Josephine was really listening. "I'll have to remember that the next time I'm feeling like I'm getting nowhere. Tell me, have you ever been to London, either one of you?"

Anna hesitated, and I started to tell about my trip to Scotland in 1993, preaching a feminist sermon in Christchurch, Edinburgh, the first woman ever to stand in that pulpit.

Anna chimed in, "What did you preach about?"

"Well, I groaned inside when they gave me three lectionary texts that didn't seem to have any possible connection to each other or to feminism. They were the death of Moses; Paul sending Onesimus, the slave, back to his master; and the man who gave a banquet and nobody came."

"What feminist ideas could you get out of that?" Anna asked.

"Well, I figured those stories had something in common, and finally realized that they all talked about the power of choice. That, for me, is one of the basic principles of feminism. Moses chose to move toward a goal in the face of opposition and despair. Onesimus chose to go back to his master and demand respect. And when nobody came to his great banquet, the host told his servants to bring people in off the street. He chose to reject rejection.

"The part that bothered me in that last story was that when the people came, he said to one of them, 'Why aren't you dressed appropriately?' In the sermon, I said 'that's an example of the sexism of the church'. It's like saying to women, 'You are welcome to come, but you're not acceptable as you are. You're not as acceptable as the males here because God is Father, and to be made in his image is to be male.' It's another Catch-22. If I question the male imagery of God and the language that excludes me, I am not acceptable to others. If I don't question it, I am not acceptable to myself. That leaves me with very hard choices to make. I often wonder if the woman who was not properly dressed, got up and left the banquet – or what choice did she make? My host canon had a little trouble with my interpretation of that one. He said I stretched the scriptures a bit to reach that conclusion. I figured if it bothered him that much, it must have struck a chord of some kind!"

Suddenly, five young women, black, brown and white, Jewish, American and Asian, full of vigor and vitality, came bouncing over the square toward us. Anna's Finnish hostess had suggested a restaurant, and we took off in that direction. It was too expensive for us. We finally found one we could afford. At dinner, we got to talking about what we hoped for on the Train.

Josephine began telling about the work she is doing in London to change the terrible conditions black women live under. "On the Train I want to work at getting a renewed emphasis on racism. I was really frustrated at the WILPF meeting. I thought they should have put that first and they didn't."

Emily was slender, Jewish and from New York. She had just had a 4-hour nap and energy was coming out her ears. "I agree with you. Human rights and racism must be the first priority. Why can't the older ones see that changed times require a different set of priorities?" She had the surety of a 17-year-old political analyst.

I, being the only "older" one there, responded. "We older people live out of a different perspective, both historical and current. You can't see life from our frame of reference and we can't see it from yours, so we need to be open to learn from each other. I say all the issues must be worked on simultaneously, each one of us choosing the one to which we can give the most energy and commitment. We need to organize others who feel the same, so that together we can make a greater impact than just one of us working alone can make. That's what I see you doing, Josephine."

Fair-haired Kirsten of Michigan spoke up: "I'm new to this political analysis talk, but that seems right to me."

Brown-skinned Sonimi, born in India, now living in London, was wise for her years. "In fighting against our own oppression," she said, "we must keep in mind Native people whose lot is worse than ours, everything taken away."

Wiry Beth of Minnesota was very much the gatekeeper of the group. One time when I had been interrupted in the middle of a sentence, she said she'd like to hear what I had to say.

Anna seemed open to hearing all the different perspectives, somewhat timid in presenting her point of view. She said little, as "Brethren" women often do.

Johanna, raised in Hong Kong and soft-spoken, seemed to have a lot of understanding of Russian life and current issues there.

Kirsten asked, "What causes war anyway? Were there two World Wars or was the second just a continuation of unresolved issues in the first?"

"I think all wars are a continuation of each other," I said. "The weapons change and the areas of conflict move from nation to nation, but the causes are all the same. Colonialism – imperialism – is one of those, nations wanting to extend their kingdoms and govern other peoples, and using land-grabbing, power-grabbing attitudes and tactics to do so. Cristobal Colon, otherwise known as Christopher Columbus, got the ball rolling when he 'discovered' America. It's ironic that his name just happens to be the first two syllables of the word, 'colonialization.'

"And look how long that kind of thing has been going on," I went on. "When I studied ancient history, we read stories about the 'marauding troops from the north before the dawn of civilization,' of walls being built all over the ancient world to prevent invasions, of fortresses being erected to hold off 'the enemy,' of countries being 'owned' first by one empire, then another. Seems like there's an inbred distrust and suspicion of people who're not like us.

"Take Finland, for example. We learned from our tour guide yesterday that it was conquered by the Swedes in the 1100s, fought over and made a Grand Duchy for the Russians in 1809, and finally gained its independence in 1917. Even then, from 1939 to 1944 in the Russo-Finnish wars, it lost most of the Karelia region and other lands to the Soviets. Catherine the Great was a great land-grabber.

"I'd like to think that's not happening anymore, but look at the wars being fought today. Israelis and Palestinians are shooting each other over the 'sacred' soil of Jerusalem. North and South Korea are at each other's throats. Protestants and Catholics can't get along in Ireland. In the East, Christians and Muslims are raging at each other. In Turkey, Kurds and Turks are fighting. Civil wars are raging in Sudan, Zaire, Zimbabwe, Bosnia, and on and on. China wants to annex Taiwan; Hong Kong's six million people are to be 'given' to China in 1997 by Great Britain. Granted, imperialist Britain stole Hong Kong from China in the first place, but why did China have the right to 'own' Hong Kong even then? Does *any* nation have the right to take over another for its own benefit? Imperialism of any kind puts nations on edge. The US is no exception. There are thousands and thousands of troops stationed in dozens of places, where, frankly, I don't think we belong at all."

Josephine's brown skin matched the gleam in her eyes. "People have too much dignity and self-respect to do nothing about it when they are deprived of privileges and lands and resources because of their ethnic background or the color of their skin. They rise up to protect themselves and resist domination. Some wars are fought to right the wrongs that have been done to people, and that's been going on forever."

"You said it, Josephine, and it's just as true today as it was in the ancient world. The Kurds are fighting for a 'land of their own' because they are hated and denied privileges in the countries of their birth. The blacks in America are told to 'go back home to Africa.' Native Americans and First Nations Canadians are the poorest of the poor because their lands were appropriated by the invading Europeans and they were savagely persecuted and killed, pushed onto reservations where the land was so poor that thousands died. It bothers me terribly that we celebrate Columbus Day in the US to commemorate Columbus 'founding' America, as though there were no people living here when he discovered the land. Right today, if some people in the US have their way, children who were born in my rich and privileged country will lose their citizenship and access to education and social programs because their parents are 'illegal immigrants'."

"Well, I'm convinced that racism is at the root of a lot of wars. There can't be peace until we change that." Josephine's voice was resolute, determined.

"I agree with you," the other Beth spoke up. "There's so much suspicion and distrust of people who are not like us. Why do we hate people who are different from us? Why do we think in 'us and them' terms, anyway? As if we're not all human?"

"The next step in that 'us and them' attitude is to think of others as 'the enemy'," I added. "Politicians are so afraid of loss of privilege and power that they have to invent an 'enemy' if there's not one easily recognizable, like the US and Russia with the Iron Curtain in between. I have a Japanese friend who tells horror stories about being Japanese in the US when the government saw them as one of "the enemy" and threw them out of their homes and into internment camps during World War II. That's a terrible blot on our history."

"Yeah, and there's that big gap between the rich and the poor in every country," Anna said. "We have this capitalistic, me-first spirit as if money is everything. People look out for themselves first and seem to close their eyes to the 'unlucky ones' around their feet."

Emily spoke up. "I think a lot of the trouble is needing to be in control, even of other people's lives. A lot of leaders want power over people and resources. We can't have peace until we begin to think about 'power-with' others."

"Right!" I said. "Lately I've been pondering this strange thought that wars start and keep going because of the basic human desire for 'a home of my own,' a homeland for the likes of me, a place for my people. Look at the Israelis and the Palestinians. Look at the Bosnians, Serbs and Croats. I think it's great to love your country, but we've got to change from clinging to that 'me-first' attitude and realize that it's actually in our self-interest to think of ourselves as one human family across all the lines of difference."

Johanna with the round face and soulful eyes looked up from the map she was reading and summed it all up, " I think you're all right, but tomorrow's another day. We've got three weeks to get these issues settled. We can't do it all tonight. Let's go back to our hotels."

It was 10 p.m. We scattered and took off in different directions. I had a sense of satisfaction, anticipating the opportunities we would have to share that kind of thoughtful conversation. It felt good to be there; I was thankful, as I walked to my hotel in the pink twilight glow of the Land of the Midnight Sun.

There were dozens of such interchanges on the Train journey. I wish I could have been a part of them all. We shared many issues that were dear to our hearts, and built bridges of friendship and understanding among our nations. We learned firsthand what life is like for people in far places. We tried to walk in others' shoes for a while.

Even so, inevitably, conflicts happened. As a consultant in human relations, some of my time is spent helping people to learn how to manage conflict creatively. I've found a particular little piece of theory quite useful. It suggests that there are three ways of dealing with conflict. A "moving against," fighting response is win/lose: "I don't want to hear another word." An "avoiding" response is lose/lose: "I'm getting out of here now." "Moving toward" is a win/win response: "Let's talk about it. I want to understand you."

One attempt at making peace, dealing with conflict, in our total community is vivid in my mind. I still feel the frustration and resignation as I walked away from it with more feelings of separation than of community.

It was the only time during the entire three weeks that the whole group was called together. We were in Alma-Aty, Kazakhstan, on a stifling hot day. Hundreds of us seated ourselves practically on top of each other on dusty grass under dusty trees in a dusty park. We must have been a sight to behold! The stated purpose of the meeting was to address the tensions that had developed on the Train. It turned out to be a time for women of color to let the rest of us know that they were experiencing racial slurs and insensitivity. The leader took firm control of what was allowed and not allowed to be said; there was to be no conversation around any issue other than race. That immediately set a tone of "moving against," of exclusion among us. I spoke once, saying that there were other tensions than those of race that I would like to see addressed, that ageism was one.

The leader responded, "That is an inappropriate comment. We will restrict what we have to say to racism."

I felt punished and shut out, aware of how immensely difficult it is to make peace. We get in our own way when we avoid genuine interaction over whatever differences cause conflict among us. I would never minimize the importance of confronting my racism; I know I have many blind spots that are all too clear to women of color, but there was no"peace" in me when that meeting was over. The leader's response was "win/lose." She won and I lost. I felt disheartened, torn apart, discouraged, and certainly without a sense of community. Feelings of separation are the first step toward war.

All of this is not to say that the Peace Train failed in its attempt to make peace. In spite of all our shortcomings and frustrations, and quite beyond them, I believe we did make a singular contribution to the very complex task of making peace in a war-weary world. Who is to say, for example, what impact we had on the decision of President Jacques Chirac of France to stop nuclear testing? Who is to say what influence we had on US President Bill Clinton's decision to sign the Nuclear Test Ban Treaty a year later and to speak out against the use of landmines? Who is to say how much the Train's message, "War is Obsolete," encouraged leaders of all nations to come to the peace tables? Who is to say how many bridges were built over chasms of race and nationality, color and gender? How many people are newly aware that there is no such thing as "a pure race," rather, that we are indeed "one family"? Our guide on the bus in Turkey said it out loud:

Today in Turkey you cannot find an original Turk. Original ones you can find only in Mongolia. If you went there and then followed the shape of the map where the Turkish people are living, you can see the way the Turks have come to Asia Minor. Just imagine, on the way they mixed themselves with all the people who were living along the way. Therefore their face is changed, their body is changed. We are all a mixture of each other.

Is not the same thing true in every country? China has about 60 nationalities living within its borders. Turkey has 40; the United States, who knows how many? The people of the world are so mobile that every race is found in every place. To try to describe a "Chinese" or "American" citizen is as impossible as to walk to the moon from planet Earth. The idea that there could be such a thing as a "homeland" for a particular race of people seems illusory here on the brink of the 21st century. Fighting wars for that purpose is unconscionable, for they exact far too high a price in human life and natural resources. Instead, we need to work at valuing our differences and moving toward understanding and respect for the people of every race and religious preference. We need to think "neighbors" rather than "friends or enemies"; "ours," rather than "yours or mine." We need to teach our children that we are "family," and the well-being of one determines the well-being of all. As folk singer Pete Seeger has written: "We are all strangers and cousins."

The Train was in the business of making visible and real that *presence* of all together as "one family." I know firsthand that there is profound mystery in the power of Presence. I learned it first in 1972 when my daughter died and my brothers and sisters and relatives and friends *came* and physically surrounded me with love and support. I knew what it meant all over again four years later when I marched with the Peace People of Ireland in the meeting of the North and South on the Bridge of the River Boyne. I experienced it again on the Peace Train where the power of presence went deep into me. I knew in my gut the truth, *"We are all one family."*

I shall never forget when we arrived in Odessa, Ukraine. The welcome was electrifying to me. I sent a fax home to my family:

We just received a welcome here that had me – and others – weeping openly. Several thousand waving Ukrainians were at the railway station crowded in behind an "official" delegation of the Orthodox Church. The Patriarch in full black dress, red stole and high hat stood alongside a woman in a headdress of flowers, wearing a brocaded gown of red and gold and holding an impressively large round loaf of decorated bread with salt to dip it in. We learned that this is a Ukrainian symbol of peace and friendship. As she moved through the crowd, we took bits of the bread, dipped it in the salt, and ate it. At the same time, other women in traditional dress moved through the crowd presenting to us red roses, white gladiolas, and purple, red and pink asters. A band spiffily dressed in red coats, black pants, black shoes, and dress caps of black with gold braid, played a lively march and then the Ukrainian national anthem. Our peace banners were waving everywhere!

We moved toward big buses which were waiting for us with women as our guides. The crowd was waving; we were waving. A stooped old man with a white beard and no teeth stood near the barricade, tears streaming down his sunken face. As I came near, I reached over and clasped his outstretched, weathered hand in my own. "Peace, peace," he cried out in English, and I responded, "Peace, peace." I felt almost guilty at the appreciation and hope he seemed to have in us as peacemakers. Children waved wildly; young people smiled and called, "Peace." An old woman bowed to me as I passed her. It was overwhelming; suddenly I was in tears!

I paused to let the moment imprint itself on my memory, marveling at the milling crowd of thousands.

Lynette put an arm around my shoulder. "What can we do with this, Beth?" she asked.

"I can only weep," I said through my tears. "Oh, how the people of the world long for peace."

The Train, with all its humanness, was like a long arm reaching out to the far corners of the earth, letting people know that they are not alone in their struggles, their misery and their hopes, that they are indeed a part of one family, our own, and that together, we *will* make a difference in this war-weary world. This was our hope as we crossed all those many borders on our way to Beijing, the words of the poet unrelenting in my ears:

I am only one
But still I am one.
I cannot do everything, but I can do something.
And because I cannot do everything,
I will not refuse to do the something I can do."[10]

5

Crossing Borders

From of old there are not lacking things that have attained Oneness.
The sky attained Oneness and became clear; the earth attained Oneness
and became calm; the spirits attained Oneness
and became charged with mystical powers...
All of them are what they are by virtue of Oneness.[1]

As we crossed the border from the Peace Train to the noisy, congested city of Beijing, our days in Finland seemed far behind us. Yet, as I stood there at the train tracks in the milling midnight crowd, my mind swept back in memory to the day before we climbed on that first train in Helsinki to begin our 6,000-mile journey. Barbara's commentary at that time played itself over in my mind.

"It has been a big task to know how to organize for the Peace Train and we have chosen as our theme, Crossing Borders. We want this to be a kind of headline as we are crossing borders. And now we are crossing borders toward the great country in which a great journey begins. We think we know what we will see, for we have heard a lot of stories and we have a lot of knowledge, but we should remind ourselves that we are traveling to areas which may be different and that we are open and we are listening. I think all the groups that are inviting us expect to be sharing with us and that we are, most of all, listening to them.

"We are also crossing the borders from being here to seeing ourselves on the Train. This is another learning experience in which we learn about the other, but also a lot about ourselves. This is the second dimension. Then, third, to come here we had to cross geographical borders and this is something." We all laughed. We knew how much time and energy everybody had spent getting visas.

"Now we are successful and we have all the visas and also very thankful to the governments who invited us and gave us permission to see their sights. But we have to remind ourselves that the majority of people who try to travel, they do not have the visa and there, too, are rough borders. You know, we are very fortunate. When I think about the majority of the participants coming from the United States, Canada and Mexico, you usually have passports, but if somebody wants to come to your country, it is nearly impossible. You have to show your bank account. You have to have an invitation letter and you [applause] you have to fill out where you live and other information before you can get a visa."

In that gap between touching the ground in Beijing and knowing what to do next, I thought, "How amazing that I am crossing this border, into a city as foreign to me as any I've ever visited. Borders – what strange, manmade concoctions they are, to mark the beginnings and endings of nation states, invisible edges, imaginary dividing lines between two different geographical units of land, walls keeping people in or out. I wish we didn't have borders at all."

I don't like the inherent dualisms borders create: mine/yours, in/out, old/young, enemy/friend, native-born/foreign – dualisms that divide us, separate us into categories that make it hard for us to think of our planet as belonging to us all and of us human beings as one family. My dream is that one day all the "iron curtains" will crumble and we will become a true "community of nations" who walk freely across all borders.

But then, standing there on Chinese soil, I felt like the foreigner I am; borders were all too real.

The dozens of borders we had crossed since we climbed onto that first train in the wee hours of a morning three weeks prior kept racing through my mind – borders of nations, nationalities, continents, religions, races, colors, ages, genders, languages, ideas, experiences and more. In spite of, or maybe because of, all our struggles, hurts, misunderstandings and human frailties, we had molded ourselves into a sense of belonging to one another. "Here in Beijing," I thought, "we will be known as the people of the Peace Train, a community linked by a common experience."

We *did* cross those borders, and I knew I would be pondering the amazing learnings I had gained from each one for a long time.

We had crossed the border into Russia twice, once from the west and once from the south. We had come into St. Petersburg in drizzling rain, buses waiting at the station to take us to our hotel. There, a brass band was playing *America the Beautiful* and then, *The Star-Spangled Banner* – "And the rockets' red glare, and bombs bursting in air, gave proof through the night that our flag was still there." The hated words rang in my ears, and I shrivelled inside at the violence, individualism and nationalism that have become "the American Way," none of which fit the scene of people on a peace journey. What's more, these songs did not include the other 41 countries that made up the Train.

Yet, the music stirred in me a sense of faraway home, of the land of my birth, where freedoms are more clear against the backdrop of un-freedom in other countries. Tears welled up at the warmth of "homeland" I felt through having others salute it by trumpet, sousaphone and trombone, especially those who had been touted as "the enemy" for so long. America *is* my country, I realized, a land of untold privileges and opportunities. It has been good to me. Like it or not, I will always be, inescapably an American.

Hotel Moskva was incredibly impressive with its semicircular marble facade, big solid windows and inviting doors. A bent old woman, looking very out of place, stood a discreet distance away from those doors. A beggar, she wore a tattered, green babushka above a mouthful of gold teeth. As I got off the bus, she took to following me, speaking all the while in Russian. I felt sick, knowing of my privilege and her lack of it. A foreigner, I could walk through those doors and find a bed on which to rest my tired body; a native-born citizen who had fallen on hard times, she could not. She began to wander back and forth in front of a row of compact cars with license plates that looked like an eye examination chart, all sorts of weird letters in that strange, Cyrillic alphabet.

As the band broke into *Dixieland,* another old woman appeared, her gray hair covered with a black babushka sporting a foppish red rose. A long, dark sweater stretched toward purple socks and worn, green bedroom slippers. Both women had bowed shoulders and sunken chests; both thin faces bore the look of suffering. The one was actively following me and begging; the other stood with a look of resignation, her arms folded across her flat stomach.

"She looks like she has endured even more than the other, had more difficulty, maybe a harder life," I mused.

Compartment mate, Patricia Hawley, was standing nearby and answered, "Yes, her face is more wrinkled, more sunken and she's thinner. She has a burdened look about her."

"Pat, these women look so old, but I wonder if they are any older than I am."

"To judge their age would be almost impossible. They could be pensioners, I think, somewhere past 60, maybe 65."

"And I'm 72. My face is not as worn as theirs, as rugged looking. I'd guess they have gone through much more hardship than I have."
Pat was somber. "Poverty hits very, very hard here in Russia."

"Yeah. That's one reason I want to attend the *Perestroika* workshop tomorrow. I want to find out what effect 50 years of *Perestroika* have had on the women of this society. Fifty years! I was surprised to read that in the workshop description. I just read *The Cloister Walk* by Kathleen Norris. She says 'the desolation of a slum reveals who we are as a nation, a people, far better than the gleaming stores of a shopping mall.'[2] I think the numbers of homeless people on the streets are an index to the quality of a nation's integrity."

"Oh, I love it!" Pat said, looking toward the woman in the green babushka. "Isn't that nice?" A Peace Train woman had just handed her a dollar. The older woman bowed to her and they exchanged smiles. It was touching; I was glad for the friendly touch, sad for the realities behind it for both women.

The lobby was jammed. Our spokeswomen collected the passports by wagon colors and whisked them off to officials who had the task of registering them. We learned that this process, which would be repeated in every city, would take a couple hours. Patience was the key. Thank goodness that a foresighted planning committee had arranged for group visas.

Visas back in our hot little hands, there was the business of finding roommates and getting settled into our rooms. Heavyset women, smartly dressed in western street clothes, suits of all colors, hose and heels, helped us find our way. Barb Anderson and I paired up and after a quick check-in, met the buses which would take us to the plenary session at Nicolai Palace.

Victoria, our guide, spoke with pride.

St. Petersburg is situated on marshy land around the Neva River and on 42 islands in the Neva Delta. The city is comparatively young, in comparison to Moscow or Kiev, founded at the beginning of the 18th century on 16 May, 1703, by the Russian Czar, Peter the First. We call him Peter the Great, whose idea was to open a window on Europe. The name of the city, St. Petersburg, was given by Peter the First after his patron saint, the apostle Peter, Saint Peter. The city was called St. Petersburg from 1703 to 1914. In 1914, the first World War started. Russia fought against Germany and they decided to change the name. They replaced the German-sounding name with a Russian name, Petrograd, the city of Peter. After the Revolution and Lenin's death in 1924, the city was given the name, Leningrad. Five years ago, it was given back its own name, St. Petersburg. Psychologically for us, it is quite difficult to call our city St. Petersburg – you know, speaking among ourselves in common conversation, we quite often use the name Leningrad, but only because we did it for many years before. Also because now, the city has a number of features which are characteristic features for Leningrad. Anyway, we will see that history is a process in which all of us are participants. Right? That's why you are here.

"Hm-m-m," I thought. "More cities of the world than not have been named for men who were flaunting their 'victories' and bolstering their egos. A little like marriage, men changing women's names to theirs, a vestige of the ownership talked about in the Bible." I remembered how I felt when I married and gave up my name. An important part of my identity had been taken away, like Victoria said.

We rounded a curve and the broad waters of the Neva lay true blue before us, a magnificent sight under scudding clouds in skies, as "blue as mine." On the far banks, stately yellow-brick buildings rose so close to one another as to appear to be a solid wall. On our side of the wide Neva, buildings were decorated with beautiful wrought iron works, which Victoria called "the metal lace of St. Petersburg." When we passed the famous Hermitage Museum, her voice swelled with national pride. "This museum is one of the biggest in the world, bigger than the Louvre in Paris, with 2.7 million items of art. It was badly damaged in the war, but they managed to restore it to its original design."

She pointed out the summer palace of Peter and his wife, Catherine the First. "Here on the left is the marble palace built by Catherine the Second for one of her many escorts, Count Orlov." Laughter rippled through the group. Catherine's reputation with men has outlasted her other "achievements."

On the right, the famous Pavlov Institute. Everybody knows Pavlov's dogs. The university here was founded in 1890 with 16 students; now there are 22,000. Lenin passed his exams here after he was expelled from Kazan University for participating in revolutionary movement. Pushkin is our greatest poet.

We passed Pushkin's home. Victoria pointed out several cathedrals that had been state-controlled museums and now were worshiping communities. Then, we came to Senate Square. The bus stopped, and she called our attention to "the most famous monument of the city."

Catherine commissioned a French sculptor to create this statue, and it took him 12 years to do it. The horse here symbolizes Russia, and the snake under the hind legs of the horse is the symbol of all the enemies of Peter's reforms. The inscription reads, "To Peter the First from Catherine the Second."'

Back on the bus, Victoria said proudly,
Our city is the second largest of Russia, the second after Moscow. They have nine million inhabitants; we have five. Now we are approaching Nicolai's Palace – your meeting.

We entered the Great Hall between massive, green marble columns, climbed up four flights of stairs and entered a large auditorium. Breathtaking. White columns, arched ceilings and a chandelier with thousands of tiered crystal lights reflected colors like the prisms of a lighthouse beacon. Women, and one man on stage gave greetings; interpreters rushed to keep up. The male speaker, representing the government, opened his remarks by saying, "I must say you are a beautiful audience and I am excited to be surrounded by such beautiful women." A twitter, half-moan and half embarrassment, went through the audience. The truth was that we were a bedraggled-looking bunch of women professionals who were serious about our mission and angry to be defined by our beauty or lack of it. As the women on the dais spoke, he ducked his head into a magazine, probably realizing that he had goofed and certainly had not "pleased the ladies."

We were tired before the meeting began. It took hard concentration to listen through interpreters who were remarkable, yet still had difficulty keeping up with what was being said without pauses. At one point, one of our group rudely shouted, "We can't hear you." Then, an Australian woman raised a question about domestic violence which was immediately re-interpreted to relate to war and international conflict. There is not even a word for "domestic violence" in the Russian language, a fact that illustrates their discomfort with this kind of question and their lack of legal recourse for victims of it.

The next day, the introductory speaker gave some firm instructions: "We ask you to address your questions only to the areas presented by the speakers. Yesterday the questions did not do that." The tension was as palpable as the shame of a child whose hands are caught in the cookie jar.

We had the choice of several workshops: disarmament, conversion and Chechnya, women and business, women and work, education, health concerns, and the *Perestroika* years. "Perestroika," one speaker said, "means 'change,' and the changes over the past 50 years have rested disproportionately on the shoulders of women."

"That's an understatement," I muttered to the woman beside me. "Not just the last 50 years. Hasn't that been true for aeons?"

"The life expectancy of women here has been about 45 to 60 years," continued the speaker, "though that is changing now. As women are giving gifts of encouragement and support to each other, they are beginning to live longer. In Russia, women are not thought to have value after the reproductive years are over; there's a kind of social death. We want to change that. Many are on the streets as a result of withdrawal of state support. They have lost access to education and health care. Some are hungry and homeless. They are the first to be laid off jobs. We have the right to abortion, and many of us are choosing not to have children."

I went to the workshop on women in the workplace. "When we study the unemployment of women in Russia," the speaker said, "we are face to face with a picture of discrimination against women. The economic impact of *Perestroika* is severe: 75 percent of the unemployed are women and they are in deep distress. The average monthly wage is 30 US dollars. To buy an apartment with one room, kitchen, corridor and bathroom is $17,000 and you must pay cash in two days. People are forced to do flexi-time and part time and that leads to instability. The number of suicides is increasing."

As we waited outside the bus the next day, Amelia and I chatted about everyday stuff, maybe to escape the heaviness of what we were learning. We talked about the little yellowed soap bars that looked like Mama's homemade lye soap of long ago and smelled like sulphur. We talked about being bitten by mosquitoes and the "5,000 little gismoes" her mother had brought along on the trip, one being an electronic insect repeller. Then we turned to essentials. Having safe drinking water was a big deal on this trip, sometimes hard to come by, and she was carrying two bottles.

"Where'd you get your water?" I asked.

"Right down there." She pointed to a small kiosk not far away. "It's tasty water, too. Last night it wasn't very good. Good, clear water today. Are you going to the workshops?"

"Yes, I am, are you?"

"Yes, I sure am. But first I'll walk you down there to get water."

"I'm on bus seven; where are you?"

"Seven? I'm on that one, too."

With our precious bottles of water, we climbed on the bus, took our seats, and sat with Eugenia, our guide, waiting for the discourteous latecomers.

"The reason we are waiting and waiting here," she said, "is that we cannot get all these 242 people under our command."

At my elbow, Pat said, "There is a shift. Some of us like to have a structure, but here we need to be a little more flexible within the structure."

"It feels like a pattern to me," I said. "One of the sure things here is that whenever a time is announced for anything, it won't be then. Some people count on that and then make us even later."

The buses finally started to move, and Eugenia brought us back to reality by summing up the previous day's workshops.

It's a very complicated time for our country, a very difficult time, called transition period. We changed a lot in our attitude to today's life and our history. For people of my generation [she might have been 45] it's a quite difficult time, because we grew up with very different ideas in our heads compared to today. All things considered to be important when I was 15–20 years old, now we have another attitude toward those things.

Moving south toward Kiev later that day, we reflected on our impressions of Russia and what we had learned. Some thought the sessions seemed staged, with almost rigid formality, that they were giving us "the party line," that they were guarded, rather than engaging in genuine interaction. Others thought that there was a genuine desire to give information. I thought we were insensitive to their leadership, and I wished for more time to interact with individual women about their own lives.

When we crossed the border into Ukraine and got off in Kiev, a great old-world city rose about us. Had it not been for the changed atmosphere, it would have seemed as if we had not left Russia – warm greetings, bread and flowers as symbols of friendship and goodwill, a band playing, women singing.

At the sessions, the same depressing facts, and to those were added the Chernobyl disaster. We were once again reminded of the horror at the time it happened: fires out of control, 4,000 people dead, mass evacuations, a grim picture. It was heavy, hearing about it from those who were living through it. On the other hand, here we were, face to face with women of remarkable spirit and commitment, determined to help people rebuild their lives and their nation, actively working to correct the grim situation of post-Chernobyl disease, death and poisoning of the land. Hope and perseverance rang through their stories. We saw wonderful demonstrations of spontaneous and generous caring.

I shall never forget walking with Zina on the streets of Kiev, encountering a pitiful, bowed old woman, her clothes in tatters, her bare toes bald through cloth slippers so torn she had to shuffle to keep them on her feet, losing them with every other step. Without hesitating, Zina went to her, embraced her, put rubles in her hand, and spoke tenderly. As we turned away, Zina's cheeks were wet with tears. "There are so many," she said, "and there is so little we can do to help; 145,000 rubles is one US Dollar here. A loaf of bread costs 50 rubles." I brushed my own tears away as we walked on.

I was equally shaken at the workshop on women's health. A dentist spoke of her work with the children of Ukraine, echoing concerns voiced by Zina earlier: "We have two and three-year-olds who have no teeth at all. By the age of 11 or 12, many of our children have 70 percent of their teeth extracted or diseased. The lands of the farmers are poisoned lands. The crops carry large amounts of radiation, so that the incidence of thyroid cancer has risen from 4 cases in 1985 to 400 in 1995. One promising thing is that Japan now has a program where some of our children are taken there to spend several months at a time, to rest and recover away from the polluted areas here. We hope to get help from the United States with similar programs. We want to work with you for the complete eradication of nuclear weapons everywhere."

I learned that all sorts of efforts and groups are working to bring about change: The Council of Working Women, Ukraine Leader Foundation, Ukraine Peace Council, Council for the Protection of the Children of Chernobyl, the Green Party, the Society of Nature Protection, The Women's Community Center. The government of Ukraine has set up Committees on Motherhood and Childhood Protection, on Education and Health. NGOs are active in lots of areas on a wide spectrum of issues. I felt humble in the presence of women of such determination and generosity. Not only had they lived through the bombing of their city in World War II, but now, a second time, they were rebuilding their country, this time after nuclear disaster.

From Kiev, the Train moved southwest across a wide valley, through lush fields with flocks of geese and ducks in puddles and on ponds here and there. Rich corn fields and gardens slowly gave way to dry desert land, which gave way in turn to fields of corn and sunflowers that looked parched and thirsty. A major oil refinery belched black smoke into the sky. We passed through villages full of pitifully poor, rundown shacks, people with a look of stoic suffering on their faces, a railway station where a man lay asleep on the pavement at the feet of people waiting for trains.

At 4:00 a.m., we were awakened by our hostess, who finally got through to us, in her limited English and our non-existent Russian, that we should be ready for passport check in Moldavia. I suddenly felt extremely deficient in my knowledge of geography and history, couldn't remember ever even hearing of Moldavia, and I knew that no stopover was planned. Now I know that Moldavia, also called "Moldova," is a tiny country the size of the state of Maryland, the sandwich filling between giant Ukraine to the northeast and Rumania to the southwest, the shortest route between Kiev and Bucharest. Whether or not we intended to stop, our Train had to go through it.

In spite of the fact that we never set foot on it, it became the subject for a poet's pen. We crossed Moldavia's borders not once, but four times, in and out going south, in and out coming back north, and every time, it's the gospel truth, it was four o'clock in the morning. This fact inspired Mims Butterworth on the Blue Wagon to write a poem which got to be a mantra chanted in good humor every time Moldavia's borders came into view.

Peace Train Nightmare

Is that Tatiana at the door? Breathe deep and count to ten.
It's 4 o'clock in the morning, so it's Moldova again.

Though problems in Bulgaria may be well beyond our ken,
We know one thing: at 4:00 AM it's Moldova again.

There's always a new rumor, about where we'll be and when,
But at 4 o'clock in the morning it's Moldova again.

One thing we have in common, be we Baha'i or follower of Zen.
If it's 4 o'clock in the morning, we're in Moldova again.

I think we're getting testy. Could it be the estrogen?
No, it's just because it's 4:00 AM and it's Moldova again.

We think we're making progress, but no matter where we've been,
By 4:00 AM each morning, it's Moldova again.

We're 234 women and about a dozen men.
Can't one of us deflect our train from Moldova again?[3]

Rumania's border check was next, and it was a border check to outdo them all! I awoke that hot August morning to a sun that had pierced the sky with a blood-red, angry streak. The Train was stopped still, no grinding-wheel melodies. We had been told earlier that the wheels had to be changed from wide to narrow gauge in order to travel through this country. I was like a child at Christmas, wondering then how the train got under the tree, wondering now, how on earth they could change the wheels with all of us on the train?

I dressed in a hurry and dashed to the end of the car where Letitia was standing. "I want to get off and watch how they do this," I said with motions. She shook her head and pointed outside the car. We were 10 or 12 feet off the ground in a railroad yard surrounded by rows and rows of rusty iron wheels! We had been hoisted into the air by ancient-looking, green hydraulic lifts. The train had been cut in half; both sides now up in the air. Men in greasy coveralls were on their knees, loosening bolts underneath the newly painted red, white and blue *Pectopah* cars. Smokers loafed nearby. A great crane lifted one set of wheels high into the air, lowered them down, pushed the others out from under the cars, and brought the new ones into place for the workers to attach and tighten. And it wasn't just the wheels. The whole iron undercarriage was unbolted and replaced.

"I'm putting myself into the hands of perfect strangers," I thought as I watched. "I hope they take their work seriously and get those nuts and bolts as tight as they need to be." Four hours later, the jerk, jerk, jerk of reconnecting, and we were on our way across this country a little larger than the state of Ohio, 306 miles from east to west and bathed in brilliant sunshine.

When we arrived in Bucuresti (Bucharest), hundreds of people greeted us at the station and an "official" delegation, elegantly dressed, offered the great loaf of decorated bread and the traditional salt, along with red and pink carnations. Mine was warm pink, like the smile on the face of the woman who gave it to me. As we moved toward the buses, guards held the people back. I wanted contact with them, and wondered if it was courtesy or the need to control that kept us separated.

On the way to the meeting place, our guide sang a haunting Rumanian song full of pathos. I wanted more when she shifted to *I Could Have Danced All Night*, and asked us all to join in.

"Bucuresti is a city of three million people," she began. "It is an old city and in this day we are having a lot of troubles."

Our meeting place that day was quite a contrast to the grand halls of St. Petersburg. It fit the picture of deprivation and poverty and "troubles" the guide talked about, nothing ornate and "high-government" about it. Walls around two sides of the room were wooden, brown. To our left, windows ran the full length of a wall; behind us, dark gray. The floor was gritty with the dust of a dry and thirsty land. There was a sense of being among the common people here, a struggling people, hard to understand even through a translator who seemed to be having as much trouble as we were. Passion was not lacking in these presentations. It became clear to me that the issues that confront women in one Balkan country are much the same throughout them all. With the withdrawal of the resources of state in the wake of the change from Communism to "the market economy," the same electric shock burns through the entire region. For the women, "market economy" or "democracy" means that the privileges of health care, food, lodging, education, comfort and recreation are only for those who have money and property.

When someone raised the issue of women's equality with men, the executive secretary of the National Women's League responded. "There is an ancient Nordic mythology. At the beginning, there were two trees floating in a river. The gods intervened and turned them into a woman and a man, to whom they gave equal powers and equal rights. That's the way it is supposed to be. Actually, in Rumania today, 75 percent of married women are exposed to verbal violence from their husbands. Some are beaten if they protest; others are afraid to protest. The Commission on Elimination of Discrimination Against Women is working with courts to give these women some redress. Shelters have been started with the financial support of corporations and the Department of Corrections. It is a huge problem here."

A woman representing the Association of Democratic Women in Rumania added, "Men are violent because we women are considered the weaker, fairer sex. We must act strongly to give them a new idea. If we are united, we can find the necessary strength to erase this scourge that affects us all."

Maria Corda of the National Abolitionists' Organization said, "We know that pornography contributes to this violence. We've had some successes in passing legislation making it illegal, but we are not free of it. It is often concealed and circulated undercover, even though violators are severely punished under the law."

One speaker said, "Our work is directed toward old women alone. Certain manifestations of violence are against old women, especially lonely, homeless old women. We are working to provide shelters for these women."

We met the next day in the Parliament building built by the infamous Ceausescu in the 1950s, a sharp contrast to the day before. A massive building of Stalinesque architecture, it had the feel of a prison. The doors actually looked like prison doors – heavy metal, circles in squares within a panel about 8 feet high. The building felt as heavy as the burden it had placed on the people during its construction. It looked out on a controlled, geometric scene. No room for freedom here.

Lynette and I stood at the top of long steps looking down on what was supposed to be a replica of the Champs Elysées in Paris. Box-like buildings lined streets that were rutted and in need of repair. Blocks of broken concrete jutted out of the sidewalks.

"This place has the feeling of having been damaged extensively," Lynette said.

"It's depressing," I agreed. "Even the flower beds look oppressive." There were some thirsty greens, a bit of red surrounded by a gray planting of some sort, and big piles of dirt waiting to be put into lawns or other flower beds.

I knew I could not even imagine the horror of the peoples' burdens and powerlessness. "You know, this place was built while people starved at its feet, thanks to the greed of Ceausescu. To think he dominated Rumania for 24 years, bleeding the people to death the whole time!"

Inside, we walked through wide halls between massive marble columns, on floors with intersecting circles and squares, brown on beige marble. A red carpet led the way into the inner sanctum, which was guarded by dour men standing stiffly at attention in their navy blue uniforms. We were led into a huge dining room where small, round tables were set with white linen cloths and red napkins. Long tables were loaded with food as beautiful as it was good, rosettes here and there, tiny baskets of tomatoes with cheese filling, red pepper decorations over platters of fish, salmon, roast beef and pork, salads of all kinds. You name it, it was there. Tantalizing desserts, a chocolate mousse so rich that after four bites I could eat no more. It was all delicious, and it stuck in my throat as I thought of the poverty that lay outside, and the members of our group who were not "in."

After dinner, we passed through a hall where two wall pictures jumped out at me, one of a woman pleading in front of a hideous monster; the other, three women with resolute, tearful faces holding identical, nude babies in one arm while, with the other, they pulled at protesting, child-size replicas of themselves. I shuddered.

I was even more sickened later when we visited the Patriarchata Cathedral built in 1656. A rope divided the people from the heavily gilded altar. Icons were everywhere. A young priest in his black dress strolled about, apparently governing what people do in there. A soldier stood at ease with his gun resting on the floor near a casket draped in gold cloth, past which people were moving in a long line. Several old women knelt there, kissing it; the young priest called to them impatiently to hurry along. An old priest, with a long white beard, a long black robe and gold stole, was sitting in a darkened area close to the casket, three young men kneeling at his feet. He touched each one on the forehead with a gaudy red cross, and reached toward me as I came along. Another shudder, and I made sure I was beyond him.

The control of women in that place was palpable. For me, the separation of people from leaders and the sense of abuse of power in the name of the Sacred were all too reminiscent of my own sexist Protestant church. I've often thought, during the past years, that "Going to church is damaging to my health as a woman." I could hardly wait to get out into the open air and breathe. Being an ordained clergywoman and feeling that way about the church that ordained me troubles me a lot.

It was my day to feel sickened. At the workshop on "Women and Violence," we were told that 80 percent of the Rumanian people live below the poverty level; families with two, three, or even four children live in one room; prostitution is on the rise. During the 1980s, there were three women in every maternity bed in the hospital; one million abortions in 1991; few women in politics; a grim picture.

Later, on the way to the Village Museum, US consumerism blazed everywhere. "McDonald's Hamburgers" covered the whole highway. A building that bore the marks of bombing held a sign in bold English: "Live Life to the Max, Pepsi!" Hollywood was there, along with Kent cigarettes, Panasonic, Marlborough, Kodak and another, "McDonald's in Rumania."

"Yuk!" I thought to myself.

The Village Museum was a redeeming place for me, a whole delightful park full of Rumanian history. I left the group and wandered about alone among buildings showing how the people lived hundreds of years ago. A high, rickety, homemade-looking windmill fascinated me. I stuck my head into tiny little storage houses that reminded me of playing as a child in the dark root cellar on the farm. Vines were intertwined around wooden fences carved into intricate designs showing pride in one's work. Across barriers of language, using smiles and motions, I made friends with Nicoleta, a mother who sat with her beautiful, black-haired, four-year-old son, Soare Silviu Gabriel, on one of the porches. When I took their picture, his black eyes changed from questioning to excited. I got their names and address and promised to send the picture to them.

Near an art display under a big tree, lace doilies hung on a line, and a gray-haired man played a tiny musical instrument that sounded like a siren calling people to a land of enchantment.

The next day sounded another hopeful note: there are 41 active NGOs in Rumania. One called "Dignity" works for the protection of women and families. Lawyers are available to help in cases of domestic violence. There is a National Organization for the Abolition of Torture. Both boys and girls are given free education for eight years. At a workshop on "Women and Health," the speaker concluded, "Many remarkable women are working for change here, to bring about peace and freedom from poverty and disease."

As we left Bucuresti, the Train moved through stunning, high mountain scenery shrouded in mist, with occasional glimpses through the clouds of villages built on tiers on the steep mountainsides. I stood at the window of the fast-moving Train, the words of *Finlandia* ringing in my ears, giving thanks for eyes to see all this beauty and for the privilege of being here, meeting women who, in the face of almost unsurmountable odds, face life with strength, courage, and determination.

On the border of Bulgaria, I was off the train in time to see the wheel-changing ritual from underneath. Some of our women walked in the field of purple and yellow flowers that stretched out lazily beyond the rusty iron wheels. A hungry-looking mongrel slouched about looking for something to devour.

Surprisingly, we arrived early into Sofia, where hundreds of Bulgarians greeted us on the train platform, more hundreds jammed behind gates holding them back. I enjoyed talking in motions with four 11-year-old girls: Tanya, Eudora, Tildora and one whose name I can't spell or pronounce. They presented the bread of friendship and the salt in which to dip the morsels. An old woman who spoke no English smiled and put a marguerite, a large daisy, in my hand. Crowds milled about us. As we waited for the buses, we sang with the guitar: *Finlandia, Gonna Ride 22 Days on the Peace Train and Study War No More, She's Got the Whole World in Her Hands, The Rose.* A Bulgarian woman sang a funny little "Chicken Song."

The singing touched deep places in me. "We *are* all a part of one another," I thought, as the lump in my throat spilled over in tears onto my cheeks.

The plenary session was held in a plain, unadorned auditorium. Above the speakers' platform, a picture of a dove in flight hung above a map of Asia. Several of the speakers were from the former Yugoslavia and spoke through interpreters. The first gave a welcome and added, "The Peace Train symbolizes solidarity; that is important to us, since most of our people live very poorly and need encouragement of all kinds."

The second speaker was openly anti-American. "Politicians abuse peoples' humanity," she said heatedly. "They sell us capitalist ideas, and capitalism destroys life. It lives by the labors of millions of people. The government should stop using money that belongs to the people. Our leaders proved to be traitors. They sold Bulgaria to the USA. Now US imperialism is spreading its dirty cloak over all of Eastern Europe. We oppose all the embargoes imposed on other countries and territories. We bear the burden of the embargo on Serbia and Montenegro. We should put an embargo on the USA to show how it feels." She had a point. Capitalism *does* bring many woes, and certainly we in the USA don't always know the effects our actions have on others.

A woman from Belgrade said, "For some, war is misery; for others, it is status, power, and money. We need to stop war wherever it is happening and for whatever reason. Every Wednesday a pacifist/feminist group keeps a vigil against war in the center of the city. In Communism there was equality; now, the role of women is getting worse. Thirty percent of our women are abused or battered. We have organized a Center for Girls where they can get counseling and have opportunities to learn in workshops. Girls from refugee camps can join in projects and live in homes."

The next day in the workshop "Organized Crime in Bulgaria," the speaker began by saying, "Crime is a world problem. Organized crime is on the rise in every part of the world, and it's all connected. Bulgaria is a crossroads of Eastern Europe, so our problems are multiplied. Unemployment is increasing and this forces people to criminal action – stealing, lying, even joining organized crime. It is difficult to be a woman here; it requires courage and strength, because women are frequently the objects of sexual violence and exploitation."

In the question/answer period, Ellen of Germany spoke: "We must begin to see the connections between violence against women and pornography. Rape is considered to be a bounty of war and that must be stopped. In this present war, at least 60,000 women have been raped. There was actually a mass rape shown on TV; Serbian soldiers shown pornography as a part of their preparation to fight."

I thought of the current lawsuits by Japanese women in the United States who were used as "comfort women" in the second World War. Nobody knows how many were raped and tortured in that war, nor in the first World War, but it is certainly in the thousands. It is way past time to declare rape a crime against humanity.

The heaviness of all we were learning was put to rest for a moment our last night in Bulgaria when a spirited and energetic folk song company entertained us with a concert. Women sang in unison; a men's chorus accompanied by a virtuoso accordion player stamped their feet in lusty rhythm. Haunting melodies in minor keys shifted tunes just a little off key, as if pulling the notes out of their sockets, making the ends of phrases full of pathos. Marching songs and plaintive melodies were juxtaposed. Every now and then, a song ended with a shouted "whoop" or "heee," and we broke into enthusiastic applause. The concert was gutsy, a singing out of their joys and struggles, griefs and hopes; I felt as if I had touched the souls of the Bulgarian people and was one with them.

In Sofia, we boarded eight big, shiny modern buses for our 11-hour trip to Istanbul. Violetta, our guide to the Turkish border, spoke good English and joked a lot. When several buses pulled out before our air-conditioned one, she said testily, "We should have been first."

"You trust our driver, don't you?" I asked from the front seat.

Saucily, "I trust myself! I know the way." I liked her spirit. Later, when we were stopped at a checkpoint, an officer appearing from a very unofficial-looking lean-to said to her,"You're late."

"We were stopped because we were speeding, and we were speeding because we were late," was her speedy retort. She seemed quite satisfied with herself as we got back on the buses: "Smile at a policeman and always agree with him," she smirked.

My knowledge of the Balkan Peninsula was sparse, and I was intrigued when she gave us some of the history of the area. She pictured it as old enough to make the United States look like it's still in its infancy.

Sofia is located on the Thracian Plain. Thrace was the ancient Greek name for the large region on the Balkan Peninsula that stretched from Macedonia north to the Danube River and east as far as the Black Sea. Under the Romans, Thrace included only the southern half of this region.

The mountains of Thrace contained valuable deposits of gold and silver. Its broad plains were used for farming and for raising horses and cattle. Some historians believe that Greece owes the foundation of its music, mythology and philosophy to the people of early Thrace.

Thrace people were savage Indo-Europeans who liked warfare and looting.

The following day, our new guide, Aman, contradicted her. "The Thracians were a peace-loving people," he said. I wondered if this was like our American Indian saga. I was taught as a child that the Indians were a savage, warring people. I now know that they turned "savage" only when they were attacked and driven out of their homes by my European ancestors. In one of the logs Columbus kept about his "discoveries of the New World," he says of the natives, "Your Highnesses may believe that in all the world there cannot be better or more gentle people."[4]

Violetta went on to describe the invasions, wars and occupations of the area as it was tossed like a ball, back and forth between the Persians, the Athenians, the Macedonians, the Romans, the Russians, the Greeks.

"The same old story," I thought. "Can there be no end to these wars, these 'conquests,' these fights over land, this racism, these distrustful and unjust relations between peoples?"

During the Middle Ages, there were about 14 monasteries in Vitosha; nowadays only two of them have been preserved. Sofia is situated on the Sofia Plain at 550 meters above sea level. There are five mineral springs right in the city, more than 500 in the surrounding territory, and they range from very cold to tepid to very hot. We have learned some things about the Thracian people by studying the treasures that have been found. Some people were digging in their yard to build a well and they found this Thracian treasure – 185 objects, predominantly of silver. They are now exhibited in the Museum of History in Sofia.

I thought of my father's frequent comment: "Every place in the world has its own special beauty and treasures." Stunning blue mountains rose high on either side of us as we entered a wide valley.

Violetta spoke of Bulgaria's fame as producers of attar roses from which perfume is made, of tombs and buried treasure that have been found "all over the Thracian Plain." She said Bulgaria was given its name by the princes of Bulgar who founded the state and that King Boris the First, in 865, made Christianity the state religion "to stop the differences between the Turkish religion that had one god and the Slavs who worshiped a lot of gods and goddesses." I doubted if that edict made peace among the people, for we are often fixated on the belief that our own religion is the only "right" one. Three times the Bulgarian people were baptized – first by the Byzantines, next by the Roman Catholic Church and then by the Eastern Orthodox Church, "depending on what government was in power." I considered myself lucky that I was born in a country that holds fast to the separation of church and state!

Violetta then reminded us again that wars are fought for the possession of land.

In 1878, Bulgaria became a self-governing region in the Turkey of the present. It got officially divided into two parts, principality of Bulgaria and eastern Rumania. The Bulgarian population was very unhappy with this artificial division, and they fought most severely against it. Finally, these two parts united in 1995.

Traveling southeast, we began to see signs to "Turkiye" and "Istanbul," and little flickers of excitement rose up in me. I felt as if I had been lifted out of a history book and into a present waiting to be explored. The valley through which we were traveling reminded me of the Shenandoah in Virginia, except that it was wider, the mountains higher. Fertile farm lands were dotted with trees, golden grain fields and green meadows. Unlike my valley, there were a lot of yellow brick and stucco homes here and there. Heavily wooded areas hugged the modern, 4-lane highway. In the villages, men with picks and shovels dug in ditches. A man forking hay on a high load instantly turned me into a young girl on the farm watching Daddy, scared that he would fall off of one of those high loads.

Violetta broke my reverie.

This is one of the biggest agricultural centers in this part of the country, very well developed. Silk clearing is very famous here. Probably we'll see some of the trees, the leaves of which feed the silkworm from which we get silk. Mulberry trees.

Here again, we can see feta cheese. [She was pointing toward a big sign.] We eat a lot of cheese with everything, especially in summer. People only rarely eat meat; every day they eat cheese and tomatoes and cucumbers, a lot of vegetables and lots of vegetarian foods. Here they are burning a field and then they plow the land.

We had a pit stop halfway to the border, and it was just that. Stationed near that Asian hole in the ground was an angry woman who demanded money and closed the outer door on me until I borrowed the 5 lei from Hasha and gave it to her. I did not begrudge her the money. In fact, I felt she deserved a hundred times that amount for enduring the incredible stench that met my nostrils from a hundred feet away. But I was hard-pressed. I naively wanted her to trust this foreigner to bring her the money later, even though I understood only too well that "trusting" someone does not buy bread or pay the bills.

The wide valley widened more as we moved through vast acres of corn and thirsty sunflower fields. The buses came to a stop at a fence where a white arch rose high above with "Turkiye" in bold, black letters. I was excited. Since Bulgarian buses were not permitted in Turkey, we piled out onto a wide slab of concrete framed by kiosks and relinquished our passports to three official-looking men who emerged from a tiny booth marked "Headquarters." A big Toyota sign dominated the landscape, a smaller Ford right beside it, Nissan, too. Honda. BP Gas. Shell. Mobil. Oil was flowing all over the place. Between Toyota and Nissan, a big "Islam," and near it, on a building "FBI." What a mixture of worlds!

To escape the heat of the burning sun, I took shelter in the shadow of Turkish buses waiting to take us the five-hour journey to Istanbul. Tempers were on edge. An officer screaming in German at Annelisa from Italy, elicited from Mary Ann an amusing and philosophical observation: "Well, there you have the world scene. A Turkish officer yelling at an Italian in German." We said good-bye to Violetta, and Aman took over as our guide.

The first thing I noticed was that the bus driver had his own door, something I'd never seen, and he jumped into and out of it several times as if to call attention to the privilege. The modern highway ran between flat fields of potatoes, alfalfa, rice, and cotton. Sheep herders guarded wide, unfenced acres of corn and sunflower fields. Horse-drawn carts ambled here and there. Cattle munched in a field of hay. We passed a cart loaded with white crushed stone, pulled by a burro held in check by an arched yoke. Into and out of villages, we saw workers in orange suits, markets with watermelons, potatoes, produce of all kinds, dark stucco and brick homes, an ancient orange church with a stork nest on a balcony, street shrines with pictures of the Virgin on the front. Milky mountains rose in the distant mist.

Aman stated with finality, questionable accuracy, and fractured English that "the first signs of human beings was in Asia Minor, which is the Asian side of Turkey which is all but three percent of Turkey. The rest is on the European side." He had an interesting concept of the origin of wars. When the cave dwellers discovered that they could *grow* food instead of *hunt* for it, that "outside the caves there is life," they built houses "to imitate the caves."

They built them on hills or mountains and they got to be villages. Of course, the people were afraid. First, they were afraid of wild animals. Then, they were afraid of enemies from people who were living at the village next to them. And then, because it was normal to be attacked by these people, there were some wars.

Simplistic as it was, I thought his theory might have some validity. Might the present racism that is sweeping the world be rooted in primal fear of other human beings who are "different"?

We were approaching a city set on a hill, and Aman gave us a bit of a history lesson.

Now we come to the first city center of Turkey, in the northwestern corner. In second century AD, Hadrian, the famous Roman emperor, stopped here. He liked this area so much that he established the city and gave it his own name, Hadrianopolis. But today its name is Edirne.

Because of the enemies, the primitive people built on hills or mountains; or else surrounded the city with stones which were built on each other and were the walls at that time. Other major city walls you will see when we are close to Istanbul because the old city of Istanbul is between the city walls of Byzantine times. Traditional cities in Turkey are built along historical trade routes, especially the silk and spice routes. Asia Minor is like a bridge between the eastern part of the world and the western part.

There are 700 ruins in Turkey which are mostly from the Western civilizations, mostly the Greeks, but the Hittites also left things behind them in the wars. Before the Greeks, there were some original people and nobody knows where they came from, but they made colonies between the two antique rivers, Tigris and Euphrates, and all these areas between the two rivers was called Mesopotamia, which is for some historians the cradle of history.

I chuckled to myself, suddenly aware that places I had heard about all my life, as I listened to Bible stories being told, were right here under my feet. It made me want to go farther and farther east into this amazing country.

Aman told the story of a Greek legend of a knot tied by King Gordius of Phrygia which an oracle revealed would be undone only by the future master of Asia. Alexander the Great, failing to untie it, cut the knot with his sword. "To cut the Gordian Knot today is to find a quick, bold solution for a perplexing problem," he added. He told of wars and more wars over the centuries, always some new invading people fighting over the land and resources.

"The same old story," I thought. "Will human beings ever get this vicious cycle stopped? Will this Peace Train make even a small dent in that territorial frame of reference?" My ears perked up when he began to link us to the Christian religion.

During this time there came to be another problem. This time it was not the danger coming from outside, an enemy, but it was a completely unexperienced thing, the Christian religion. There were only two legal religions, the Christian one and the one that was the paganist religion which we call today mythology, which is stories; only that we still read about them, but they are only stories and really not the religion of that time.

I wanted to say, "Whoa! That mythology you dismiss so easily was the genuine expression of faith at a time before the Divine Feminine was swallowed up or actually destroyed by the patriarchal elevation of the male as King, Judge, and Ruler of the world." Being a visitor in his country, I stayed silent, wondering if those women way back then also remained silent out of fear of being misunderstood or discounted or accused of "stirring up trouble." I wondered, too, if I am silent when I need to speak up and challenge assumptions that are often presented as immutable truth by male religious leaders.

The new religion, Christianity, was a very dangerous thing for the people who were living and practicing the Jewish religion at that time. When the Romans had seen that many people were accepting this new religion, it was prohibited. Those who continued to accept the Christian religion were punished, either there were martyrisms or they were sent away to the Greek island of Patmos. That island is the only island of the Aegean that doesn't have sweet water to drink, only salty water. It is where St. John, the Evangelist, was sent in the Revelation part of the Bible.

There were missionaries of the Christian religion going through Asia Minor and St. Paul was one of them. He made three journeys and he did this after the crucifixion in 32 AD. From then until 330, the Christian religion was cut off. Constantine the Great, one of the last Roman emperors, came onto the throne and established it as the only legal religion of the Roman Empire.

As a youth long ago in my church, I had studied Paul's missionary journeys, the persecutions and deaths, the hiding, the danger to Christians. But suddenly this story came alive in a whole new way. Here I was, hearing it being told in the land in which it had happened! I found myself thinking, "How glibly men use religion to justify repression, to keep women and others under their control! Terrible!"

The next day, when I heard a woman in Istanbul speak of "going over to Ephesus to do some shopping," I did a doubletake. Was I in another world and time? Ephesus? Ephesus is a place in the Bible, not a city where I can make a day trip to buy something!

The Turkish people are like a soup. You put in onions, carrots, tomatoes and mix them all up. That is what you will see in Turkey, all the colors and all the human beings of the world. There are no conflicts among the people here. The women are mostly good-natured. We live in peace. There is a small terrorist group that flares up and needs to be put down occasionally – the Kurds in the southeast corner.

"How remarkably shortsighted men of privilege are," I thought. "That 'small terrorist group,' which you dismiss as unimportant, a pesky flea bite on the flesh of the leaders of church and state, is a *people* rising above acceptance of themselves as victims, demanding that they be treated with dignity and respect. How disgustingly easy it is for men of privilege and power to put a name to the 'troublemakers' and hear nothing of their dreams or anguish!"

There is a famous sentence which is said by Aga Turk, the founder of the republic: "Peace in the country; peace in the world." It's mentioned as the symbol of his mentality and it's the reality that accepts symbolic events. Turkey has never participated in any war after the First World War.

Today Turkey has a big problem at the southeastern corner in the Kurdish area. This terrorist group attacks always at night and mostly the small villages at that area. If they cannot get any money from that village for themselves, they take and kill whatever it is, whether a man, woman or child or animal even. But it's only a local war. We cannot say Turkey is participating in war with another country.

Turkey doesn't like anymore to be in wars. But you can read in newspapers, Turkey is ready for a war with Greece; Turkey is ready for a war with Bulgaria; with all the neighbors; but it is only written in the newspapers. The reality, there is no easy possibility to push Turkey into a war. Therefore, it remains since 1918 or 1923, a place where there is no war anymore. Especially Istanbul is probably the luckiest city of the world, because the last war in Istanbul was the year 1453. Since that time Istanbul hasn't been taking part in a war anytime.

"What a curious kind of reasoning," I thought. "Is this one man's way of denying what's happening? Or is it his yearning for peace?"

Aman brought out a little bag of goodies, gummy bears and licorice wheels all around. I chewed licorice as we crossed the broad plains in the midst of blooming sunflowers, and passed through the little town of Silivri on the Marmara sea, a beautiful blue sea that stretches to the south and connects with the Aegean. Aman told us that five years ago there were 80 kinds of fish in those waters; now there are only five – pollution. Mother Earth is hurting everywhere, it seems.

Aman told us with pride that Istanbul is the single city of the world which is established on two continents. Downtown is the European side. People rush from Asia to Europe in the morning and back to Asia in the evening. *Istanbul is the biggest city of Turkey and is very dirty, and there are many people who are extremely dangerous because among these 12–14 million inhabitants, only 2 million are living since two generations in this city. The rest are coming from differ-*

ent villages of Turkey and they have come to earn much more money in Istanbul, which they couldn't. So unfortunately, many of them have started stealing.

Istanbul is one of the newest cities of Turkey. Compared with Ephesus, established in 13th century BC, Istanbul, the 7th century BC so it's a very new city.

Amazing! San Diego flashed through my mind as a baby just beginning to crawl.

Istanbul today, well, it's a wonderful place, a very beautiful place. But if you come to the daily life in Istanbul, unfortunately you are no more of the same opinion – these buildings so close to each other and air pollution which is unbelievably high. Probably sometimes in winter evenings, it's the dirtiest city of all the world. Sometimes when you go out, it's not fog, it's smog that you see. You cannot see the cars driving the other way, it's so dark and gray. And it's so humid in summertimes, the humidity comes up to 95 percent, which does not allow you to breathe. Sometimes it will be announced not to go out of houses because the air is polluted.

Most expensive houses of Turkey are at both shores because the air is not polluted over there. There is wind; there is water. The wooden houses of the prosperous are renovated and restored in a beautiful way; rich people of Turkey have houses there and they live there.

Our hotel today is just at the inner side of the city walls. Whatever is in these city walls is the old city. It's on the main road connecting the entrance of the old city with the very center of the old time, by St. Sofia, the famous old Byzantine church. The same road leads you, it's 7 kilometers long, leads you to that historical point, the famous Ottoman government palace.

The city rose around us on seven hills: concrete buildings, built on top of each other; a sea of houses in every direction, red roofs with high-rises behind them, spread out all over the dry, deserty ground; a lot of buildings in process, partially built.

The market beside the road was crowded with heavily draped Muslim women buying beautiful fruits, bananas, peaches, grapes.

Arriving in Istanbul was a thrill I will never forget. It was easy to see what Aman meant about that mixture of peoples, and with that, the mixture of minarets and high-rise apartment buildings, dress and transportation. It was like going back and back in time, through a very mixed-up museum of history.

Narrow, cobblestone streets were lined with shops featuring elegant woven carpets, jewelry, art works and souvenirs. I had to have a cup of tea served in those glass cups on the sidewalk. I got so depressed seeing only women's eyes looking out from under their heavy, black, draped clothing and veils, that I bought a bright green, embroidered and jeweled pillbox hat, worn only by men, and wore it on the tram to go downtown sightseeing. For my own sanity, I had to make a protest against the expectations laid on women by the men in our lives, whether they be governmental, religious or personal, Muslim or Christian.

The next morning, my first priority was my throbbing left eye. My medicine had been missing so long that the pain was severe, and I was frightened. I went to Dr. Brigitte of Germany and asked if she had Pred Forte 1% in her medicine trunk. I didn't want to risk using anything else. She didn't, and graciously offered to help me find a pharmacy. Neither of us knew the Arab word for "pharmacy," so we spent an anxious hour trying to make people on the street understand what we were looking for. We tried every word we could think of, "medical, pills, drug store, apothecary…" Finally a woman exclaimed, "Oh, *eczane,* here, here." We searched the store signs and finally found one open at 8:30 in the morning. Brigitte explained what we needed and what a rush of relief I felt when the man understood. I paid $3 for the replacement of the $24 prescription I had bought in the States, and used it while I was still in the store. It relieved the pain almost immediately, and my eye was not damaged. When I think of Brigitte, I see an angel of mercy.

In the plenary session, Rishnev Soufan made a brilliant presentation on the History of the Feminist Movement in Turkey. "We are very young in this struggle. Before 1980, women's questions were always in terms of legal equality. After 1980, we examined the split between the private and the public sphere; 1980 to 1987, there were small groups, mostly elite and academic, discussing feminism as an ideology. A turning point was establishing a publishing house with space of our own, and we began to examine the need for political involvement. We had campaigns in 1987 to 1990. One march against women-battering had 4,000 women, the first time male violence was shown, and we were criticized for it severely. We showed that it was not only individual, but a tool of male dominance. We referred to feminism now as a Movement. It gained some legitimacy, and people were forced to take women seriously.

"In 1989, we had a campaign against sexual harassment, and established the connection between male violence at home, on the street and in the workplace. Our symbol was the purple needle. It meant 'the shame of harassment is not ours.' In 1990, we got the one-third clause outlawed. That meant that judges could [no longer] reduce the penalty for rape depending on who the woman was, a wife or a street woman.

"Our third campaign was for women's solidarity. We said we would not allow women to be used against one another. We failed to get the civil code changed that man is the head of the household, but we ran a campaign against repression of ethnic minorities, the Kurds, and 11 of us went to prison for a month to support women in prison. Kurdish women are torn between oppressions. We want them to start groups of their own and join us.

"Now we encourage women's participation in the public sphere. We publish a journal; we have a Ministry in Social Services for Women and our prime minister is a woman and very supportive."[5]

A lively question/answer period followed this plenary presentation, including differences between First and Third World understandings of feminism, the fear of backlash or co-optation, the impact of Islamic fundamentalism, the problem of the "hot Kurdish war," and creative ideas of ways to challenge the male system. One woman said that "Islam teaches that there is someone between yourself and God, punishing you in the name of God."

That evening we crossed a border that truly astounded me; we traveled *across town from one continent to another* to have dinner on the Bosporus, the waterway that connects the Black Sea with the Marmara and provides an entryway to the great Mediterranean. I knew about it, but until I got there, I did not understand how literally it separates Europe from Asia in the same city, the only city in the world that spans two continents. The Bosporus is a little strait only 19 miles long and two miles across at the widest point. It is named for two Greek words, *ox* and *ford*, meaning a place narrow enough for cattle to cross. A Greek legend tells that the goddess, Io, changed herself into a cow in order to cross the Bosporus!

The cries of the *muezzin* in the evening air and streets full of heavily veiled women in black were keen reminders that we were now in Muslim Istanbul and the days of glorious Catholic Christendom in Constantinople were ancient history. The elegant dinner, followed by Turkish music and vigorous dancing, once again pulled me toward the street and those of us for whom there was "no room in the inn." The whole evening I alternated between feeling pleasure and anger, shame and powerlessness to bring about any change in that reality.

The next day, the plenary and workshops forged in me a deep sense of connection with these women. They are like beacons of hope in a very cruel world, working against odds and forces that boggle my imagination – Fundamentalist Islam and sexism. Still, they are moving toward the goal of getting control of the decisions that impact their lives, overcoming the deep distrust of the "other," whether it be skin color, religion, privilege or lack of it, which, as one speaker said, "seems to be rooted way down deep in the human psyche." Where laws are made that affect themselves and their children, they are insisting on being heard. They pay a high price for their devotion to the cause of freedom and equality. Their courage and stamina are a continuing inspiration to me.

The monuments, minarets and mosques of this big, bustling city were eloquent reminders of Turkey's 9,000 years of history, during which people of different origins came in waves and mingled with those already settled there, each time creating a new culture. It was, as one brochure described it, "a symphony of sounds, smells and people in the most unlikely combinations of appearance and action."[6]

In a way that was deep and mystifying, it connected me to my conservative Christian roots and the Bible stories that were an integral part of my young and growing life. I didn't want to leave this country so soon; I felt as if I had only a fleeting glimpse of its magnitude, only a tiny taste of its great feast of cultures, religions and daily living. I wanted to stay forever and go east as far as the rising sun.

During the early stages in planning for the Peace Train journey, we had been told that we would go by ship from Istanbul to Odessa. I had looked forward to this, and was disappointed to learn that the cruise had been cancelled because the company had gone bankrupt. The only thing left to do was to retrace our steps, back through Bulgaria, Rumania and yes, you guessed it, Moldavia again.

We crossed the border into Russia from the south and came into Voronezh, where there was a six-hour "rest stop," then on to Saratov for a stay of three hours, to delay our arrival at the border of China.

Saratov – now there's a memory! I got my first glimpse of the great Volga River, about which I had taught children to sing "Yo, heave ho!" when I was a music teacher aeons ago. In my mind then, it was about the size of little, meandering North River in my native Virginia. Seeing it for real took my breath away, so wide that I thought at first it was a big lake or a tributary of the ocean. When a bunch of us rushed to the water's edge and Zina negotiated a boat ride, one of my wildest dreams came true. And the icing on the cake was having the boat dock at a secluded place where several brave sisters and I went skinny-dipping. Oh, the feel of that cool Volga wetness on my bare skin!

Our time in Odessa, Ukraine, on the Black Sea, was to have been from 10:00 a.m. to 10:00 p.m. We learned after we got there that the Chinese government had other plans for us. We were not permitted to enter China, as they had agreed, on August 23; we had to enter two and a half days later.

No explanations. Our leaders seemed as baffled as we were, and we knew better than to ask for reasons. The Chinese government had made a decision; we obeyed.

What a difficult situation for the Odessan hosts! Here were 242 people on their hands for a couple days more than they had expected. They rose gallantly to the occasion and with generosity and ingenuity, gave us experiences I shall never forget.

The War Memorial, a so-called "peace park" where the Ukrainians threw out the Nazis, was our first stop. We visited a camp home for children whose parents were in prison. Then the buses took us to the Potemkin Steps, an engineering marvel in concrete, leading down to the beautiful, blue Black Sea. The 190 steps are measured in groups of 20, divided by wide landings. From the top, you can see only the steps; from the bottom, only the landings. American sailors in dress uniforms swarmed about. "What are you Americans doing here?" I asked a friendly looking fellow.

"Oh, just cruising, looking around to see what we can see. We're on a mission to keep the peace. What are you doing here?"

"I'm here on a Peace Train with 242 women and a few men from 42 countries. We're on a mission to make peace." He looked baffled.

"We're the ones who make peace," he said.

"Wrong," I said. "You're the ones who make war. What right do we Americans have to be 'looking around' over here to see what we can see? Would you like it if the Ukrainian military people were doing that in the United States?" He shook his head as if to say, "Well, here's one of these crazy peaceniks who make no sense." He went up; I went down.

That night our stranded troope was entertained by a performance of The Renaissance Ballet of Moscow in the famed Opera House. I was completely enchanted, to be in the midst of a full house of Ukrainians enjoying beauty and culture right in the middle of their great problems and struggles. What a privilege! It was one more reminder that people everywhere live in hope with remarkable spirit; they sing and dance right in the midst of pain, right through a lot of turmoil.

The next day we crossed the border into Kazakhstan, a place where vast deserts are dotted with tiny yurt villages so much like the sands around them that they can be missed by the naked eye. I felt as if I had entered another world. Yurts, circular tents made out of felt or skins on a framework of poles, are the homes of nomadic peoples who live off the land. Camels roam free in the fields under blistering sun. For many years, Kazakhstan was the nuclear testing ground for the Soviet Union, and is now reaping the effects of radiation and poisoned lands.

After traveling for days across flat plains, at 12:00 noon on August 24 we spilled out of our air-conditioned Train in Alma-Ata (Almaty), the capital, and into 100 degree Fahrenheit temperature. This time, in response to their welcome of flowers and bread, some of our women gave a circle presentation with dance and song.

"*Spaciba, spaciba!*" they applauded. "Thank you, thank you."

Gulsara Tiencheeva, an attorney in the School of Law, opened her comments with a warm welcome. "There is a Kazakh saying," she said. "'May you feel the joy of the nightingale at dawn.' This women's program was organized by our NGOs without any intervention from government. There are 300,000 activists in the NGOs of Kazakhstan and there is a women's political party. We want an end to nuclear testing in our country and in China, because we believe it is genocide for our people if this continues. There is in Kazakhstan the 'Goddess of Life,' *Mayapa*; we want her star to shine over the earth. For this to happen, we must work together for women's human rights and to save the earth."

Svetlana Shakirova then traced the history of feminism in Kazakhstan. "The Congress declared political equality between men and women in 1917."

"And in the United States we keep on defeating The Equal Rights Amendment!" I thought. "And we think we're advanced?"

Svetlana went on. "But traditional agreements about marriage are made when girls are in the cradle and marriages at early ages are common. Feminism is taken by some to be nonsense or as prejudice against men. The draft constitution makes no distinctions between men and women, but all the words used are masculine, while meaning 'women are included.' It is an infringement on women's rights, because, while it says any citizen can be president, citizen in Russia is masculine, so, really, only a man can be president."

"Do they still think of themselves as being a part of the USSR?" I wondered.

"When we approached an official and asked about women in the constitution, he said, 'I love women very much.' In Kazakhstan, we need a revolution from within.

"The fight for feminism is like a fight with windmills. We still picture women as mother, wife, housewife, prostitute or a prize in the hands of a tycoon. We dream of a time when our sex means no more than the color of our eyes. We are making some progress: we have introduced into textbooks gender-neutral stories. We have many NGOs now focusing on women's rights, and we have a newspaper for girls."

The next day, at a workshop on Feminist Art, artists spoke about their work. One had lived with a family in a yurt for a year. In blues and golds, she pictured life in a place with no windows, only open sky above, and brilliant stars. Another artist had taken her cue from ancient Kazakh petroglyphs, and on a gorgeous piece of silk embroidery, pictured a man being changed into something else.

We were given a fashion show with regal costumes that accentuated the golden-brown skin of the models. One wore a black, red-jeweled, flowered cloak over a slinky aqua gown; another, gold damask over black with a fancy white yoke. All the while, drums, flutes and two strange, long-handled string instruments set a tone of sadness, gaiety, pain or joy.

The highlight of the entertainment for me was a concert by the Uighurs, who have lived in central Asia from ancient times. They are known for their music and culture.

"If you want to understand a people, understand their music," the leader told us. "As everywhere, women carry visions of life and give the culture to new generations. Uighur women endured many difficult times, were often given as gifts to the men of foreign countries, and still they kept their music alive. Uighurs lived on the Silk Route and girls were used to carry goods on camels across these roads. Some of these died from the strenuousness of the journey." One song with piercing tones spoke of girls being sold by parents who had no money, who, when asked why, said, "It is the destiny of Uighur women."

One song and dance full of pathos depicted a girl watering her garden flowers with water she had carried a long distance from mountain springs. A woman in a purple fluorescent cloak over a slinky, green, flowered gown and green pants, wore a brown fur hat with a red crown over long, black braids that hung to her waist. Her dance was as slinky as her dress. The leader said this dance was to show that "Uighur women have elasticity and can roll away from men if they need to."

They ended the concert with the statement, "Music has no borders; we will now all dance together." And that's just what we did. All over the audience, we got up and, oh, how we danced, joining hands and hearts around the world!

That evening, I went with Ellen, Amelia, and Mary to Panfilov Park to stand for a few quiet moments in Zenkov Cathedral. On the way, I paid $10 for a two-minute phone call to my kids. I was feeling too far away. I called daughter Jill and got a machine. Disappointed, I called daughter Marta. When she heard my voice, she shrieked, "Beth! Are you all right? Where are you?"

"Faraway in Asia in Alma-Ata, Kazakhstan. How's everybody? How's Eric?"

"We're fine. Eric's doing better." I later learned this was not so; he was really very ill. They were protecting me.

"Did he get the house?"

"Yes."

"Call him. Call Jill, tell them I"m fine. I go into China tomorrow."

Click! We were cut off. I took a deep breath, said a prayer of thankfulness, and thought, "How absolutely amazing it is that wires can cross what seems like a million miles and put me in touch with those kids I love so dearly."

As the tracks moved us steadily eastward toward the great country of China, I was ready to continue the journey. Hours went by, and word came down the lines of cars that we were to destroy all books and materials about China, and to take no more pictures since we were approaching the Chinese border. It was late afternoon when the great blue body of water gave way to flat, brown desert plains.

"I can just imagine Genghis Khan storming down through here," Pat said, as we gazed out the window. All of a sudden, someone pointed in the direction of a long row of low buildings, so identical in color as to be almost indistinguishable from the sands surrounding them, and shouted, "That's China over there!"

Something in me jumped alive. Was I really going to be in this country that had seemed inaccessible to me since childhood when I had heard those stories of our missionaries being forced out? Was this really China that I was seeing, this vast brown, empty desert land? It was somehow not the China I had envisioned, full of almond-eyed people and red and gold signs. At this moment there were no people to be seen. Yet, this barren, unpeopled plain, stretching as far as my eyes could see, had my heart racing with anticipation, dampened by just a wee bit of trepidation.

We came to a stop near a little cluster of beige-colored, concrete block buildings, and knew we were at one more checkpoint, about to cross the last geographical border for the Peace Train. Here we would say good-bye to the Russian train which had become "home" to us; Russian trains were not permitted to enter China. For the remaining three days of travel into Beijing, we would ride the train appointed by the government of China, staffed by Chinese attendants, and accompanied by one whole coach filled with Chinese security officers.

When the doors of our Russian train were opened, I cringed. I looked down to no platform, but rather, ground that was uneven and sloping downward. To get from the Train to that ground had to be a mighty big jump – ominous. I hoped I could do it without getting hurt in the process. Buses holding a maximum of four people with luggage sat alongside the train waiting to transport us to the "holding area." Inside the Train, tension rose as we huddled over our luggage in the stacked-high aisles, urged by Chinese officers to get off, instructed by our own tour guides to stay on until further notice.

The banners and welcoming groups of other borders were starkly missing. Outside each door stood a stone-faced Chinese officer in stiff uniform. He didn't move a muscle as I gritted my teeth, clumsily maneuvered my luggage over the edge, jumped down, reached above my head and caught the suitcase someone was handing to me.

"No big drive to be gentlemanly here," I thought, as I turned to help the next woman. "We can hardly call this a warm welcome to China."

6

Strange Welcome to China

The bigness of China makes you wonder.
It is more like a whole world than a mere country.
All beneath the sky, 'Tianxia,' was one Chinese expression for their empire; another
was 'All between the four seas,' Sihai.[1]

We can always fool a foreigner. Chinese Proverb [2]

The Chinese government's unilateral changing of minds about permitting stopovers in Urumchi and Xian sent an electric current through me and the whole Train. I had so looked forward to spending time in the famous marketplace in Urumchi, the first Chinese city we would visit. Urumchi, however, was just north of Lop Nur, a region in which a nuclear test was detonated during our time on the Train. It was rumored that the Chinese government did not want to risk having their people see anti-nuclear demonstrations, or whatever else these strange Peace Train women might do. We would not be stopping there or in Xian, home of the famous clay sculptures, as had originally been agreed. In fact, during that nearly three days of travel, we would have only two 20-minute rest stops a day on railway platforms.

It was downright eerie to me, to have anticipated being among a people who are one in five the world over and seeing absolutely no one. We were being held behind barred gates high above streets which were eerily empty, guards with guns at ready in circular elevated watchtowers above us. I found myself wanting to scream into that vast emptiness, "You don't understand! We're women on a peace journey. We are not enemies!" Strange welcome to China!

From that first view of flat sands stretching as far as the eye could see, the new Chinese Peace Train traveled eastward through Tien Shan (Heavenly Mountains) of dizzying heights and dozens of deep, dark tunnels. Caves punctured the sides of the steep inclines. We moved across the North China Plain, crossing and re-crossing the Huang-Ho River, named Yellow because of the yellow mud it collects and carries for hundreds of miles, sometimes called "China's Sorrow" because of all those who have lost their lives in its path. I began to be aware of walls and more walls, sometimes fitted into the ditches at the bottom of rising hills, sometimes retaining rubble from obstructing railroad tracks. Here and there a lone man knelt under his cone-shaped hat, placing brick by brick in the blazing sun. Sheep and goats grazed on hills so steep they looked like horizontal wedges about to fall off. My first view of The Great Wall was a heap of muddy brown bricks and rubble.

The Chinese call their country *Chung Hwa Min Kuo,* Central Flowery People's Nation. The English word, China, comes from the word, Chin, the name of an ancient Chinese ruling family.[3] This place we call China *is* as big as the sky. Its history is as complex and convoluted as its geography and culture are beautiful and vast. It's almost a travesty to speak of this country and its people after being there for three short weeks. It's like trying to spoon the Gobi Desert into a nutshell, like an ant attempting to walk the full length of the Great Wall. China's written history starts in 1300 BC with primitive writing on bones.[4] That history is so ancient as to confound my young, Western mind.

Almost all of China's life and people were hidden to me. Eighty percent of the population are peasants stuck in back-breaking work and poverty. From the forbidden Train windows, I got only those few fleeting
glimpses of them, cultivating unbelievably high, tiered mountain slopes or
bent to the work of building the omnipresent walls and ditches in the burning sun. Hidden were the happy family groups and gatherings, the special
celebrations like Spring Festival and Chinese New Year. Hidden well away
was the gulag, the hellish Labor Reform Prison system administered by the
Public Security Bureau. I knew it was there, because I saw it through the life
of Harry Wu, a native son of China, who spent 19 years in the torture and
cruelty of it, then exposed it to Western eyes in his heartrending book,
Bitter Winds. Carolyn Wakeman, who collaborated in the writing, described
the book as "an invaluable personal record of the persistent, barbaric abuses
of human freedom in our time… (also) a testimony to the extraordinary
courage of the human spirit. The atrocities, horrors, and abuses endured
by prisoners in the gulag are beyond endurance for many and hideous
beyond belief."[5]

No wonder China is touchy about "foreigners." In the 1200s, the
Mongols swept in from the north and established their rule. In the 1300s,
the Chinese revolted and established the Ming Dynasty. In 1644, the
Manchus invaded and set up the Ch'ing Dynasty which lasted until the
republic was formed in 1912, all the time troubled by rebellions and "foreign interests." Japan defeated China in the Sino-Japanese war of 1894 and
afterward, when China's rulers felt their independence was threatened,
attempts were made to kill all foreigners and native Christians. That's what
the Boxer Rebellion in 1900 was all about. It was led by a Chinese secret
society known to foreigners as "the Boxers," to Chinese as "Society of Har-
monious Fists." It was secretly supported by the Empress of China. An international army, including United States troops, defeated the Boxers. In the
20th century alone, China has known nothing but turmoil and struggle,
tyranny, cruelty and witch hunts. It is hard for me to imagine what it would
be like to be tossed about from one rule to another, to have "the enemy"

among my own people, never knowing who that was, changing every time I turned around. The Chinese have a saying, "Everything will change again in ten years."[6]

The amazing book, *Wild Swans*, by Jung Chang, chronicles three generations of one family's living through that chaos and anguish. Chang tells the acutely moving story of her grandmother, born in 1894, whose feet were bound when she was two years old.

Her mother, who herself had bound feet, first wound a piece of white cloth about twenty feet long round her feet, bending all the toes except the big toe inward and under the sole. Then she placed a large stone on top to crush the arch. My grandmother screamed in agony and begged her to stop. Her mother had to stick a cloth into her mouth to gag her. My grandmother passed out repeatedly from the pain. The process lasted several years. ...For years my grandmother lived in relentless, excruciating pain. When she pleaded with her mother to untie the bindings, her mother would weep and tell her that unbound feet would ruin her entire life, that she was doing it for her own future happiness. In those days, when a woman was married, the first thing the bridegroom's family did was to examine her feet. Large feet, meaning normal feet, were considered to bring shame on the husband's household.[7]

At 15, Chang's grandmother became the concubine of a warlord general in the town of Yixian, a town "built like a fortress, encircled by walls thirty feet high and twelve feet thick, surmounted by battlements" (p. 27). Chang tells of life under Japanese rule from 1938 to 1945, in Manchukuo when her mother was taught in school that "there are two republics of China – one hostile, led by Chiang Kai-shek; the other friendly, headed by Wang Jingwei, Japan's puppet ruler of part of China" (p. 34). She tells of being ruled by different masters from 1945-1947, when the people became "slaves who have no country of your own" (p. 101). The Japanese had surrendered following the United States' bombing of Hiroshima and Nagasaki, and actions of "officials" had severe consequences for the entire family. The morning after the surrender, Chang's mother opened the front door to see the bodies of a Japanese woman and two children lying dead in the road. A Japanese officer had committed hara-kiri; his family had been lynched.

The Soviet Red Army took over and the people were grateful to be rid of the Japanese. Her mother joined the Communists. The Russians formally recognized Chiang Kai-shek's Kuomintang (National Party of the People) as the government of China. Stalin had agreed to withdraw the Soviet Red Army from that area within three months of victory. Civil war erupted between Communists, with Mao Zedong as leader, and Kuomintang under Chiang Kai-shek. There was corruption everywhere. In the Kuomintang, disagreement with the policies led to accusations of being a Communist, followed by arrest and torture. From 1958-1962, Mao led his "Great Leap Forward" in an effort to show that China could outdo the United States in industrial output. He decreed that making steel was more important than growing rice, and stilled any protest with torture or death. This resulted in the unspeakable horror of a famine that took an estimated 30 million lives. Chang tells a story to illustrate the utter horror of that famine.

Years later I met an old colleague of my father's, a very kind and capable man, not given to exaggeration. He told me with great emotion what he had seen during the famine in one particular commune. Thirty-five percent of the peasants had died, in an area where the harvest had been good – although little was collected, since the men had been pulled out to produce steel, and the commune canteen had wasted a large proportion of what there was. One day a peasant burst into his room and threw himself on the floor, screaming that he had committed a terrible crime and begging to be punished. Eventually it came out that he had killed his own baby and eaten it. Hunger had been like an uncontrollable force driving him to take up the knife. With tears rolling down his cheeks, the official ordered the peasant to be arrested. Later he was shot as a warning to baby killers (p. 310).

The "Cultural Revolution" began in 1966, when Mao used the latent violence of the young, known as the Red Guards, to destroy "the four olds – old ideas, old culture, old customs and old habits"(p. 376). That seemed strangely inconsistent with what I was taught about the Chinese, that they revere the elderly and the old. All intellectuals, including artists, scholars and musicians, became suspect; teachers were tortured and named as enemies of Mao; great treasures in museums and private homes were destroyed.

Distrust was continually being built between China and the West. Films were used to show how decadent the West was. As a child, Chang was told to "Think of all the starving children in the capitalist world!" She thought of the United States as a place of miserable disease and poverty (p. 326). Ironically, as a child in the United States, I was hearing about Christian missionaries being thrown out of China or disappearing there, told to eat everything on my plate, to think of the starving Chinese.

Mao's craze for power and adoration was so great as to drive leaders to foster distrust among the nation's own people. Name-calling and "exposing" neighbors and friends has been encouraged in China throughout the century: "reactionary bourgeois authorities," "class enemies," "capitalist roaders." Political parties in power nosed about for "enemies" or "dissidents," even within families. Small wonder that Tienanmen Square was covered with blood and death in the demonstrations of 1989. No wonder at all that the government moved the Women's Forum out of downtown Beijing to avoid whatever might be done by these "foreigners" from all over the world.

My time in China led me to see it as a country of contrasts and contradictions, much like my own United States and every country I have visited. There are immaculate marble halls for those of privilege, wealth and status, and sooty streets filled with debris, spittle, poverty and filthy smells for those without privilege. It is a country of tall mountains and short people, of high rises and low hovels, of soft smiles and hard looks, a land of welcomes and walls, locked gates and open doors, caves and modern hotels, police officers who appear out of nowhere to say "No" to whatever you are doing, and warm, generous people genuinely wanting to be friends. It is a place where there are separate ticket lines and fees for foreigners and natives. One Chinese woman said, "We have one face for Chinese; another for foreigners." It is a great land, so rich in culture and history, in art and literature, as to make my United States look like a nation born yesterday. I was as caught up in its magnificent variety and grandeur as the Peace Train was swallowed up in the blackness of those hundreds of tunnels.

My own life has been enriched by the contributions of China. I live by the concept of *qi* (chi), a Chinese belief that life force is centered in the lower abdomen, circulates through the body, and can be directed to other parts of the body. And who could ever resist the pungent warmth of China's *baiju*, rice wine? I am touched by the fact that 2.6 billion people have the same love of China and pride in its accomplishments as I have for the country I call "home."

It is highly symbolic of what is happening in China that the Fourth World Conference on Women was invited to be held there. It seemed incongruous at first. It was only in 1970 that the footbinding of women was outlawed, and still today infant girls' necks and backs are broken by midwives at birth, or amniocentesis which reveals a female fetus is often followed by abortion. The one-child law and the traditional valuing of boys over girls is a stark reminder of the violence against women and girl children.

At the same time, China wants to be seen as a world power, a trading partner with the nations, a country to be reckoned with in the United Nations, and is as open to new ideas and ways of doing things as the United States. To tell the truth, as I told my friend, the government which extended the invitation may have had no idea how great the numbers would be nor how far-reaching the influence of the NGO Forum and Fourth World Conference on Women would be. In my short stay there, I realized that the Chinese government and its officials were as foreign to me as I to them. The people of China are not to be confused with the government of China, a fact as true in every nation as there.

The generosity and helpfulness of individual women in China was immediate and unreserved. When I got to Huairou and tried to find batteries to replace the wornout ones for my dictating machine and camera, I had great difficulty. Finally, I went into a place where a delightful young woman by the name of Tong-Whai, in her booth in the shopping fair, said she would *go* and find me batteries. She was surprised when I said I would go along. She spoke English I could understand, and even taught me a Chinese word or two: *Xiexie* (thank you, pronounced "she-shee") and *Ni Hao* (hello).

As we went upstairs and down, through a humongous shopping center, she asked about many things. "What is life like in the United States where you live?" "Why are you at this conference?" "What are you doing here?" I enjoyed our conversation immensely, invited her to come to visit me, and gave her my card. I wouldn't be surprised if she does just that. Tong-Whai is an English major at the University of Beijing, working part-time to make money. When I said, "thank you, *Xiexie*," she bowed; "It is my duty as a good host in China to help you." She must have read the same banner I saw: "Be a good hostess. Be a credit to your country." After an hour and a half of searching, we found the batteries. She was as pleased as I was. For her to have failed to help me would have meant loss of face for the Chinese government. When a student fails, the fault is the teacher's.[8]

Alongside the friendliness of the people was the surveillance and "security" harrassment some of us experienced while attending the Forum and Conference. It made my skin creep. Not only were there uniformed and sometimes armed officers at every village entrance on the way from Beijing to Huairou; they would appear at my elbow anywhere without warning, letting me know that whatever I was doing was not allowed. One day, I was marveling at the beautiful, carved marble steps in The Forbidden City, when a young man, walking by with an older woman, stopped me and asked, "My mother would like to have her picture taken with you. Would you mind?" Just as the camera clicked, a stern officer stepped forward and sternly asked us to move on. As I strolled alone through the gardens of the Temple of Heaven, I ducked behind a tree just in time to obstruct the view of a uniformed officer who was taking my picture. This happened more times than I could count. At the Forum, I would suddenly become aware that walkie-talkies were being used to record my conversations with other women. One day, five of us were trying to hail cabs, when a police officer stepped forward, shook his head and shouted, "No! No! Too many." He held up four fingers. The law limited the number of persons in a cab to four. Our intention was to use two cabs; his assumption was that we were violating the law.

One day, when I really wanted to be alone, I walked the streets of Beijing just to see what I could see. Huge, plastic tarps were draped over the clutter of unfinished or unsightly construction, in fact, over anything the government or people did not want seen by strange eyes. Old men squatted on doorsteps in dimly lit or dark alleyways surrounded by tiny living spaces all crowded in together. In one, a woman bent over a bucket, cooking dinner. A barber gave a haircut on grass covered by a white sheet, near a channel of water. In a dark alleyway, rodents played in garbage dumps. On a mound of green grass, men crouched intently around a game of checkers. Workers labored under shoulder poles carrying heavy baskets heaped high with everything imaginable. Rickshaw drivers pedaled precariously balanced loads of household furnishings, vegetables, fruits, nuts and breads. An old man bowed a plaintive tune on an ancient-sounding, two-stringed fiddle held between his knees. A cab driver, with practiced skill, spit the juice of *binglang*, betel nut, through his teeth onto the slimy floor. A small child's mouth dropped open when he saw me. Staring from behind his mother's skirts, he called out, "*ni hao!*"

The waves of bicycles, carts, pedicabs, trucks and cars on the streets of Beijing were a breathtaking study in cooperation and driving skill, especially if you are in or on one of those moving vehicles. Ever so deftly, they wove in and out, barely missing each other on turns that made my heart skip a beat.

Feeling adventurous one day, I decided to save a little money and ride in a pedicab to the hotel. No roller coaster ever gave the rider more thrill than I felt racing down the main street in the midst of careening Chinese wheels! It reminded me of the time in Bangalore, India, when I rode in a rickshaw to find a continuing education center. I wouldn't have missed it, but when I got off at the hotel, my weak knees reminded me that a once-in-a-lifetime experience may need to be kept that way. I had wanted to be "among the people." Well, there's no better "flesh and bones" way of fulfilling that wish than a pedicab ride!

The Chinese have a saying: "If you laugh, you will live long."[9] It was sad, and understandable, that I did not see more people laughing. Even the children seemed like puppets on a string, controlled and very proper.

The Chinese err on the side of sacrificing all individuality for the sake of the state. They take pride in *chi ku,* the ability to endure suffering. Americans, at the other end of the spectrum, are so engrossed in individual freedoms and "what's-in-it-for-me" attitudes that we think we owe our country nothing, and we want no interference from government into our personal lives. Individualism seems to be an ingrained trait of our national character. Even in marriage and psychotherapy, according to the writers of *Habits of the Heart,* "A deeply ingrained individualism lies behind much contemporary understanding of love," and "the full significance of the therapeutic view of the world lies in its expressive individualism, an expanded view of the nature and possibilities of the self."[10] By contrast, China's sense of the centrality of the state and the peoples' commitment to "the whole" seemed strangely overdone to me. I saw absolutely no sign of resistance to authority. Do both countries need to seek a middle ground?

It was in the dead of night that the Peace Train pulled into the Beijing station. Just before our arrival, rumors had run willy-nilly down the length of the 15 coaches; we would be met by Chinese security officers carrying blankets, just in case we disembarked naked. Where such wild ideas got started, no one seemed to know. It may have been only the natural result of the hotbed of uneasiness, suspicion and fear spawned by the constant surveillance of officers on the China train.

The station was dark and dingy, black with the soot of many trains. Suddenly, after three days of seeing empty station platforms, we were surrounded by Chinese people, elbow to elbow. I huddled in my Train group like a lost child waiting for something to happen, to receive instructions as to what next. Finally, Esther directed us to the buses that would transport us to the meeting place. There, we would register for the Forum and receive the packets designed to guide us through the maze of bus schedules, hotel locations, plenary sessions, workshops, tents and folk activities that would fill the days of the Forum.

By this time, it was well past midnight and fatigue with the intensity of a flu bug was creeping up from my toes to my head. That didn't keep me from realizing that the Chinese had worked hard to prepare for our coming. Flags in rainbow colors were planted alongside the highway. Over them, huge banners waved out the red and gold message in English and Chinese: "Welcome, Fourth World Conference on Women."

At Workers' Stadium, tall signs, alphabetized in a half-dozen languages, towered over the heads of intense registrars seated behind tables that stretched the length of three sides of the huge auditorium, surrounded by boxes of programs, application forms, instructions, picture name tags on long chains, and who knows what else. In one corner of the room, program booklets printed in several languages were tossed into a massive pile. Thousands of women queued up to gain access to the tables, their faces a mixture of the tension and excitement I felt inside me. It had been such an uneasy process to get to this point, and on the other side of the table were the women who had the power to say "No, your name is not on the list." My tension mounted as I was refused at several different tables; then, finally, relief – I got the nod that I was "in." I burrowed through the pile for a program printed in English, then headed, bone weary, to the buses that would take me and a couple hundred others to the luxurious and modern 21st Century Hotel.

There, another hurdle. On a jam-packed mezzanine, we were asked to name a roommate. I was waiting my turn in the line, when a young woman I didn't know pointed toward me and said, as if this were the last straw, "I'll take this woman." So it was that May of Switzerland and I escaped the masses, lugged our heavy suitcases up 17 flights and collapsed into bed. It was 3:00 a.m. of my first day in Beijing.

I slept away the morning, then decided to beat the crowd and go early to see what would be going on behind the scenes at the Olympic Stadium where the opening session was to be held. I had not yet caught on to what it meant to be in China. For two and a half hours, I shifted from standing to sitting to standing again on the curb under a drooping pepper tree, just outside high iron gates where stolid security guards paced back and forth, back and forth, guarding the Stadium entrance. This was as "behind the scenes" as I was going to get until they decided to open the gates. The heat of an over-friendly Beijing summer sun beaded my brow and poured sweat down my back.

After a while, other women came and milled about me. A group of Chinese women nearby glanced toward me, then away, chatting with each other, obviously about me. Finally, one of them came over, and in very understandable English asked if she might have her picture taken with me. That led to six or eight other women wanting to do the same. I got a kick out of that, in spite of the fact that I knew that my only claim to fame was my white hair and skin. Their smiles touched me, though, and made the waiting less prolonged.

Buses rolled in; dozens of young teens poured out, dressed all alike in tight-fitting, shiny blue leotards, carrying white stick-doves on long poles. One by one, they put them on the ground in a pile and threw themselves down beside them, not looking at all like the energetic dancers they would become a couple hours later. Other buses arrived and a hundred or more young men in navy blue leotards gathered in formation, holding rectangular shields that flashed silver on one side and dark blue on the other, the props for the beautiful fan dance we would marvel at later. A group of small almond-skinned children in orange and brown released their nervous energies by testing their dance steps. By now hundreds and hundreds of us had gathered, and dozens of buses lined the highway. Everywhere I looked, some group was arranging itself in readiness to move at a moment's notice. It struck me that they were doing this completely on their own, with no apparent adult supervision.

What a sight we all were to behold, dressed in all the colors of the rainbow and the native dress of dozens of nations – kimonos of Japan, flamboyant gowns and headdresses of Africa, elaborate golds and reds of Thailand, Indonesia, China, folk colors of South America, bluejeans and T-shirts of the US, pantsuits of Europe. Inside the gates, above the stadium, flags of the nations hung limp in the heavy humidity, and huge balloons high in the sky mirrored the colors and insignias of the flags, announcing the world-wide character of this gathering. The crowd became restless; activity burst in every direction. In spite of the oppressive guardedness at the gates, the excitement in me rose to a pitch.

Suddenly, as if given the nod from on high, the guards pushed open the iron gates and waved the crowd to enter. With an adrenalin rush, I surged forward in that sea of women, feeling the thrill of being in a place and time where history was certainly in the making. The first dusk of evening was settling on us as we streamed toward the stadium, eagerly anticipating the opening of the NGO Forum of the Fourth World Conference on Women.

Suddenly, a shout pierced the air. My insides curdled; a shudder ran through the crowd. "Foreigner! Back!" In the time it took me to glance around at the olive-skinned mass pressing me, I realized that I was the culprit; my white hair and Caucasian skin made me stick out like a sore thumb in that crowd.

A second time the voice shrieked: "Foreigner! Back!" Blazing almond eyes fixed on my round ones, and a finger thrust upward, cutting a passage-way in the crowd like a sword. Confused, embarrassed, I struggled backward against the current toward the stairway to the upper level of the bleachers. There, dozens of foreigners were scrambling for a place in a line that led to another security point. I joined them and my turn came. The guard held out her hand: "Invitation, Please." I groaned inwardly, pointed to my Peace Train button and the Forum dog tag with my picture on a chain around my neck.

"They told me at the hotel that they ran out of invitations and this is all I need to get in."

"Wrong! Sorry"! That awful shrug again. Rules are rules. She motioned me out of line. I did not move.

"No, I have come too far. You cannot turn me away."

"Back!" She glared at me and turned to accept a dozen invitations from outreached hands of women pushing through the gate. I stood my ground, very much in her way.

"I will not go away. You must let me in." We both heard the pleading in my voice, near tears. To my amazement, her shoulders slackened and her voice softened.

"You stay here. I'll be right back." She locked the gate, took off through the crowd and, before I knew what was happening, came back and handed me an invitation. Immediately, then, she took it back, unlocked the gate and waved me in.

Trembling all over, my knees gone to jelly, I found a seat among the impatient stream of "foreigners," and sank into it. I was back in the Chinese Embassy in Los Angeles. My welcome to China was true to form. I was a foreigner then and I was an "outsider" now, and that would not change during my stay in China. I was to be reminded often of the irony of that as I moved in and out of Beijing and Huairou under those beautiful white banners with gold and red lettering I shall never forget: "Welcome to the Fourth World Conference on Women, Equality, Development, Peace and Friendship."

I was touched to see that to the three dimensions of past world conferences – Equality, Development and Peace – the Chinese women had added a fourth, "Friendship." It was a powerful statement about the difference between the people of states and the leaders of states, between governments and NGOs! How fitting that in a country that has had a tidal wave of abuse of women, a worldwide network of organized monitoring groups were meeting in the shadow of world governments, who themselves were meeting for the cause of justice for women and girls around the world.

7

Governments and NGOs

We hold these truths to be self-evident,
that all men [sic] are created equal, that they are
endowed by their Creator with certain unalienable
Rights, that among these are Life, Liberty and
the pursuit of Happiness. That to secure these rights,
Governments are instituted... deriving their just powers from
the consent of the governed.[1]

When I told a friend that the United Nations Fourth World Conference on Women was being held in China, she asked,"Why on earth would the government of China, of all places, with its feet-binding of women and its female infanticide, not to mention its human rights violations, invite thousands of feminist women to hold a conference there?"

"That's easy," I said. "The government of China wants the country to be seen as a world power. They didn't get the Olympics, so they'll take second best, the women. And what better place for women to meet than in a country that needs to see women differently, to be told that girls are valuable? Asia is the only continent which has not been host to the world's women. And I'm sure that the government of China had no idea how much impact the Conference and the Forum would have on their women and their way of life. It's like they've opened Pandora's Box and don't know it yet. Governments aren't always very smart."

I was struck by the simple explanation of Aman, our guide in Turkey, as to how governments came into being in the first place.

In the Archaic Time the people banded together and created some rules for community living which were for the safety and protection of the people against enemies who threatened to overtake them. Then they chose leaders to supervise the keeping of the rules, and that's how governments got started.

"And from that time to this," I thought to myself, "is a long stretch of centuries when empires have risen and fallen and, far too often, governments' dedication to the people has eroded into self-seeking, powermongering, land-grabbing and fear of loss of control, which lead inevitably to war."

It is a fact that governments are essential to the well-being of nations. It is also true that, at this point in time, they can't be trusted to have the best interests of the people at heart. Indigenous people, especially women, the world over suffer pitiful conditions, the result of heavy imperialistic tracks made by governments deep on the pages of history. Greed for natural resources, land and fame motivate those in power to claim ownership of others' lands and peoples. The country of Hong Kong, for example, has just been "given'"by Britain to China; Taiwan may have to fight a war to stay an independent state. Ireland has endured "troubles" for years under Britain's domination. The tribes of Africa are spawning wars faster than they can be stopped. The United States, Australia, and Canada pushed natives off their lands and claimed sovereignty, and are still violating treaties made in good faith. It's everywhere, this governmental penchant to "take over," control, dominate. The misery of women's lives and the pitiable statistics decrying the lack of progress made over the past 20 years in correcting that misery, testify to the fact that governments do not see women's issues as a priority. That's why we need NGOs – Non-Governmental Organizations.

The term NGO came into being to describe those women who would not stay at home in 1975 because they were not "official" governmental delegates to the First World Conference on Women in Mexico City. That conference, sponsored by the United Nations, launched "The Decade for Women." The UN Forum for Women became a parallel conference. The women who attended that NGO Forum believed that governments need to be watched by the citizens; they got into action, monitoring and lobbying their governments to create legislation and agencies to change the status of women. In 1980, Amsterdam, Holland, hosted the Second Conference and Forum; in 1985, the site was Nairobi, Kenya, Africa. There have been many conferences in between, focused on particular aspects of women's lives and the issues that affect them, and NGOs have been active in them all.

NGOs are a little like the insect-like marine animals called copepods. Copepods are so tiny as to be barely visible to the naked eye, and at first glance, seem insignificant. But their impact on the marine food web and chemical cycling in the oceans is profound. Chuck Colgan, a researcher in marine biology, claims that "They are the primary components in the transfer of energy and nutrients between microscopic plants and larger animals in the seas, an interaction with global importance."[2] I think NGOs are like those microscopic plants, of global importance. They generate energy between individuals and systems of government and provide essential nurturance for continuing life.

Recently, a friend and I were talking about what is happening in this modern ocean of women and girls. "It's too much," she said, "so overwhelming that I don't even want to hear about it. I feel too small to do anything about it."

I know the feeling. It reminds me of one of the slogans of the Forum and Conference: "Think Globally. Act Locally." It's like the proverbial stone thrown into water. I can't know how much impact my little actions have on the web of injustice and war, but I do know that millions and millions of such "little actions" are having a profound effect on the people and governments of the world, like those infinitesimal copepods out there in the ocean.

I belonged to NGOs long before the term was coined: FOR, Fellowship of Reconciliation; ACLU, American Civil Liberties Union; On Earth Peace Assembly; NOW, National Organization of Women; Amnesty International; Oxfam; San Diego Economic Conversion Council; Witness for Peace; WILPF; MADRE, For the Children. "MADRE," the Spanish word for "mother," is an organization of women helping women in all parts of the world to better the lives of children.

The NGO Forum and UN Governmental Conference in Beijing brought those life-giving copepods into a huge vat of struggle and hope. The stated purpose of the Forum was "To bring together women and men to challenge, create and transform global structures and processes at all levels through the empowerment and celebration of women."[3] It was, by its very nature, a place where the difference between peoples (NGOs) and governments stood out in stark contrast. The Forum, with all its vitality, energy and courage, connected women's issues, concerns and actions to all the women of all the nations. It mobilized women to lobby their governments to endorse and take serious action to improve the lives of women and girls, which is the heart of the official document called "The Platform For Action." The Platform is far-reaching and thorough, endorsed in Beijing by 189 countries, an action that in itself is a miracle, a cause for hope. It puts teeth into needed change, demands reversal of the pessimistic figures describing improvements and steps forward during the last 20 years.

Václav Havel once made a comment about the difference between optimism and hope. "'Optimism' is the belief that things are going to turn out as you would like, as opposed to 'hope,' which is when you are thoroughly convinced something is moral, right, and just, and therefore you fight, regardless of the consequences. In that sense, I'm full of hope but in no way optimistic."[4] I am full of hope about the possibilities that are inherent in the Platform for Action. When I see the passion, determination, and sacrifices that are being made by courageous women all over the world, I have hope. I'm even guardedly optimistic.

We had been promised that "the government" of China would not watchdog our activities at the Forum, that the Forum grounds would be considered under the jurisdiction of the United Nations. Frustrations ran high on that August 31, 1995, the first day of workshops. It was not enough that "officers" with their tape recorders seemed to be at everybody's elbows, apparently listening in on conversations or "reporting in" what they had heard. Security points were as thick as tar pits and just as hard to get through.

Out of the 126 workshops scheduled for the 9:00 a.m. slot that first day, I had chosen"The Campaign Against Female Genital Mutilation," given by The Egyptian Organization for Human Rights. I wanted to see what progress had been made in that area since the 1985 NGO Forum in Kenya, when I attended several workshops focused on struggles to get the practice outlawed.

On its long, dangling chain around my neck, my "dog tag" boldly displayed my picture and my "number. " It was clear no one got anywhere without this "ticket." Duplicating my experience of the night before, I re-discovered that it was not enough. Security points dovetailed into more security points; long lines queued up for the airline-like purse-probing and electronic surveillance. My frustration knew no bounds. Two and a half hours later, I finally reached my eleven o'clock choice, "Effects of War and Armed Conflict on Women," put on by the General Palestinian Women's Union.

My frustration was multiplied by that of thousands of women, which resulted two days later in an action taken by the head of the China Organizing Committee. She met with governmental officials and threatened to bring the entire Forum to a close if they continued such activity and did not live up to their earlier agreements. Talk about courage and pluck! The next day, the security points were gone – the tape recorders hidden in pants pockets, used only surreptitiously – and the Forum grounds were teeming with Chinese men in plainclothes!

Way back in January, there had been strong protests when the Chinese government moved the Forum out of downtown Beijing, ostensibly because the Workers' Stadium "was not structurally sound for such a large group," reportedly, because they feared protests in Tienanmen Square. The Stadium would have accomodated the 27,000 women who were registered and could choose to attend the plenary sessions. In Huairou, the largest indoor meeting place was the main conference hall which seated 1700 people.

The day before Hillary Rodham Clinton was scheduled to address the Forum, I was surprised at the intensity of my determination to hear my "First Lady" speak. I felt ashamed that President Clinton had not considered these events of enough import to be there in person. I thought he should have joined the many heads of state who did. I was also glad that Hillary had resisted the opposition to her coming.

A big outdoor stadium had been prepared that would seat all who came. The evening before Hillary was to speak, Mother Nature looked on the affairs of "mice and men" with amusement. Steady rain began to fall, foiling their best-laid plans.

At 4:00 a.m., I groaned as I plowed through a downpour to meet the bone-rattling bus to Huairou, armed with my trusty umbrella. At 5:30 a.m., I joined the hundreds already standing on the wide steps leading to locked doors, the umbrellas a tapestry of beautiful bleeding color. Hillary's talk was scheduled to begin at 9:00. More and more women filled the steps and pressed in until we were a soaked mass, every umbrella emptying its full load on the person next to it. I was drenched, feet, hair and clothing. My dress clung to me like the wet women pushing against me. Hours went by, and the streams of women and water stretched past the landing onto lower steps leading to the street. With every move, soft, sucking sounds of feet squished in soaked shoes. Even in the heat and humidity, I began to shiver. We talked about everything imaginable; we joked about the rain; we sang songs; more hours went by. Nine o'clock had come and gone and a testy frustration stirred the crowd. A voice in Chinese-accented English came over a loudspeaker: "Ladies and gentlemen," (if there were any men there, I did not see them) "please, no pushing or shoving. People might get hurt." Indeed, I did feel uneasy, shorter than anyone near me, at the mercy of anyone who might give me a shove, wet as a fish and on slippery steps with nothing to hold on to except my soaked umbrella.

Then it happened. More than a dozen Chinese men cut through the crowd like a bunch of knives, blade to handle. Firmly linked arm in arm, they shouted "Security" and pushed women aside to get through. The line moved immediately in front of me. One of them stepped squarely on my foot and pushed me off balance. The ranks of women caught me and kept me from falling, but not before I had looked him straight in the eye and felt a sudden surge of anger. The crowd stirred as if there were an undercurrent of reaction among the women. They had done it to us again!

"It's another Catch-22," I said to the tall African woman next to me. "They seem to think they have a right to do anything we can't stop them from doing."

"Terrible!" her accent made it sound like music.

It was nearly 10:30 when the admonition of officials came over the loudspeaker: "Please move slowly so as not to trample anyone." The doors to the inner sanctum were pushed ajar and the mob poured into the auditorium. In minutes, those 1700 seats were filled and the aisles were bulging with women standing. I got a seat in the next to the last row of the front section and glanced around to the row behind me. My first thought was, "I don't believe this!" The man who had stepped on my foot was right behind me, and the whole long row was filled with seated Chinese men! Then I *was* angry! I heard myself saying aloud to no one in particular, "The nerve of these men to take 30-some seats when hundreds of women either can't get in or are standing in the aisles! It's not only sheer discourtesy, but what about that promise the government made that there would be no security officers on these grounds?"

I turned to face the men, pointed at my foot-stomping offender, and raised my voice: "Security. Up! Out!" A whole row of heads shook NO. At that moment, a Spanish woman standing in the aisle, more vociferous and angry than I, shouted, "Up! Up!" In minutes hundreds of women's voices had joined the protest. The decibel level rose; eyes all over the room focused in our direction. It got intense and it got loud. Gradually, the stolid refusal on the men's faces changed, first to discomfort, then, outright fear.

They shifted uneasily in their seats, obviously wanting to get up and run, and not moving a muscle. They looked so vulnerable and helpless that I felt a fleeting twinge of sympathy for them, very fleeting. Greedily, not wanting to lose my seat, I said to a standing Spanish woman, "They aren't going to move until somebody in charge tells them to. Ask that security officer on the stage to tell them to go." She took off, and I saw her speaking to one of the "officials" standing there like marble statues.

Five minutes later, as silently as puppets on a string and without any apparent instruction, the whole line of men got up and disappeared. The group quieted and the seats quickly filled with women. On one level, it seemed like a petty disturbance. I had not "turned the other cheek." On another level, I was tired of being "nice," letting men get away with mistreatment of women, and I had a certain smug satisfaction in having had a part in this demonstration of woman-power.

It turned out to be short-lived. The authorities in China are not to be outdone by a bunch of demanding women. While we were led in wonderfully lusty singing to while away more time, the men were apparently plotting their response. Just before Hillary appeared on stage, and too late to do anything about it, the aisles which had been cleared of women to satisfy fire restrictions, were filled with those same men! The best we could do was to get them to sit down or kneel so as not to obstruct our view to the stage.

Hillary's skilled analysis, forthright comments, and warm, empathic spirit inspired me. She made visible the women who were not there, and she insisted that "women's rights are human rights."

I had learned years ago that many governments think and behave as if "government" and "people" are synonomous. In 1982, I went to Nicaragua with an NGO, Women Against US Intervention in South America. While we were there, a newscast told of two helicopters that had been shot down over Nicaragua, and of a man from Alabama who had been killed. The pilots were wearing United States uniforms, the helicopters marked "US Army." Even so, the United States government immediately announced that they were not US planes or pilots.

We were meeting with a group of women who supported each other in their grief as mothers and wives of war martyrs. A woman named Carmen, the mother of seven children, was grieving four who had died in combat, another imprisoned and tortured. She knew of the death of the Alabama soldier. What she said hit home to me: "I know you are the people of the United States, and not your government, but you *are* responsible for your government's actions. They need to hear that you oppose what they are doing in Nicaragua. And, if you can, please tell the mother of that man from Alabama that I will grieve with her over her son's death." Her great spirit struck a chord in me that still resounds. She separated us as people from our government, did not blame us for the action, but she held us responsible to let our voices be heard in protest.

"You have free speech in a democracy," she said. "Use it."

A couple months ago, I watched a video called *Gate of Heavenly Peace.* ("Tienanmen" means "Gate of Heavenly Calm.") It documents the brutal story of the Tienanmen Square massacre, and tells of the time the students and their supporters appealed to the governmental authorities for an audience and conversation. Chosen representatives took the message: "The people request an audience with you."

The response came back: "What an absurd impossibility! Are we to have conversations with ourselves? We *are* the people!" The bloodshed that followed proved just how wrong they were.

China doesn't have a corner on that fallacious thinking, however. Even in my own democratic country, one of my duly elected representatives never votes the way I want him to vote, and it isn't because he doesn't know my views! He seems to be deaf to other voices and views than his own. The government itself keeps important information from the people, which is anything but just or democratic. Government agencies and their corporate contractors spend jointly between five and six billion dollars a year to classify documents as "Top Secret," "Secret," or "Confidential." About 1.5 billion pages of documents have remained classified for 25 years or more. What kind of democracy is it when a government official as unprincipled as former President Richard Nixon says, "The system of classification in the United States has failed to meet the standards of an open and democratic society."[5]

That's, of course, before he was found guilty of the same kind of cover-up.

Senator Daniel P. Moynihan says, "Secrecy rules conceal and protect not only military or intelligence secrets, but also the blunders of agencies and officials. The partial opening of the security archives of the Soviet Union have produced stunning disclosures about U. S. government actions. We find ourselves relying on archives in Moscow to resolve questions of what was going on in Washington in mid-century. This is absurd."[6] No wonder that in my democratic country right now there are groups who distrust government. Sadly, they allow their distrust to degenerate into violence and terror.

Women know that the cult of secrecy and lies that plagues both public and private life in this world society must be broken. For these reasons and more, NGOs are critically important at this juncture of the world's history. Governments must be monitored and held accountable for their actions and inactions. We grassroots citizens need to support each other in this hard task.

NGOs are now active in every nation of the world, filled with people like you and me, people who keep their eyes and ears open to what is going on around their feet and in their governments. They make their voices heard, as we did in Beijing, telling it "like it is," demanding change. I have never heard of an NGO that has "top secrets" or withholds information deliberately from its members. Members of NGOs do not think they are synonymous with government. They learn from their mistakes, rather than trying to cover them up. To my knowledge, NGOs tell the truth. I heartily wish that governments did the same.

One of my favorite NGOs is MADRE, For the Children. It's an organization dedicated to easing the burdens of the poor, oppressed, marginalized and victimized peoples in many countries, especially women and children. In speaking of the hope of the peasant population in a village of 450 families – 4,080 men, women and children in Guatemala – Vivian Stromberg, the Executive Director, wrote the following:

For the indigenous people of Zapotitlan, Guatemala, life is brutally hard, but their hope perseveres in the dream of a simple health clinic.

To oppressors, hope is a dangerous thing. That's why they go to such lengths to squash it. [Hope]... threatens the standing order of things, something the US-backed military regime in Guatemala City just won't tolerate. The military is more interested in guns than medicines, in violence, power and control than immunization.

The army maintains a constant, threatening presence. Military vehicles rumble through the streets. Men with machine guns rove the neighborhoods in silent menace. Homes are broken into. Villagers mysteriously "disappear." Mutilated bodies are dumped into anonymous mass graves.

And yet, amid this chaos and terror, terror our own US government chooses to ignore, the people of Zapotitlan still dream of a better future. They haven't given up.[7]

At the Forum, it became clear that thousands of like NGOs have not given up. The hope and determination that surged through those thousands of women does indeed "threaten the standing order of things." It is seen as "dangerous" by totalitarian governments who want to do as they please without accountability to anyone, a sure path to tyranny.

As they did in China, NGOs work two ways in their own countries, with and for the people and as a monitoring conscience for the governments. They are the yeast, a living, moving organism in the dough of governments and society. While governments spend much of their time and energy preserving the status quo and protecting those who are in power, NGOs are Holy Termites working to undermine unjust structures, eradicate repression, torture, war and all violations of human rights. They are no longer willing to accept "what is" as just, inevitable, or unchangeable. No wonder the Chinese authorities were uneasy.

Governments, in contrast to grassroots organizations, are superstructures linked in a massive network of secrecy, intrigue, self-interest and lies. They are very often blind to actual living conditions and life situations created by their actions. They are sometimes systems of torture and hate, fanning racial hatreds into "ethnic cleansing," condoning rape by blaming the victims, or, worse, promoting it as "earned spoils of war," as in the former Yugoslavia.

In 1989, the government of China, to limit dangerous population growth, instituted in good faith a one-child policy. The trouble is that they still value male above female, acting as if women and girls are expendable. The rate of female infanticide has risen sharply, creating a situation in which, by the year 2000, there will be no wives for 60,000 Chinese men of marriagable age. If that weren't so awful, it would be laughable. Didn't anybody make the connection between killing girl children and having no women to marry?

A workshop leader at the Forum told of a "traffic ring" that is even now stealing girls as young as six or eight off the streets of adjoining countries, selling them to young men of China who force them into marriage. This means they become slaves to Chinese husbands and mothers-in-law, refugees with no right to citizenship. I lost sleep after that workshop, and I still feel outrage and tears when I think of the horror of it.

Governments do a lot of dissembling, covering up mistakes and pretending that all is well. NGOs tell the bold and awful truth as they see it, and they see life as it really is because they live among the people who are living it. When my own government officials visited El Salvador years ago and came back denying the atrocities and poverty I had seen there with my own eyes, I was shocked. They had not seen the El Salvador I saw when I went to stand with the people in remembrance of the hideous butchering of five priests and two women two years before, carried out by soldiers trained in my own USA. They had been limousined from airports to official halls through areas of the elite and wealthy. I went by public bus, and saw streets full of squalor and need. I have walked with women living in the slums and mud huts on the outskirts of Nairobi, Kenya; on the streets of Calcutta, India; under bridges in San Diego, California; on poisoned lands in Kiev, Ukraine. And governments are still busy pouring money into military might, preparing for the next war, indulging in the big business of selling weapons, building the "brotherhood" of war. Governments somehow do not seem to realize that what hurts one nation hurts all nations; if we poison the land in Ukraine and put radiation into the air, sooner or later we will all reap the same harvest of disease, malnutrition, poverty and death. With the rise in immune-related diseases all over the world, including the USA, are we indeed already reaping that harvest?

China's facade made me sad and angry at the same time. As had happened in Nairobi in 1985, the Chinese government had exiled or hidden, goodness knows where, the "objectionable" people, the homeless, the ill, the poor, the imprisoned. At the entrance to every village, stationed guards kept us from seeing "real life." It was reported that prisoners had been executed just prior to the coming of international visitors. The ever-present rust, blue and white plastic blankets kept "reality" from our sight. The eyes of governments are remarkably nearsighted. They need the corrective lenses of NGOs to help them see their people in the naked reality in which they live.

The Chinese government controlled the number of participants by refusing visas to thousands of women around the world and limiting to 5,000 the number of Chinese women who could attend. The *China Daily*, the official newspaper, refuted the life experience of Tibetan women and even threatened those who were telling the truth. It denied abuses in orphanages that have been documented beyond refutation.

I learned firsthand that *China Daily* is a propaganda machine. One day during the Forum, Marisa, our "exercise guru," and I were waiting in the same line. She called out, "Beth, I see you got quoted in the *China Daily*. You must have been interviewed."

I was astounded. "Not me, Marissa. Nobody interviewed me."

"Well, they quote you. I brought you a copy of the paper."

I was curious. I opened it to read, "Beth Glick-Rieman of the USA said she was surprised at the spaciousness of the home of the manager of a village cooperative she was visiting. She assumed that several families lived there."

"Well, I'll be darned, Marisa. They got my name right. Somebody must have read my dog tag and put into my mouth the words the government wanted the people to hear. So, this is the media in China. Outright misrepresentation. At least in America, I'm not important enough to get misquoted in the newspapers!" I wanted nothing to do with *China Daily* after that, and I realized how very important it is to the government of China that the United States be impressed with what is happening there.

It's a little like the Pentagon in the USA denying any responsibility for the Gulf War Syndrome plaguing hundreds of soldiers who served there. After a great deal of pressure, newspapers have just announced that, "The CIA admits that its errors may have led to the demolition of an Iraqi ammunition bunker filled with chemical weapons."[8] That event exposed tens of thousands of US troops to nerve gas and debilitation they will live with the rest of their lives! Not to mention the wave of disease and death unleashed on unknown numbers of Iraqi children and adult citizens!

Denial of the truth undermines the credibility of governments, and tardy admission of guilt does little or nothing to change the burden people must carry as a result of those actions.

The more absolute the power, the more likely it is to be abused. As Lord Acton said, "Absolute power corrupts absolutely." Like the fear instilled in the toddler by a parent's voice too loud and threatening, governmental repression, injustice and control deaden the creative life and thought of a people, and hold back the day when peace and justice may govern life on the earth. That day will never come until the voices of women are heard and taken seriously.

8

Listen to Women
– for a Change

We were drawn into one another's presence.
We began hearing one another to speech.[1]

Whole means putting back together history and nature,
split apart by a patriarchy that assigned history to men as prized
and nature to women as denigrated.[2]

The air around me still resounds with the stories of women, some told in Helsinki, many told on The Peace Train and many more told in Beijing, stories full of suffering, action and hope. Some were about privileges and commitment to personal growth and responsibility. Some were about giving a voice to the voiceless, the poor, the oppressed. Some were about putting an end to the craziness of war and preparations for it. Some were about saving our Mother Earth, her creatures and her plants. Some were about open confrontation of the evils being perpetrated against women and girls.

It began in Helsinki, before the Train was on the tracks, as women clustered together, learning to know one another, crossing the boundaries of color, nation, race and language. I joined some of the groups and found myself traveling to far distant places.

All together, these stories are building and maintaining a network of support, encouragement and possibility within which we can work in our own small corners for change. All together they present a microcosm of the lives of women throughout the world. I invite you to listen in as these women speak in their own voices about what life is like for many women and girls in this world.

Lynette of Australia had dark hair and smiling eyes.

Beth: Lynette, what is it like to live where you live, and have you lived your whole life there?

Lynette: I was born in Australia, in a country town called Temora. I have lived my whole life in Australia. There are six states and two territories in the country. I come now from Canberra, the city of the national government. There is a lot of awareness about women's issues there, a stark contrast to the many areas I've been through. I stay very busy. I have a husband and two daughters. Family life is very important to me.

I work full-time in the public sector spearheading a program in management development for senior managers under the federal government. Prior to that I worked in the Parliament for the Attorney General. I am also involved in many community activities. The main one, leading up to Beijing, is a National Steering Committee for a Coalition of Australian Organizations for Women. We received some nominal federal funding for the purpose of getting representatives from our 70 NGOs to the Beijing Conference.

Over 300 women from our NGO sector are going to Beijing. It is the first time a national coalition of this kind has been created. Previously, these groups have been working in isolation. Now it is amazing how we communicate with each other. The coalition puts out a newsletter that goes out to each organization every two months, and they have the opportunity to send back information to be sent out in the next newsletter. More importantly, we have a fortnightly, fax service that goes out from the federal government to the NGOs. It is an activities report that lists every government inquiry that is going on, any decisions that are pending, any positions that are opening, any conferences that are being held. Every two to three months we have a telephone link-up with the NGOs to see what their needs are and what is happening or not happening in preparation for Beijing. They fax back to us this information. Then the National Peak Women's Council, an advisory body to the government, uses this network to know what the women's position is on any given issue.

Beth: What attitude does the government have toward the NGOs?

Lynette: A cooperative attitude, because we at the moment have a Labor government with a strong platform in social justice. They have a high regard for NGOs.

Beth: What is their attitude toward women?

Lynette: We're lucky. This particular government has a healthy respect for women. In 1972, they appointed a women's advisor to the government. Since then, the prime minister has always had a women's advisor at the cabinet level. She is elected into the cabinet and then appointed by the prime minister to handle the women's portfolio.

Beth: Tell me about how you got to where you are. What was your life like when you were little?

Lynette: The town where I was born was a very traditional, Anglo-Saxon community, all white. We had a gold rush and Chinese workers came to work, also, an influx in the early 1950s of European migrants, mainly from Greece and Italy. There were no native tribal people in our area. The churches were a mix, Roman Catholic and Protestant, mainly Anglican or Church of England. Irish Catholic nuns came in and set up schools.

My mother worked managing a retail store until she married and had children; then she stayed home. Very few married women in Temora worked outside the home, and that was true all the time I was growing up. My father never allowed her to work. She obeyed, and was totally dependent on him for income, so there really wasn't any choice.

Beth: What was it like for you to be a girl in that home?

Lynette: Very difficult. I am a very independent person. From a young age I was a free thinker. My father had the attitude that I was to be seen and not heard. I had an older brother and a younger brother. Any conversation at the dinner table the boys were deferred to. It was quite a restrictive environment, especially in education. Primary school is eight years, junior high four years and senior high or college, two years. Then you go to university. When I finished junior high, my father refused to pay for the next two, so it was clear I had to pay my own way. I worked in a little candy store to finish high school. My father was quite annoyed that I chose to do this. Later, when I graduated, he was proud of the fact.

Beth: Would he have done this for your brothers?

Lynette: He would have paid for them, except they chose to go into apprenticeships for a trade. The interesting thing about this is that I did pave the way for my sister who was 12 years younger than me. It was never a question that she would go on to university. He refused to pay for me, and I couldn't pay for it myself, but when she came along, he paid for her to go, so I think I paved the way.

Beth: Did you have some specific interest that you wanted to follow?

Lynette: I was interested in history and I was anxious to be a teacher, but I wasn't able to follow that up.

Beth: What was life like for you being a teenager?

Lynette: I had quite good teenage years. There was not a lot of money in our family so we made entertainment for ourselves. I played sports, was in the school hockey team; everyone played hockey. We read a lot. We had a really good library in our town, and we were encouraged to read. We didn't have television, so I think we were more imaginative. I had good girl friends. We listened to music, sewed clothes for each other, and just had fun times.

Beth: Besides education, were there other times for you when being a girl was a disadvantage?

Lynette: Probably not, because I was pretty mouthy. I always stated my own position. I had some pretty strong friends, a group of girls that in and out of school supported each other and became a network. We did a lot of things girls were not supposed to do. There was certainly clear delineation between what girls could do and what they couldn't, but we didn't challenge it then because we usually did what we wanted to do. One of the things was that if we wanted to go to the movies on a Saturday night, we weren't allowed to go by ourselves; one of our older brothers had to go with us. It was fine; it was a two-way thing. My brother used my friends as his girlfriends so he wouldn't have to search. It wasn't materialistic growing up but we had some fun times.

Beth: Sounds like you felt pretty free. What did you do for fun?

Lynette: We played tennis, went to school socials. Some girls had a record collection, so we got together and listened to music. It was pretty wholesome, a lot of fun. It was pre-alcohol and pre-drugs and that was good. I was born in 1949.

Beth: After you got out of school, what did you do?

Lynette: I moved to Canberra and sat for the public service entrance exam. I got accepted and took that training knowing that my parents couldn't afford to pay for any other education. So I started work at the age of 18, worked as a secretary in public service, worked my way up for 23 years before I left. I married during that time and had my daughters.

Maternity leave came in 1972. I was the first woman in my particular work area to return from maternity leave and that was when I came up against my first harassment. The male workers felt that it wasn't right for a mother to work, that she should be at home with the children. For two years prior to my going on leave, I had been in a high level job, not permanent, but continually acting at a high level. When I came back, I had been put down two levels. It was almost as if they considered my brain had been on holiday as well. They also decided to send me on a two-week training program in Sydney. My baby was nine months old and they expected me to say no, that I wouldn't go. I knew this was a test because if I had said no, and I was the next one to go into the manager's position, I would have lost that career opportunity. So I discussed with my husband what I should do, and he actually took annual leave from his job and came with me and brought the baby. At lunch times during the training, I went out and fed the baby and then fed her again as soon as the course was finished. We did that for two weeks. I knew that had I refused to do that, they could have refused me the returning conditions that other women had fought so hard to get and I would have blown it for the other women, too. But I really had to have my husband's support to do that. He has always supported me; he even supported my working when the girls were very young.

Beth: Would you call your marriage egalitarian, equal in all respects?

Lynette: Very much so. We worked hard at it in the initial stages. When we married, neither of us had very much money. We were both keen to work and right from the start the household chores were automatically split between the two of us.

Beth: How did you decide who did what?

Lynette: It was very easy. A perfect example is ironing. I had ironed a shirt in a hurry, and he made a comment about a wrinkle in it. I said, "If you don't like it, do it yourself." So we've now been married 25 years and he's still doing all the ironing. I just added my ironing to it and as we had the girls, their ironing was added to it, so now he does all the ironing for the household.

Beth: Were there other areas?

Lynette: Housework. He does the cleaning. I do all the shopping because he hates shopping. I have done most of the cooking because I love cooking and he finds it a chore. The gardening is shared, but he does the main part of it because he loves gardening.

Beth: Seems like it just flowed. Did you have any arguments about it?

Lynette: We had more arguments about family, because my mother-in-law thought it was dreadful that I made her son do the ironing. My brother who is younger than me needed some help. His wife was having a baby and she had to go to another town because of complications. They had two little children at home, and he rang me in a panic and asked me if I could come over for a week and watch the children while she was in hospital. I wasn't in a position at work to get the time off, but my husband was. So my husband took the week off and went to my brother's house and cared for the children. Well for the family, this was mind-blowing. My little niece and nephew just couldn't get over the fact that their uncle was able to do house-work. So it has been very much equal sharing.

Beth: Tell me more about your work back home.

Lynette: We are quite busy at the moment because of the French declara-tion to resume nuclear testing, working on some environmental issues as well. We still have to clear up some testing sites from World War II. The major part of Australian society is not particularly pro-active in peace and justice issues; so we are working hard to keep those issues in the arena.

Beth: Do you have regular meetings of WILPF?

Lynette: Our chapter meets monthly but we often have only about six mem-bers. We have a lot more financial members than contributing members. The lead-up to the Peace Train has been good. There's been a bit of a resur-gence in attendance. Helen Cook and myself are from the Canberra chapter, just the two of us, and some from Melbourne and Adelaide and Sydney.

Beth: Does your chapter do certain actions for peace? How do you keep the awareness of the desirability of a nuclear-free zone in the minds of people?

Lynette: One of the pivotal roles that our chapter can play is that we are actually based in the nation's capital, so we see members of Parliament and Representatives there. We are often called upon to send papers to the north, after monitoring what is going on. We tend to be a bit more of a lobbying group because of our geographical position and if WILPF nationally wants to get something into Parliament, we have a couple of parliamentarians who are members of WILPF, which is wonderful, and we have pretty good access to their offices. So it's good for us that way.

Beth: Did you have any trouble getting visas to China? I had quite a hard time at our Chinese embassy.

Lynette: I had to be careful when I was filling in the form. I had to apply personally through my Russian visa because I couldn't put the name of my employer down. I'm technically paid by the Department of Defense, even though we are a statutory authority. There was no way I could put the Defense Department on it, or the Chinese government would immediately reject it. Normally, I'm a strictly honest person, but I've had to be a bit "slip of the tongue." It opens up a whole new thing that we never think of.

Now my concern is for the Chinese women once the conference is over. They will have had the opportunity to meet with women who are not as controlled by their governments as they are. They will have had the opportunity to see what life could be under a different regime. It will be an issue, I'm sure, as to how they will return to normality. How will the government treat the women after all the visitors have left? Bear in mind that the Chinese government really had their eyes opened in Copenhagen at The World Social Summit Conference, to seeing how effective the nongovernmental sector can be in lobbying governments to effect changes in their agenda. I'm hearing they are convinced that they do not want to encourage this nongovernmental sector in China, which is quite anti their thinking. In the middle of that, there are the women who have been exposed to it and have mingled in it, and what will life be for them after? My great hope is that our going there will be able to give them some change, but I hope it's change for the better and will not make them more putdown afterward.

Beth: That may be inevitable. I wonder, too, what will happen. I think every movement ahead for justice and peace bears its penalties and price. In my own life, in San Diego, which is a major military installation, when I have spoken out against wars, I have been ostracized. When I was speaking at a Church Women United meeting, a woman stood up, came to me at the podium, and said angrily, "If your life depended on the earnings of a navy man, you wouldn't be talkin' this kind of stuff. You ought to be thrown out of here!" Then she left. The committee was embarrassed. I felt as if I had been giving too-easy answers. It clearly pointed out what peacemakers are up against when people earn their living by the military. They don't want to hear about peace. War is a good word for a lot of people in my country and peace is a bad word. That's very distressing.

Lynette: Yes. I have an interesting situation. The job I am doing at the moment, the office is housed in the Department of Defense. Across the corridor are military personnel who have been very scathing about my being on the Peace Train.

Beth: Scathing?

Lynette: Oh, very scathing. "What do you women think you will achieve? The military is the way to do justice in the world, through military might and power."

Beth: Tell me about being on this Peace Train. How did you get here and what has it been like for you?

Lynette: I got here through being a member of WILPF. I saw it advertised and sent in an application, not expecting to get on it. We were hearing rumors that there were only 200 places and they would be filled rather quickly. So I was surprised when I got the letter saying, "Welcome Aboard." Life on the Train has been mixed for me. I guess I learned more about myself than I expected.

Beth: What have you learned?

Lynette: I have always been a people person and thought I needed people around and I've operated well with people. But now I've noticed that too many people can be overpowering for me. At times I have just needed to be alone and to get away from it all. One of the things that struck me was the rudeness of the women. Some of the questioning toward our hosts in the various cities has not been particularly sensitive to the situation of the women there. I have been a little bit alarmed when some of the women have used their stories to push their own points of view which are alien to our hosts. I thought that we were there to learn and to meet with our hosts, and at times we could have been more sensitive to their level of understanding and to the economic situation they're in. I think that a lot of them sacrificed to put on some of the functions they did for us, and I think that at times we forgot to say "thank you" enough. So I guess the Peace Train has been a time of learning.

Beth: Do you think there are justice issues on the Train that have not been addressed or that have been?

Lynette: I have mixed feelings about that. I think some of the issues that needed to be addressed in the group have not been addressed. I see a very hierarchical structure, administrative structure, when I would like to think that an international women's movement would be more participative. From my point of view, I think that has been a bit of an injustice. There are a lot of skilled and capable women here who haven't been given the opportunity to participate. Decision making has been very centralized. I wouldn't want to comment about injustices against the black women on the train. I find that hard to support. I think they've been given opportunities to express themselves and to conduct workshops and to encourage others to understand. I think the women from the lower nations like Columbia and Peru haven't been given opportunities to tell their stories, and they have been through a lot in their struggle toward liberation. There is some injustice in that.

Beth: I agree. One woman told me she strongly objected to the officials' having given workshop time to a man to hold forth on his own issue of homophobia while the women of Columbia and Peru were being told there was no workshop time available for them to talk about what's happening in their countries.

Lynette: I went to that particular workshop. I am not convinced that it was needed at that time. There were more important issues we needed to address. I am unhappy, too, with the fact that the tour operators left one woman behind at the Chinese border to deal with a difficult situation in a strange country. I think one of them should have accompanied her and joined us at the next stop.

Beth: Are there other things that troubled you?

Lynette: I wished that my compartment mates would have been more considerate about sitting on my bunk when I wanted to rest. I wish I had not felt too intimidated in that situation. I needed to let them know my feelings.

Beth: What are the good things about the Train? What effects has it had? What may happen because of it?

Lynette: I think it was wonderful that we had contact with women in these countries. I have just been overwhelmed with some of the discussions and the life situations of those people, with understanding how life is for a lot of women, to know how difficult things are for them, to know the dangers they must face in order just to survive day to day. I think the understandings we will take away from the Train are great. I did not know that the lifestyles in the countries we have gone through still existed in the world. To observe some of that has improved my understanding and I hope my tolerance. So I think I will be taking away good things from the Train, maybe in general from the people, but there will always be some people who stand out, that from the start have brought special memories and I want to keep in touch with them.

Beth: What do you see yourself doing in Beijing?

Lynette: Since I am a member of WILPF, I hope to have an opportunity to show that the peace agenda is important. I want to watch the other issues as well. At the top of my agenda is equality in all levels of decision making. And I want to see education for all girl children, regardless of their age, and for all women. And health care for women and girls is certainly important to me.

Beth: Thank you very much, Lynette. It is wonderful to have this time with you.

Lynette: It's wonderful that someone wants to hear me talk.

It is often hard to find someone who genuinely wants to listen to us when we talk about our lives and what is important to us. Women often speak of the frustration and anger they experience when men seem not to listen or to value what they say. Men *do* come from a different perspective and life experience. I have often felt that my words and opinions were being devalued or discounted. It is not only men, however, who have trouble listening to women. Women themselves are not always good listeners. Some are so engrossed in their own lives and work that they seem to have no interest in hearing others.

One day, a woman from the USA sat beside me at dinner. She works as a consultant, trainer and writer, sometimes teaches teachers in elementary schools how to teach conflict resolution to children from kindergarten through the grades. She is also a journalist and hopes to get out several press releases about the conferences. I learned a lot about her, and since I do some of the same things, we could have really connected, but we didn't. Not once did she ask me what I do, where I am, what is exciting for me. Always the focus was on her. That's sad. I think being peacemakers means first of all making connections. My time with her left me with no sense of connection and I was certainly not at peace.

In contrast, there was Josephine of London, a woman whose warm chocolatey skin framed black eyes in a long face with strong jaws. She was a wonderful listener. We spoke of one of the tasks of women as being to find our voices and speak out. She told me that she is here to speak out about making racism a priority; that she believes it is the most important issue facing the world today, that the older women in WILPF don't seem to hear her or take her seriously.

I've had that same experience of not being heard. More times than I can count. The first time it really got to me was in 1975. I was an adjunct faculty member of United Theological Seminary in Ohio. One day, 20 faculty people sat around a polished mahogany table in the conference room, only two of us, women. I had not spoken often in those meetings, so I surprised myself by suggesting an approach to a specific problem we were discussing. There was dead silence for a minute; it was as if they were stone deaf. Then a male professor picked up the conversation, which went on for about 20 minutes, after which he made the very same suggestion, as if it were his own idea, and the group immediately accepted it as the way to proceed. I remember wondering if I was a little crazy.

I've since learned that this experience is common to women. All too often, when we do find our voices, men do not, perhaps cannot, hear us. In 1985, I was with about 20 women on an educational safari west of Nairobi following the Third World Conference on Women there. We were in a small farming village near Lake Victoria, Kenya, sitting in the blistering sun under a tarpaulin stretched between bamboo poles. We had just eaten with our fingers the porridge that had been served so generously on broad leaves.

Tall, black Letitia was speaking in broken English, gesturing with leathered, calloused hands that had the look and feel of being close to the soil. "We will go now to see our tree plantings. We got them through foreign aid from the United States. We had some trouble at first. They sent a representative to meet with us so we could tell them what we needed. But that man spoke only to the men, and our men didn't know what would grow here because they never do the farming. If they had talked with us women, we could have told them that what they wanted to send would never work. So we did a lot of work planting trees that died the first year. This time, though, we finally got through to them and we think we will have success. We need these trees to help stop erosion of the soil."

Twenty years later, in Huairou, I attended a workshop on "Women's Sustainable Alternatives for Managing Natural Resources," given by The Network of African Rural Women's Associations. Men are apparently still not listening to the voices of women. A woman from India asked, "Why is it that we can't get men to pay attention to what we know and say? We are the ones who work the farms. We know what works and what does not. We know how to bring about change if only we could get the men to listen."

Tayba of Sudan, whose dark eyes matched her skin, wore an air of friendliness, a flowing scarf over her black hair, and the glow of a new bride. Our time to talk was hemmed in by meetings.

Beth: Tell me about your life, Tayba, what it was like to be born where you were, to be a girl there, and what is your life like now as a woman?

Tayba: I was born in Sudan in the national capital, Khartoum, and grew up in a big family.

Beth: How big a family? I was one of 12 kids.

Tayba: You can't believe it, there were 15 kids, but I come from a family of thousands. We have extended family like cousin and cousin of your cousin. My father is married to four women and we live in a big house. Each woman has her own house. I had a very exciting life. I was the youngest of all; my father died when I was seven. Being a young girl in

Sudan is a struggle; we don't have an outside life. We definitely don't go out alone. If you're going to visit your friend, you would take along your little brother or cousin. Doing things alone is completely different and difficult for me.

Beth: Tell me about your home.

Tayba: In Sudan we wait for my brothers to come from their job and then we sit down and eat together. We have a big tray, plates full of meat or rice or salad. It was unheard of not to eat together. I don't know how to eat alone. We were taught to behave and to be responsible, especially a girl child. You are always told you have to learn how to clean the house, how to take care of sister and little brother and even older ones, you know. When my sister was 13, she cooked for the whole family.

Beth: As a girl, did you get to go to school? It isn't common, is it, for a girl?

Tayba: No, it isn't common. I liked to study, and I have my aunt who went outside the country to study. I went to government school. I got good grades. I went to university in Khartoum and heard about the African Fellowship Program which gives ten people from different African countries scholarships to study in the American University in Cairo. Luckily, in 1988, I got the scholarship representing Sudan. I finished my master's degree in administration. Then I got a job with the United Nations in Saudi Arabia. When I finished my mission, I came back to American University.

Beth: Aren't you supposed to get married at a young age?

Tayba: Yes, before you're 17. Even in the stories, when the beautiful girl grows up she will go to the prince and get married. We have medical doctors who spent years and years behind books and reading, and after they get married they just stay home. They have to take care of the husband and raise his child, and there is no other institution to help. If I went back to Sudan, I would take the role of the traditional woman.

Beth: Tell me about Sudan. Is genital mutilation practiced there?

Tayba: Yes, one of the highest rates of severe genital mutilation is found in Sudan. More than 80 percent of the women are circumcised. It's the biggest country in Africa and is surrounded by eight different countries that also practice female genital mutilation.

Beth: Is that done surgically, or is it done by the women?

Tayba: It is done by the midwife in villages. They are trying not to do it in the hospital because the NGOs are trying to make public awareness. It is quite difficult because millions of them want their women to be circumcised. If a girl is not, she's not accepted, because people whisper, "Oh, she's not circumcised." They throw bad words on her, like you are prostitute or you're something like that. So many men don't want to marry a woman who is not circumcised, and each mother wants her daughter to get married.

Beth: How old are girls when it is done?

Tayba: Usually between five and seven years old.

Beth: Was it practiced in your family?

Tayba: Yes.

Beth: Do you have memories of it, or would you rather not talk about it?

Tayba: I think I was five years old. I remember one thing bad. My cousin helped my mother carry me to the midwife, and I was biting her. I remember later I was suffering when I had my period first time; this was so painful. I had to go to the doctor and be helped, it was so painful.

Beth: There are three kinds of female circumcision, aren't there?

Tayba: One is suna; that means whatever is coming from the prophet, you know, the Koran. Mohammed doesn't encourage the circumcision because he found it as a habit in the Arabs at that time. So he said, "Don't take it all. Don't sew it. If you want to do it, do it this way, but I prefer not to do it." So they just cut the upper part of the clitoris and they don't sew. You never find female circumcision in Saudi Arabia. They never do it, even in all the Arab world, like in Jordan, they don't do it.

Beth: I did not realize that at all. Thanks for talking about it. I know our time's short, so tell me what the Peace Train has been like for you.

Tayba: A wonderful experience. I have met so many nice women and I have learned a lot from their experience. I had the sense of unity and diversity. They all want something in common, peace. It was very good, a peaceful atmosphere; you never hear anybody shouting at each other. Sometimes I felt myself out of it, that I cannot fit in all groups of people. But the concept of sharing is what's good; you take lunch with different people, breakfast, dinner. You talk to this and that, and you never feel lonely. I never felt alone.

Beth: What has the NGO Forum been like for you?

Tayba: I thought it would be like people are going to start doing action, to do the lobby, you know, to build a good network. Now we spent the whole week doing the workshops and presenting the case studies but not doing the network and what is going to happen after this? It was very informative to me to know that even American women suffer from not being satisfied, not being represented at a governmental level, high posts in government. They want a woman to be different in her way of dealing with power than men. But we lacked the action. Same thing as in the Social Summit in Copenhagen in March and in Cairo – talking about it but not getting the action.

I wished I could have had more time with Tayba, to learn more about her life and her hopes.

Pia Massie of Vancouver, Canada, was one of the young ones on the Train. She was curious about this interview process.

Beth: Pia, tell me how you happened to get on the Peace Train.

Pia: A friend of mine from Europe asked me if I would help to make a film with them, so I came.

Beth: Oh, really. So you're the team that is making a video of the whole trip? Are you a filmmaker at home?

Pia: Uh-huh. I work in all different kinds of films.

Beth: Are you employed by a company?

Pia: I have a company, but I set up a new company for each new film.

Beth: What kinds of films do you make?

Pia: Documentaries, commercial films, teaching films, television films.

Beth: Tell me about the documentaries you've done.

Pia: Well, this is one. And I did a documentary about street kids in Vancouver.

Beth: In East Vancouver?

Pia: No, all over the city, all the homeless kids that are coming into the city. And I did another documentary called *Last Wild Salmon* on the depletion of the salmon stock in Canada due to overfishing and pollution.

Beth: What are the films you've done that you've enjoyed the most? Or have you enjoyed them all?

Pia: I love making films. But there are definitely some that you enjoy more than others.

Beth: What's one that stands out in your mind?

Pia: Well, the ones that I enjoy most are probably my own films, where I write and direct them, and I know exactly what's in them. For me, one very enjoyable film of mine was called *More Homesome*.

Beth: More Homesome. That's sounds fascinating. Where'd you get the title? Is that a song?

Pia: No, not really. The letters are very close, "homesome," "lonesome."

Beth: Very close to "wholesome," too. You did that one completely? You did the writing?

Pia: Well, actually, for that one I interviewed a lot of people about what they thought the meaning of the word "home" was. Then I did the writing using some of that.

Beth: How long have you been at this?

Pia: About eight years.

Beth: I'm excited to see what you do with this Peace Train trip.

Pia: Yeah, it will be interesting.

Beth: What do you think, up to now, are the interesting things you have discovered about the people on this trip? Have you had some good interviews?

Pia: I've been doing a lot of the image stuff. We have a second camera and they're doing more of the individual stuff and picking up the details and images, and stuff like that. But just in talking with several women here, it's interesting to see how they are such different people. And also, the other thing that I found really delightful emphasizing was that the median age group was so much older than I thought it would be.

Beth: You know, I looked around here and thought "there are too many gray hairs on this Train."

Pia: It's very interesting, because I thought there would be a lot of younger activists also. But then, the most hard-core activists are older people.

Beth: Well, we have less to lose.

Pia: No, I don't think it's just that. It's that finally all the needs of today are more clear and you know exactly what's important and what's not.

Beth: I think that's true. I also think that there's not as much risk for me as an older woman to say it like it is, to work at what I don't like and stick my neck out for peace and justice.

But it's also a time element, like you're saying. We have more time, the pressures of raising families are less, my children are pretty much on their own. I still have to earn my own living. But there is something about facing the end of my life or looking toward the end of my life, and realizing that if there's anything I want to do, I'd better do it. I may not have tomorrow. I may not have tomorrow even on this Train. So to decide what it is I want my life to say when I'm gone, and then to go for it, is really important to me. And I want my life to say that I worked for peace and justice in this world.

I was reading an article in the airline magazine as I flew from San Diego to New York. This woman was talking about her life; she was 64, which looks young to me, because I'm 72. She had reached a point in her life where she said someone had asked her how she had made a choice to do what she was doing because it was very risky work. She was a Native American. And she said, "I made a choice of what I wanted my life to be about, and then I put on blinders. I didn't see anything else and went for it." That's kind of the way I feel about my own life and this Peace Train. It felt really urgent that I put on blinders to all the demands at home, the pressures on me, and there were lots of them, from family, decisions about financial stuff, my children's worries, just incredible crunches and I thought, like my songwriter son says, "I'm going to bite down hard and swallow tenderness" and go for what I think is right for me to do. So here I am.

Pia: It's important to you, what your kids think?

Beth: Oh, you better believe it. I think they're afraid that I might get sick or, might get hurt, or get whatever in China. And I said to myself, I can't live my life by their fears. If they are afraid of that, they must face into those fears. I want to live my life in the faith that everything will be well.

Tell me about some other women on this train. Or, since you're spe-cializing in images, tell me what images you've gotten?

Pia: Well, one image I got that I really loved was the Sister who's on the Train, who's in the habit. We went swimming, so I got these great pictures of her swimming and then, you know, putting her habit back on and to me it was just so beautiful, because it just showed that anyone can do whatever they want. There are no restrictions – and so much of the time we place restrictions on people based on how they look.

Beth: Yeah. Was that the nude swim?

Pia: No, she had actually borrowed a suit from somebody else.

Beth: So your understanding of her changed when she went into the water. Are there some others that you have in mind?

Pia: I've only been here a day and a half.

Beth: Oh, my, you haven't had time to collect many.

Pia: No, I'm really completely exhausted. I sleep most of the afternoons so I can get adjusted.

Beth: Yes, I've had to do a lot of that, too. I'll let you go. Sorry if I wore you out.

Pia: How'd you get on this Train?

Beth: Well, from the very first time I heard about it, I knew I had to be on it, and then they refused me. They said it was already full. That was way back in January. So I borrowed the money, wrote back and sent them a check for $2400 and said, "For some reason I have to be on this Train."

Pia: Wow!

Beth: About three or four weeks later, I got the call that I had been ac-cepted, which was wonderful.

Pia: I'm glad.

I was intrigued with the name of May Piaget of Switzerland.

Beth: Your name is famous, May. Tell me, are you related to *the* Piaget?

May: Yes, he was the cousin of my grandfather. I met him just once.

Beth: Were you impressed?

May: No, not really. I already had seen him at the television. But I would stand beside him when he was working at his desk, you know, the famous one, with all his mountain of papers, and he was so slow, so friendly, so near, that I was not impressed.

Beth: Was he friendly just with family, or with everyone?

May: I think he was friendly with everyone. He was like that. The name, Piaget means... in France, the name of a person is related to their work. *Piaget* means a sort of taxer, the one that collects the taxes you have to pay to go by car or railroad. This sort of order is a *piage*.

Beth: May, you said you had made a train trip like this before. What was that trip about?

May: I went to Scandinavia and the northern and southern parts of Europe as a tourist. It was when I was young. Now I'm a journalist for the United Nations and I'll be sending articles back to my newspaper to let people know what is happening on this Peace Train and in the UN Conference. This is a very different kind of trip. What are you doing with all this interviewing?

Beth: I'm going to write a book about this trip, so that women's voices can be heard in a new way. I'll quote you.

May: Good!

Crystal Swartile, is a First Nations Canadian whose black eyes sparkle when she talks.

Beth: Talk about what it was like to be born wherever you were and to be born a girl, what it's been like to be on the Peace Train and what you expect in Beijing.

Crystal: I was born in a little town in British Columbia. My parents left there right after I was born. I lived in lots of little towns as I was growing up, in the Yukon and northern BC and the Interior. I went to school through Grade 11 and then I dropped out and traveled around BC, moving to different places. My father is Dutch and my mother is Mohawk.

Beth: Were you set apart from other children because of that? What do you remember about your childhood and your teenage years?

Crystal: I think there were times in my life when I was set apart and I just didn't fit in. But people didn't always know and didn't see me as an Indian.

Beth: When they did know, were you excluded from certain groups because of that?

Crystal: I think for me I'm at a point in my life where it's not exclusion. It's a gift. I can be with both sides of my life and feel good about it.

Beth: What came from your Indian side?

Crystal: I work with the understanding of a Creative Being all around us, that we are to be respectful of Father/Mother Earth and of all beings. I am always looking at my life for balance. Each day what I do for myself is to look at the Medicine Wheel. I use that as a tool for myself to gain balance. I go to churches too, to get my spiritual needs met. That's where I meet my friends and accept who I am. It helps me to understand being Native, and that being Native is okay, that I'm not just native, but I'm Dutch, too, and accepting both parts of me and that's all right.

Beth: How did you get on the Peace Train?

Crystal: My colleague and I wanted to get some resource material for our organization on the status of women in Canada. I was telling this other woman who was working there that I'd like to go to China and Asia. And she said, "Did you know that the women's conference is meeting there and there is a Peace Train that's going there?" I didn't understand that, so she gave me the number of a woman I could talk to about it. Then I went to one of the meetings where the Chinese women came, and I said, "Gees, I'm gonna go for it."

Beth: What has the Peace Train experience been like for you? Did it fulfill your expectations?

Crystal: I had no expectations. I had never done anything like this. The only thing I wanted was to enrich my job on my committee. I had never taken into account what's happening to the women in the world, because of my job with First Nations people. And then I thought, if I don't understand what's happening in the world, how can I understand different people? And if my job is to find a balance in everything, I need to know that.

Beth: How has it been for you?

Crystal: It's a lot of learning. A lot of learning on politics, different words for different political settings, how to be politically correct. I was afraid that I would make a mistake because I didn't name myself correctly, like you know, if I'm First Nation, or Indian, you know, like that.

Beth: Have you felt criticized on the Train for not being politically correct?

Crystal: I've been told things just about all the time. And how can you do something right if you don't know you are doing something wrong?

Beth: That's true. And, Crystal, I'm old enough to know that what is considered "politically correct" today may not be "politically correct" tomorrow. What's more, I believe that people have a right to name themselves in whatever way they choose, and whatever that is, is politically correct for them.

Crystal: Yeah, and not be judged for that.

Beth: Were you in the Rolling School?

Crystal: Yeah.

Beth: What was that like for you?

Crystal: Mixed.

We were interrupted then and never got back to finish our conversation. Instead, I began to talk with Helen Spaulding of the USA, the oldest woman on the Train. Helen had a smooth, round, open face, graying hair and the beginnings of a dowager's hump. She was wearing a chartreuse polyester suit with a flashy flowered jacket bespangled with red roses, as colorful as her personality. When she asked me to guess her age, I said, "Maybe 80," and she laughed.

Helen: At my next birthday in November, I will be 88. (There was a proud ring in her voice.)

Beth: That's a lot of living. I'd like to hear you talk about yourself and how you've lived all those years. I heard you've been active in the church most of your life.

Helen: All my life. I've never had another job except church. I'm a Disciples woman, but I've worked with a lot of other denominations.

Beth: What did you do in the church?

Helen: I did a lot of traveling. I'll never forget one time when I had a meeting in Oslo, I flew back to New York on Scandinavian Airlines and I left my moneybelt under my pillow. As soon as I got to New York, I reported it. Well, a couple weeks later, I got it in the mail. The Scandinavian people are honest. Boy, I wrote them a nice letter! The first time I was in Russia, I traveled over to Finland and walked all over Suomenlinna Island. About 1,000 people live on that island. It's beautiful, full of woodlands and surrounded by other islands. That archipelago was formed during the ice age when enormous ice banks passed from the north to the south and left behind thousands of little islands.

You know, when Russia determined to create St. Petersburg, they took the Finnish land away from Finland.

Beth: Now that Finland has its independence, do you think they might lose it again?

Helen: Oh, I hope not. It was after World War II that the Russians declared that they would never let that happen again. They must control clear around that water. Someone criticized the President of Finland who was an elderly man. They thought he gave in too much to the Russians. But what could he do? After all, Finland fighting the Russians? That's like David and Goliath.

Helen's droll way of speaking and her strong commitment to making peace in the world stirred me. Her years of experience were in strong contrast to those of young Amelia of California. She and her mother, Mary, were together, so I interviewed them both.

Beth: Tell me how you happen to be on this Peace Train.

Amelia: My mother and I are doing a mother-daughter thing. My father's sister is here, too. We're sharing a compartment together, so it is a really interesting experience for a family.

Mary: Within our family, peace has always been a really strong issue, so it was great to be on this train to experience that. I've had a great time; I met a lot of fantastic women.

Beth: What sticks out in your mind as important?

Amelia: A workshop for me that was really good was building bridges. That's when colored women and white women came together and we built bridges. It was really quite an experience. Please take note that we are one of six mother and daughter combinations on the train and one of two mother, daughter, and aunt combinations. As Mary said, peace has always been a very important issue that we have acted upon in our family and I extend that family across the world. But the one thing I want to say here is, I am a member of Women's International League for Peace and Freedom. And the reason that I'm a member of that organization is because Mary encouraged me to join.

Mary: We encouraged each other. It's a kind of slightly reverse thing when you have a 16-year-old, as she was then, telling me that I should join WILPF.

Now meet Ellen Diederich of Oberhausen, Germany – a tall, dark, strong woman, articulate and full of vigor. Her commanding presence and astute political analysis intimidated some and inspired others. I was one of the inspired. Ellen combined her wide knowledge of the issues affecting women's lives with firsthand experience of being on the front lines for peace and justice for a long time. The songs she got us singing in our "waiting" times still ring in my ears.

Beth: Ellen, talk about your life and who you are.

Ellen: I was born in 1944, come from a working family, a minor family, union socialized background and resistance in Nazi Germany. So I grew up in a very strong political environment. In that time, the area where I lived was the big industrial area, the area of the Ruhr. This was the time when everything was bombed and my mother and father told me that I spent the nights of my first year in bunkers. One week after I was born, my house was hit by a bomb. So war was very early present in my life.

I come from an anti-fascist family, so my people were in concentration camps; we were in prison. Sometimes today I think when will it happen that people from the United States will have the same feelings many of us have?

But it might be different because we had the war on our soil. We could see the faces of our mothers after World War II, women waiting for trains bringing war prisoners back. Some were expecting their son's bodies.

When I was 11 years old, I started to think about all this. I found a book called *Shattered Home* written by a man who was a prisoner in a concentration camp. He was forced to take record of medical experiments which were made on prisoners in the concentration camp. I read this book and I was totally shocked. Shocked. Since that time I am always searching for ways this should never happen again. In a very early age, I joined the socialist youth movement. I went to the summer youth camps with internationals coming together. When I was 15, the first Easter marches against the atom bomb took place in Germany. So I joined the Easter march. I had a role model, Bertrand Russell. I saw this man sitting on strike just in front of the British nuclear scientific research place, the most famous thing in Britain. The antinuclear movement started there. I was very impressed seeing Russell, who was in his 80s in that time, calmly sitting. This was what I was searching for, nonviolent action.

Beth: Did he lead those? Why are they called "Easter"?

Ellen: Ya, every year held on Easter. I was very active in the socialist youth and I was thrown out of it because of participating in the Easter marches, which was very interesting, because the year before, all our leaders and party members, they were in the front row. And one year later they had a new program saying they wanted the remilitarization of Germany, things like that. So we were thrown out. But the very deep reason was because there were also communists in the Easter marches. All my critical thinking started then, at 16.

Well, what else? I did an apprenticeship in a lawyer's office and then married very young. I was 18 when I married and when I was 20, I had two children, and I was a housewife for seven years or so.

Beth: Were you politically active at that time?

Ellen: When I had time. I still went to the Easter marches with my husband and sometimes with the children. We were very involved in actions against the Vietnam war.

Beth: What kind of actions?

Ellen: Demonstrations, sit-ins, whatever.

Beth: You and your husband?

Ellen: Ya. Then in '68, the student movements, it was a combination. My big industrial area has a strong tradition of labor movement, of anti-fascist movement, and so it was an interesting combination together with the student movement. We founded the first anti-authoritarian kindergarten. Then I started to read a lot of things about education and living together in collectives. It was the time when we thought we should have free sexual relations so nobody should own anybody. So we gave up the small family. We didn't see that hundreds of years of experiences and feelings are in our bones and that we really couldn't stand this. I mean if my husband was in the next room with another woman and I was there, whoosh! After half a year, all the marriages broke and my husband and I also got a divorce. Then I fell in love with a man who was a scientist at university and in two weeks I decided, I leave this place and I go to him. I took my children.

Beth: Your husband didn't quarrel about your taking the children?

Ellen: No, no, no. Well, then I jumped into a new role of the university scientifics and I thought, "What are they talking?" They didn't have names anymore, only "He's a sociologist, he's a tech ..." And I got silent. I couldn't talk anymore. The man I was together with then was the youngest professor of the university, very smart, very nice and so all the women students... It was a hard time, anyway.

Beth: You mean they were all infatuated with him?

Ellen: Yes. Then I started to think that I would also go to the university and to study, to use the university for my interests. I had a high school degree; then I started to prepare myself for the university and after a while I did it and I started to study and this man and I broke our relationship. This was very difficult. I didn't have any job, and then the children and work and political work and so on. I found four other women to share the work of the children and we studied together and lived together in one house. This was a very good experience for me. I couldn't have done all of this alone. I had to work. I got a scholarship from the trade union for my studies but it wasn't enough for three people, and my former husband never supported us financially.

Beth: Isn't there any law that requires him to support you ?

Ellen: Yes, there is, but he was a freelance graphic designer and could always say he didn't have the money.

Beth: What was your work then?

Ellen: Well, I studied and from the very beginning I had a school at the university in the evening, teaching adults. Those ten years were very intense in the way of emancipation. I was also in the peace movement. In the middle '70s , the women's movement started. If you are single mother in a capitalist society, you really see what this society is about.

At the same time, there were a lot of changes in the political movement in Germany. The Red Army started and the state would answer with very strong restrictions, I mean they would beat you, prison, isolation and all this kind of stuff. I felt very close to some of the people because I knew them from earlier times. I never agreed with their politics, using violence as an instrument of politics.

I was very shocked about the human rights violations which took place, so I got involved in the Bertrand Russell Foundation. They set up several tribunals. The first one was on Vietnam, the famous Vietnam tribunal. The second one was on torturing in Latin America. And the third one was on human rights violations in Germany. In that time all over Europe it started to get really very rigid – '76, '77. I was secretary, besides my other responsibilities.

So there were three wings: Peace Movement, Human Rights, Women's Movement. Then I started to go to other countries. I have been many times to Italy. Every year we have the International Women's gathering in Italy and this is where I learned the most. Italian woman have influenced me very deeply.

One day I discovered I was not myself. I was living in the image of a man. I was involved in a Protestant student organization, something like that. They gave me the opportunity to go to a lot of European countries, North Africa as well, and see the level of the women's movement in that time, so it was very interesting. So I started to go more international, all the time watching demonstrations, and I was always very committed and very involved.

When I finished my studies, I started to work in the family's magazine in Berlin, a very good magazine called *Courage*. Very political. Very feminist. It was really a voice for the feminist movement. Then I discovered that to be only for women was kind of narrow. I had the feeling I was torn between the socialist movement and the women's movement. So I thought, where am I? Can I bring the family perspective into the socialist movement like what the Italian women would call double militancy? So for a while I worked in both parts. It was very hard. Most of us were coming from the left movement organization, so we had a Marxist perspective and never forgot that there was a working class, working women. As long as we don't take serious the problem how women can raise their children, the feminists will never be a movement of the masses. So this was different from the United States, I think, because we really came from a different perspective.

At the beginning of the '80s, a new wave of the peace movement started. We had the first really huge Women's Congress for Peace in '79; there were about 1000 women who came together. We invited Helen Caldicott and she came and said, "Here in Germany, you are on the front lines of the battlefield." I mean Germany, both parts, was the country where most of the nuclear stuff was deployed, east and west. We were right in the middle.

In '81, the Scandinavian women were calling for the first women's peace march. We marched from Copenhagen to Paris, 1400 kilometers, calling for nuclear-free zones with every mayor of every city or parliament. Declare your city nuclear free. Declare your area, nuclear-free zone.

Beth: This was 1981?

Ellen: Yes.

(Ellen reached for a thick photograph album and opened it on the table between us.) I'm doing a book on women's peace actions in which we took part and I'd like to show you some of the photographs. I dedicated the book to the women from Ravensbrück, the women's concentration camp where 98,000 women were killed. On one of our trips I met these two women who survived Ravensbrück. They were from the Czechoslovakian village of Levice where the Nazis killed every man and every boy. They even took the bones out of the graves and smashed them. The title of the book is *War Does Not Have the Face of a Woman*. This is the other thing I'm concerned with, small style conflict.

Another reason I started with the peace movement were the faces of our mothers after World War II. This picture from Nicaragua shows these women waiting for a train which brings former war prisoners back from Russia; waiting with their sons, husbands. See the faces. You can see the war.

Beth: You can see the agony in them.

Ellen: Then we learned that men laugh when they sell weapons. This is a picture of the management of an arms company. See the men laughing? We made a poster out of this, very famous now in Germany.

This picture is myself in Vietnam. Vietnam was really turning us around, so this was the poster for the first peace marches. In '81, we marched from Copenhagen to Paris, the next year from Berlin to Vienna, and the third year from Dorfmann, which is in our area, to Brussels, NATO headquarters. This was the year that NATO made the decision to deploy the Cruise and Pershing. The peace marches were really something very interesting; we painted all the streets. I've been several times to Greenham Common outside of London.

Beth: So have I. It's a powerful experience to be with those peace women.

Ellen: It is. I love what the Greenham women did with the mirrors, holding them up in front of the police weapons. The other thing I thought was very important was the peace march organized by the women of Scandinavia, into the former Soviet Union. This was in '82, the first time that women broke through. They were on a train and they had several stops. In Minsk they had big marches; it was the first East-West common peace activity into the Soviet Union. All along our route we did things simulating what would happen if a nuclear bomb would hit. Then we would read a text telling how to inform the people all along our road. And we had a theater play with us, the role of women in war.

And here we are again today, winning the Silver medal in arms export. We are now number two in the world. We have, for instance, given as a present to Turkey, 530,000 machine guns plus ammunition, so they can struggle with the Kurdish people.

Before the Nairobi conference started in 1985, several governments tried to keep out the question of peace because they said, "Too political for women. They should not talk about this. This is something they should leave to political leaders. They should stick to women's issues," whatever they understand that women's issues are. I think peace is a woman's issue. So we were about 40 activists, women peace activists from different countries, who came together and said we will have a peace tent. We rented a room and we tried to create a place and a time where women from so-called enemy countries could negotiate. So in that time we had the war between Iran and Iraq; we had Palestine and Israel which is still going on; we had the cold war USA-USSR, we had of course negotiations between France and women from the South Pacific, and many, many more.

Nairobi meant for most of us, even if we had to talk about terrible things, something uprising. One got the feeling that women from the smallest islands to the highest mountains have started to move, to do something, because we will not accept anymore that wars must go on and on. Did you know that in this century more people have been killed in wars than since Jesus Christ was born?

We started to learn about the effects of nuclear testing, especially on women who are breast feeding. Nairobi was also, I would say, a women's summit. I belong to a group of about 50 women, who went to all the summit meetings where there were no women, no persons of color. In all the summit meetings there were just old white men getting together and saying, "We are the summit meeting."

The Nairobi conference showed us how women would do a summit, 40,000 women according to how it is in the world, about 65 percent women of color, and so we started to negotiate. Obviously we were very dangerous because after three days the order came from the Kenyan government to close this peace tent because we were criticizing and we were calling the United States imperialistic and other countries too, not only US. It was thanks to Nita Barrow who was the chair of the conference that because she gave the statement "If you close the Peace Tent, then I close the Forum," that we could go on. When I look back now, I see we still have testing going on, but there are some changes.

I remember in Nairobi there was a very moving, heartbreaking discussion among women from South Africa. I cried when I heard Winnie Mandela talking about it's necessary to have guns in the street in South Africa. There is a change in South Africa there, fortunately. Mandela is free, and others. But they are still under constant worries about the economic function. We have other changes like Northern Ireland, and the Soviet Union is now a different country.

On the Peace Train now we traveled into Bucharest, you know, the country where the vampires came from, Transylvania. Well, I had the image that not only in Bucharest, but in all these eastern countries, another kind of vampire has arrived. You could see on top of the houses in Bucharest, Coca Cola, McDonalds, all these are there now. Another generation of vampires. What does this mean to women and to peace issues?

I have been in Yugoslavia ten times in the last two years bringing humanitarian aid from Germany. I don't know how people, women, can survive in these countries. I would like to give you one sample. In a country like Rumania, 80 percent of the women who get pregnant have abortions. What does this say about the future vision of women? A loaf of bread costs 60 cents in US currency. Everybody in the world knows US dollars. Sometimes I have the impression that the stories of Bosnia will start again. So many people lying in the street. We saw children's labor; we saw cheap prostitution. We saw especially old women, sitting in the street with a little bowl of tomatoes or four dried fishes – trying to sell *something*.

I've been many times to the former socialist countries. I've always traveled through them because I didn't like their qualities. But what about these countries and traditions, are they a danger to world peace? I never,

ever had expected this poverty to start again. I mean it was like something from the last century. And now, how do we stop it, how can we help the situation of these so-called countries in transition period?

This is one of the big questions, I think, for peace right now. Keep this in your mind please. One nuclear submarine means that 230 million children in the Third World cannot get an education. And they're still going on building them. And as we said in Nairobi in the peace tent, even if we don't use the weapons, they kill people because you can't use the weapons to keep people warm in the storm. This I think we have to repeat until the words become ashes. We have to repeat it and repeat it and repeat it.

At the time of Nairobi, we had the insanity of Star Wars. I just saw a documentary some weeks ago about all these images of Star Wars – unbelievable. And I know that 95 percent of all the scientific work in the United States goes into the military. What does that mean for peace, for creating the secure future? The citizens who invited us to visit them are very brave and we have to be very courageous. We have to make our sons and daughters ready. We have to have peace; also you get healthy if you are a peace marcher. Another thing is we as women have to be in the media.

Beth: What have you been doing since Nairobi?

Ellen: After Nairobi, we took a peace train to Northern Ireland to support the women there to start the debate again. We went to different places, for instance to Stuttgart which is the center of the advanced war technology. All the firms are concentrating there; it's a big arms factory. We organized the peace tent in Stuttgart.

And this is a picture of Fazia, the one I lived with for 15 years. She was in concentration camp as a child and she survived. She is black German. Her father was a African diplomat and her mother is German. She is a famous singer in Germany. She was in the peace tent and she saved the situation a hundred times with her singing.

We brought the peace tent to Belfast, in Northern Ireland, but we couldn't set up there; it was too dangerous. So we switched every day to another place. After Nairobi we discovered that we know very little about daily life of women in other countries. So we decided to take a peace caravan, a peace bus. We visited women's workplaces: farms in the Soviet Union, kindergartens. We followed the route of the Germans in World War II, so we visited a lot of former concentration camps and tried to speak to women who had survived. We demanded a stop to all nuclear testing, the suspension of all acts of war, the scrapping of all nuclear weapons after the year 2000.

Beth: Did you know that between 1945 and 1962, over 200 nuclear tests were done in the US alone? Do you think we can get that stopped?

Ellen: We're certainly working at it. We asked for the release of the thousands of millions of dollars that have been spent on armaments to be spent for the independence and equality of women, for development of peace. Powerful stuff.

In the socialist countries we brought exhibitions and films; we wanted to have an exchange. At the peace conference in Prague, we said we would come if we can establish a women's center. After two or three days, when the man from high Soviet stepped into the women's center and asked, "What are you doing here?" we knew we had gotten their attention. That was a breakthrough.

We visited several parliaments also. We always tried very hard to break into the former socialist countries but we never came as enemies. In discussions, we tried to figure out what is the background of our lives, what are the experiences, how to break through the enemy picture.

Then in '87, the first world women's conference in the Kremlin – 40,500 women, the first time the Kremlin hosted so many women from all over the world. It was during Gorbachev. One year after Chernobyl and Peace Caravan, 120 women were in the Ukraine and we were very frightened what could happen to us. Fazia and I did the whole trip. She is one of the women who accompanied us three years to different places. Unfortunately, now she has cancer, breast cancer. The Nazis did medical experiments with her and her heart is very weak, and now she always has water in her lungs. It's not good.

We interviewed a lot of women about their experiences in war. We wrote peace in all the European languages of all the countries we came through.

We did a lot of work in El Salvador, and I was very touched to see the women's prison there because they are outside during daytime and can talk to each other and visit with their families, quite another thing than prisons in Germany are.

In Washington, in the Peace Center, the Committee of the Mothers of the Disappeared in El Salvador were awarded the human rights award of the Kennedy Foundation but were denied visas to come to Washington to take it. So we decided, if the mothers can't come to the US, we should bring them to Europe. I organized the trip, and for two months I was traveling with three of the mothers in ten European countries visiting parliaments. We visited dozens of solidarity groups. We met a woman who spent 35 years of her life in exile and then after Franco died, she could come back. She was 92 years old and it was very moving, the Salvadorans and her.

We met Carmen Campos; one day her daughter who was seven months pregnant was picked up and she went to the police asking for her. She was raped by seven soldiers. They cut off her breasts. They smashed her eyes and threw her out. They thought she was dead, but a taxi driver found her and she was saved.

Anna's four-year-old daughter was run over by a military truck. And Maria was taken by the death squads and later put in prison. She gave birth to her child in prison and now she is in the United States informing the people in the US about it.

I've been to Yugoslavia the last two years. Mostly the old women remain in Croatia in refugee camps, because the younger have gone to Germany, to US, all over the world. We gave a lot of humanitarian aid to Croatia. We had 30 trucks and 500 tons of medical, but we were stranded for a week. They arrested one of our negotiators and tortured him terribly and then we decided to go back and we sent the stuff to other places.

Beth: Ellen, you have spent your whole life in the cause of peace.

Ellen: Ya, and I would like to give you two examples from one very big hope I got. Every day for about 14 days, hundreds of thousands of children left the school every day in Germany protesting against the Gulf War. Nobody had organized it. It was the first generation to grow up frightened of environmental disasters like the Gulf War. So this was something well done.

The other thing which really made me very hopeful in the last month was a breakthrough on treaties. I learned that the women's movement has really done a lot in the last 20 years. For the first time in history, it was possible that we were able to inform the world about what happened to women in war, all the cases of rape. At first it was very difficult to report, then the big media took it and made it public. Now the work of women on violence against women has made the connection.

Beth: That gives me hope, too. Every success we have makes some difference. What are you doing now?

Ellen: I work in The Women's Peace Archive in Germany. My salary is paid by The Foundation for a Compassionate Society in the US. We have one store in Rome and one in Germany called The Four Directions. We sell jewelry and crafts, furniture from Mexico, clothing from Guatemala, and in Germany, toys, jeans out of a factory in Tyler, Texas. We have a political cultural center, a school and the peace archives, all in one place. We do political fashion shows, the models mostly refugee women who live in our area. Some are second generation refugees from Chile, one from Kurdistan. They speak about their countries, like India last time, we explain about the women who produce the silk in India. We want to make peace attractive.

Megan Hutching of New Zealand is the age of my daughter, Marta, and has the red hair and peaches-and-cream complexion of daughter Peggy. I felt drawn to her quiet, responsible leadership as spokeswoman on the Red Car, and asked if we could sit together on the bus ride from Istanbul.

Beth: Megan, talk about your life, what it was like for you to be a girl in New Zealand, and how do you happen to be on the Peace Train?

Megan: I was born in 1957 in Warkworth, an hour's drive north of Auckland. That's the largest city on North Island. I was the youngest of six, four sisters and a brother eight years older than me. It was on a dairy farm. I don't remember much except that I had a happy childhood. My oldest sister

Robin, 17 years older, was away and my mom was horrified to be pregnant again. She was afraid people would think it was Robin's child; so she had her walk up and down the streets of Auckland so people would know.

Beth: Did you ever feel unwanted?

Megan: No. I was lonely sometimes. There was a creek in the middle of the farm and I used to help with cows at milking time. We had a big garden, fruit trees. The bathroom was an outside toilet. The kitchen was small. I liked school and was good at it.

When I was 10, my father had heart attacks and we had to sell the farm. We moved to Kerikeri in the north of a bay of islands, population 1500. In 1815 it had been visited by Anglican missionaries from England. The oldest building in New Zealand is an old stone church there. My oldest sister lived there with her husband and two children. It was a citrus growing area. My father worked in an office for a building firm. I worried, became conscious of my own health. I left home at age 15, had to go to Auckland to school. I boarded with a woman the school found. It was nice living with her, but it was a miserable year. The school was large; I didn't know anybody and saw my parents only at holidays, two weeks in May, three weeks in August and six weeks in the summer at Christmas. I was lonely for my friends in KeriKeri. I went to university in Auckland, got good marks but didn't enjoy the subjects, so I dropped out after two years. My parents were angry but got over it. I didn't go home as much for a while. Our family is close.

Beth: What would you say are the values your family lived by?

Megan: Be honest, considerate of others, careful of money, don't overcommit yourself. Family is important. No matter what disagreements we have with each other, when one has trouble all are there. It's been hard on my sister-in-law, hard to feel a key part of the family group. We are noisy, great laughers. I like to travel. I spent time overseas, in Australia, Greece, England and down through the middle of Italy, Florence, Siena. It was a strange feeling to climb the leaning tower of Pisa.

In 1985, I went back to university and finished my BA in history and archaeology – loved it. I worked in the university library, shelving books part-time. I finished in 1987, and got my master's degree in history three years later. An important source of New Zealand history is oral stories, so I did an 18-month project. I did interviews with immigrants, people in the local suburbs in Auckland and people in arts. This was to build up the archives, to add to the written sources and manuscripts. The Historical Branch of the Department of Internal Affairs is now publishing a *Dictionary of New Zealand Biography*. Two volumes are out and one is in process. In 1990, Auckland had a celebration of 150 years since the start of the colony. New Zealand became independent of Britain in 1908. Captain Cook had "discovered" the country in 1792. A few Europeans did trading with the Maori people. In 1812, missionaries started coming. Edward Biggon Wakefield of Britain sent his brother to buy land from the Maoris, then sold it to the people who would set up villages like Wellington. The British government didn't like this. In 1840 there was the Treaty of Waitangi when the Maori people ceded sovereignty of land to the British Crown. That was when thousands of English came.

Beth: It's that same old story of one nation taking over another, isn't it? How did you learn about the Peace Train?

Megan: A friend belonged to WILPF and invited me to the group. I went and liked what they did. I met older women with wide and deep knowledge of social justice issues in New Zealand. They were anti-war people during the war and were very welcoming. I've been a member of WILPF for ten years.

Beth: Tell me about your WILPF chapter.

Megan: The chapter covers the bottom half of North Island, the Wellington Branch. The meetings can be frustrating, lots of talk, business wanders around and there's not much action. Most of the work is done outside the monthly meeting. I organize actions, like May 24 – International Women's Day for Disarmament. I write minutes and do some correspondence.

Beth: What kind of correspondence?

Megan: Writing to France's prime minister, Jacques Chirac to let him know we are against nuclear testing. And our newsletter comes out four times a year.

On the opposite side of the world from the United States, there is a country called Republic of the Philippines. I had known for years that it was an island nation. What I did not know is that it is not one island, but, astoundingly, 7100 islands. Filipino children are told an old legend, that their land was formed when a giant threw a huge mass of rock into the sea. The rock broke into dozens of pieces, and each one formed an island. Actually, only 11 of these are considered major islands. Most of them are bits of swampland or jagged rocks sticking out of the sea and do not even have names.

A small Filipina on the Train had cocoa-brown skin and dark eyes that held a gentle, intense look. We will call her Ana. She works in the Women's Development Program for the National Episcopal Church in the Philippines. I asked her about her work there.

Ana: Up to now in the church, women cleaned the church and did the washing of vestments. Now we are teaching them how to participate in decision making. We want to see them become self-aware, to be able to facilitate meetings, to build their skills in communication and conflict resolution. We try to build their self-confidence.

Beth: Are there areas of your work that you especially enjoy?

Ana: Community development. I facilitate community organizing, and that includes educating women to what is going on in the Philippines, the health programs and cooperative projects.

Beth: How did you learn about the Peace Train?

Ana: I was co-sponsored by the Peace and Justice Office of the Episcopal Church, USA, in New York, The Church of Sweden Mission, and the Episcopal Women's Foundation.

Beth: What has it been like for you on this Train? Do you think that peace has been lived out? What do you think we mean by peace?

Ana: I mean harmony and justice. I don 't feel discriminated against on the Train, but it has been divided by those who can and those who can't pay. Dividing us into classes over dinners is a justice issue. Everybody doesn't have equal access. Our lifestyles on the Train have been mostly social and that is shallow. I wish we were more sensitive to lifestyles of poor women. It is hard for a woman from a poor country to watch women have beautiful wine and dinners we can't have. And there's been so much consumerism. We forget that the more we spend, the more we exploit others' cheap labor. Nuclear disarmament seems to be a big issue on this Train.

Ana spoke with the authority of having lived with the deprivation and need of the poor in her country. Her earnestness made me feel ashamed of taking for granted the privilege and abundance I know every day.

Hasha is a Muslim woman. At the time I asked her for an interview, she was crocheting a *Kufi* (headdress) for her son, her earnest, dark and solemn face ringed with a colorful turban.

Beth: Hasha, tell me what you remember about your young years.

Hasha: I was born in New York in 1955, but I grew up in Baltimore. What I remember about kindergarten was that a sweet lady, Smallwood, my teacher, always smelled good and there were turtles in a ceramic pool. I had a good time in school. When I was in about third grade, a girl from kindergarten came in and read us a book, and I was amazed she could read like that. I had a hard time learning to read because I hadn't had any preparation, not many books in the house. We did have a couple of ABC books, but I had little interaction with my mother, and that has lasted all my life.

I told her one time, "I'm gonna kill myself. My brother gets to do what he wants to and I don't." It bothered my mother and she kept asking me, "Didn't you say you were going to kill yourself?" I played with boys and one girl, and made mud pies with my girlfriend. My father was a funny person. He liked me and played with me a lot. High school was a growing experience. I had to take an hour's ride on a city bus. I majored in psychology in Gaucher College.

Beth: Why are you here on the Peace Train?

Hasha: The Islam temple works for peace. I'm an activist. I teach people they are not negroes. "Black" and "negro" and "colored" are all slave terms created by the white man. I'm on this Train to educate people to think of themselves as being Moorish Americans, that they don't have to buy in to the supremacist attitude of the USA people on this Train. I want to be shown respect for our people and our contribution to the human family. We suffer a lot because we don't have meetings on the Train; everybody suffers because of that. A person in our wagon turned up her nose at me, and those things need to be talked about.

At the Forum, I spoke with Irana from Holland, very fair, with sky-blue eyes and graying hair.

Beth: Tell me Irana, what has stood out for you so far from what has been going on, from being in China and here in the Forum?

Irana: It's not my first time here. I lived here in China from '89 to '92, then for a while in Hong Kong. Every time I come again, I get more irritated by the way the Chinese are handling things, especially these events.

Beth: What irritates you?

Irana: Well, for this particular conference it's the site they chose. It's not that they couldn't find anywhere else. It's a way to get this whole conference out of the way, not in town where the women might cause trouble.

Beth: What kind of trouble?

Irana: We have some security people next to us. I'll just say it is for the reason that they don't want any interactions between this conference and the people.

However frustrated I was with the constant interruptions, these small, fragmented interactions often led to important connections that continue even now, two years later. I caught a moment with Johanna Kao of Hong Kong, the young map reader in Helsinki. She was like a sponge soaking up every juicy bit of the activities on the Train.

Beth: Johanna, how did you get into peace activities?

Johanna: My mother was active in the anti-war movement in the '60s and '70s. I grew up believing I could make the world a better place, that we are here to give each other strength, support, vision and hope. Working for peace is one way to do that.

Terry Wolfwood, a Canadian, talked about how she helped to make the wallpaper decorations in the train and how impressed she was with the women in the countries we visited. We had just left Odessa, Ukraine.

Terry: Those women are into total reconstruction of destroyed societies, and yet they had such a dignity and a commitment. I felt that we were never anywhere long enough to do them justice.

It was hard to listen through translators. I found out that some of the translators had never translated in public before, but we were impatient with them. We interrupted them and corrected them and shouted at them, and spoke while the other languages were being spoken, and I saw this mirror of the imperialism of the English language.

But I learned that these women have a sense of the solutions to rebuilding their societies. It's not like they're waiting for somebody to come from outside to help. They want our solidarity, but they know the solution to rebuilding their society is within their own lives and within their own society. The most we can do is to prevent our society from hindering that reconstruction. Our work and our help to these women lies not in their countries but in our own with our own government. The Peace Train is a mirror that was held up for us to see our own faces.

Beth: What did you see in that mirror?

Terry: Most of the Peace Train riders, the largest group, came from the United States of America. The mirror of cultural imperialism on the train was very strong. We often assumed in our patriarchal way, that there is only one answer and only one way to do things. I said at one workshop on the Train that the success of the patriarchal system is dependent on the internalization of its ideology by the oppressed. If we as women consider ourselves oppressed by that patriarchy, we must always hold up that mirror to see how we have internalized it. We see that in our not waiting for a translator to speak, not waiting for the end of the talk, not waiting, as many people in this world do, for a quiet time to think something over before we respond. Many indigenous people in the world have a period of silence between speakers as a form of respect. We didn't do that because we had the

First World model of instant gratification and always the right to be right and the right to speak.

Beth: Terry, what will you take away from this Peace Train experience?

Terry: A great sense of humility. Humility about belonging to what is really a small percentage of the world's population, and consuming most of its resources, producing most of the armaments by corporations which are still based primarily in the United States and a few in other northern countries and Japan, controlling the economic lives of people all over the world. Through that control, women are being continuously impoverished. Women are being left out of the global economy or they are being abused and oppressed by it. If there is anything that we need to take away from the Peace Train and Beijing experience, it is to see what we can do in our own homes, in our own countries, to change that oppression. To start it at home.

Look at this banner. It says, "Listen to Women – For A Change." More than anything else, I think, women need to listen to other women for a change.

Blonde, copper-toned Lisa Hofman of The Netherlands had an authentic openness and vitality about her that caught me immediately. She was a part of the official delegation to the UN Conference.

Beth: You were born in Holland, Lisa? All I know about Holland is that it's famous for having windmills and the most beautiful tulips in the world. As a child, I learned the story of the little boy who saved the town by putting his finger in the hole in the dike. I know that dikes are built because most of the land is below sea level, and windmills are used to drain water from the land. Tell me more. It's part of The Netherlands, right?

Lisa: Right. Holland is the dominant province of The Netherlands. There are about 15 million people in the 12 provinces. Netherlands means "Low Countries." Some people call us "The Dutch." I was born November 1, 1950, in Heemstede, near Haarlem in North Holland. I live in Utrecht, but I work in Brussels. Belgium is just to the south of us.

Beth: Tell me about your work.

Lisa: I worked for a long time in an NGO, "The Foundation Against Trafficking in Women," paid by government subsidies under the Ministry of Welfare. There are many aspects of trafficking in women, but it always comes back to the same problem – an international problem. There are always women at the door who need support, and always limitations to solving the problem. I wanted to move to a bigger sphere of women's issues, so in February I moved to the bureaucracy and started as a staff worker with the Green Party in Parliament, which includes all 15 countries in the EU [European Union], in women's issues. It was a big adjustment, even though moving meant getting to work on the international level and that is exciting.

Beth: What exactly do you do?

Lisa: I bring reports and resolutions to put pressure on the commission. The work in parliament is done by 18 committees. The Women's Rights Committee is one. It was established in 1984. It's not given as much money or importance, but still, it is a recognized committee. There was a decision that there be a working group of six commissioners watching the movement toward equal rights and mainstreaming women's rights.

Beth: What gives you satisfaction?

Lisa: I wrote a resolution to the NGO Forum in Beijing suggesting that if China did not comply with our conditions, to move the Conference to Australia. I lobbied for it and defended it in parliament. China, Tibet, Taiwan and lesbians and prostitutes approved it. Now we have to see if it has impact at the Conference.

I feel insecure working in parliament. I don't know the structures and am just learning how to lobby. In March, I will lobby for reproductive rights, anti-discrimination and quotas.

Beth: What has been your experience on the Peace Train?

Lisa: Great. There are so many powerful women on the Train. Doing things together makes good connections. I am often in between keeping privacy and borders and taking in all these wonderful opportunities and conversations. I was homesick last night.

Beth: So was I. The pulls toward home are really great sometimes.

Lisa: But the Eastern world is becoming real; women are not a place on the map. I like making comparisons of my life to theirs. I love being so different, dancing and singing, then coming back to the train and going "Wow! It's home." Strange, not being able to speak to people and feeling so at home with them. I did have some trouble with this one anti-lesbian person, when I told her I was lesbian. But I think that when any woman defines herself and claims it and finds her voice to be heard, every woman gains.

Brown-skinned Manel of Sri Lanka was short of stature and tall of spirit. She spoke with the intensity of having witnessed too much horror.

Beth: Manel, tell me what your life is like in Sri Lanka.

Manel: I am a Sinhala language teacher and also taught history of Sri Lanka and India to students ages 15 to 17. I am 43 years old, married in 1975, and the mother of five. My husband is a lawyer. I was engaged to another man who was in the leftist movement in 1971. He was abducted and killed. In 1975, I met my husband, who was also a political detainee. I wanted to study law but got married instead. He works with peasants and farmers and community-based organizations like trade unions.

From '89 to '91 we had a tyrant dictator. There was a youth uprising, and he called in vigilante groups, covered their faces and came in and burned nearly 60,000 young people. Others were detained in camps without recourse. Everybody lived under fear. We wanted peace and justice. Women often got together, weeping for sons and husbands.

Beth: How did you get connected with WILPF?

Manel: In 1989, my husband took a job with the United Nations Human Rights Commission in Geneva, Switzerland. I went with him and met the women of WILPF. That broadened my vision of the world. In 1991, we had a women's day slogan: Eliminate Violence. In 1994, we have more than 300 grassroots members. In 1995, we demonstrated against the World Bank's policies toward developing nations.

As the Train moved along, I got little pictures of the lives of my compartment mates. Barb Anderson of Canada commented one day about her life as a child: "My father always did his own laundry and ironing. He had been in the Air Force. Mom wouldn't let him in the kitchen. She had grown up in a log cabin. I spent summers on my grandfather's farm. My grandmother played organ in the United Church; piano at home. We had musical evenings. I'm a videographer, and I'm working with a team to make a video of the Train, especially looking at Canadian women."

Barbara had a quaint sense of humor. She told me of a time when she and her husband added their dog and cat to the census. The cat was a child Barb had prior to marriage, and the dog was a product of an affair Bruce, her husband, had during the marriage. They declared these "children" to be very slow, with severe disabilities. Someone in the government actually called them up to ask if they had adequate facilities, including transportation, to care for these "children," and they told him that "their special needs are well met." Barb's voice had a giggle as she told this story.

Mary Ann Matoon, a Jungian analyst from Minnesota, said one day: "I never married. My aunt lived with us and she didn't get pushed around, so I knew I had a choice. I grew up in Nebraska in Beatrice, 40 miles from Lincoln. Small farms began disappearing in the '60s, people moving to the cities. There were 22 churches, one of them Catholic. There were Mennonites in the surrounding area. Anybody named Olson, Johnson, Swanson or Marsh could get elected. My parents were involved in community life while I was a child."

Pat Hawley, a calm, serene woman, was a Lutheran pastor in Minnesota. She was on the Train for R & R, she said, so she spent a lot of time in her bunk reading books about the areas we were visiting. Pat often made comments and gave information that added a lot to my understanding and knowledge of the areas we were visiting. She was pleasant, with the remarkable ability to stay cool, not to get "steamed up" about anything.

Novim, a Kurdish woman in her early 50s, is a refugee who now lives in Sweden. When I learned from Ellen of Germany that she had asked her for an interview, I asked if I could join them. A translator helped us to understand her broken English.

Novim: We were all the time in many councils listening to films about war, not against war.

Translator: She means all the violence shows and the news and films and media and video. It's like a propaganda *for* violence, not against it.

Novim: And this violence against peace and against woman. I think woman in Europe, they do very big things. Women for peace organization and women for peace and freedom and committees, and they do good. But the important thing is they want more strong. I don't know why now they are not organization but movement. War is not finished. War is beginning of war I think. Yes, turn out to be weapons to Turkey. Why not to Yugoslavia and not Turkey?

Ellen: Because the military industrial complex which has lost the enemy picture when East-West was changing, needs new fields to train and to go to export weapons again. I've been ten times to former Yugoslavia in the last two years and we have been transferring a lot of humanitarian aid. We were asked questions about every kilo of flour we were sending down but the arms business people, it's very easy for them to import. It's unbelievable. It's the biggest arms market in the world now, even if they have an embargo on certain aspects. It's really very, very simple and this is my experience from Yugoslavia. I'm not going to send any kind of humanitarian aid anymore. I'm not working in this field anymore. I will struggle in my country against the arms export to Turkey or wherever and this is really what we have to struggle and fight for and they will not like it.

Beth: And in the US as well. I couldn't sleep when the Gulf War started, I just couldn't believe my country was getting into that, and I felt helpless to do anything about it. I joined a protest march, wrote poetry and wept. Getting the arms race stopped feels impossible, because big business gets in there, and it *is* big business. War is big business. I want to put my efforts now into organizing against torture. It is absolutely abhorrent to me that my government, with my tax money, promotes the teaching of torture in the School of the Americas in Fort Benning, Georgia. 60,000 soldiers from Latin America have been taught terrible things there. Then they go back to their country and torture people. It's ghastly. I saw with my own eyes what that can mean when I was in the church in El Salvador. Pictures of the killing of the priests and women lined the walls – horror beyond the imagination, dismemberment, gouging, butchering. I keep wondering how long it will take the world to realize that we can't teach war and the tactics of war and expect to have peace. I want to be working against the terrorism that the military teaches. The whole world seems locked in this huge business of making money on the backs of people like you Kurds. I want to do what I can to change that.

Novim: Three months ago parliament was founded in The Netherlands, a Kurdish Parliament.

Beth: Do you think this could be a step forward to let the world know more about the Kurdish question?

Novim: I speak my opinion, what my opinion is. This parliament is okay. Good. But they have a lack because not many Kurdish organizations or Kurdish parties are with them. I think if they could come more walking together I think is good, but only for Turkish question. It won't be parliament in exile for all parts of Kurdistan and all democratic movements with the parliament. This is success.

The other question I have is the people's party, I mean PKK has now chosen Germany as what they call the second battlefield. So they are struggling as I find it a very violent way in Germany every night. We have house burnings; we have burnings of travel agencies; we have burnings of Kurdish people; I mean they have started to struggle, and I think there must be other solutions than that. It's another kind of nationalism.

The other point is what I really don't like in the struggle of PKK is that they really are in the drug business. I have several friends in the PKK and some of them were in prison because of this. They support their own struggle with selling drugs and destroying other people's lives, and they also have a big thing into prostitution. They control prostitution. In Hamburg in Kurdish area, the prostitution is controlled by Kurdish men. It's really awful. I have a lot of fights with my Kurdish friends about that. They say we need to get any kind of money to support the armed struggle. And I really don't accept and can't go with that.

Germany is very big land. We need a friend today. We don't need enemy. Germany is not our enemy. But Germany has good relation with Turkey giving them money, strategic and importing weapons to Turkey.

Ellen: Ya, Germany gave to Turkey as presents 530,000 machine guns.

Novim: Ya, and this is wrong of Germany. Is terrible. I think is enough for Germans starting two wars. I think German people and German government must think, what it means, war for them. And sometimes, the PKK, I think, they do very bad things in Germany against Germany. Turkey and Iraq and in West do not have sympathy with us Kurdish people. We Kurdish people have been in Europe before 30 years. European people sympathized with us. Weapons. Drugs. Toxic Waste. Buy and selling women and children. That is the slavery of today.

Beth: Yes, it doesn't matter which country it is, men are buying and selling women and girls everywhere all over the world.

Novim: I don't know what I can say. This for me is terrible. I was tortured in my country and escaped. If I go back, I will be killed. I dream this.

Molly Moore Rush of the USA has a name that doesn't seem to fit her; she never seemed to rush. I was very drawn to Molly, partly because she and I had the same want for more community in the Red Car, and she had affirmed my leadership in attempting to achieve that. Her brown eyes in a pleasant, round face, and her soft, gentle and unhurried manner invited relationship. She was also clearly focused and determined when it came to issues of justice and peace.

Before I met her, I knew that she had known my nephew, Ted Glick, one of the Harrisburg Eight who had spent time in prison for protesting the

Vietnam War. She and her husband and two children had slept on a black woman's porch to support them at his trial. Her nun friend was arrested and spent a week in jail. "We aren't going to change things," Molly said with feeling, "until ordinary people get arrested, not just priests and nuns."

Beth: Molly, tell me who you are and how you came to be such a peace advocate.

Molly: I was born in Pittsburgh, Pennsylvania, baptized "Mary" because the priest said Molly wasn't a saint's name. My family was on welfare when I was a kid. I wanted to get married and have kids, so I had four children. My mother kept the children, and I supported her.

Beth: How did you get to be an activist?

Molly: When I was 28, in 1963, I joined the Catholic Interracial Council in Pittsburgh. By accident, I met Don Mullen from Ireland. He came to Pittsburgh and introduced me to the film, *Gods of Metal.* He had been organizing for the closing of The School of the Americas, using Father Roy Bourgeois' film *School of Assassins* which was funded by the Maryknolls. I kept in touch with the protests of the Vietnam War and that's how I met Ted. Also I'm connected with NCIPA in Pittsburgh.

Beth: That's the National Committee for Independent Political Action. I'm connected with that, too, and Ted is National Coordinator, a writer and editor of their bulletin. I know you have been in many different kinds of activities for peace and justice. Tell me about them.

Molly: I went on famine walks when Bishop Tutu marched with us. We marched to a beach where bodies had never been buried. There are connections between famine and justice and peace. I did another walk to commemorate "the longest walk" in the 1830s, when Native Americans had been forced on a long walk to a desolate place. Soon after that, tribal leaders sent money to the Irish who had been forced off their land. Action From Ireland (AFrI) placed a plaque on the Lord Mayor's house commemorating this. In 1993, I went to St. Brigid Conference. She was a strong advocate for peace and justice. I visited St. Brigid's Well in Kildaire where she had the position of Bishop. AFrI used Brigid's story to focus issues. During the Gulf War, I had high school students in a mall weaving a St. Brigid carpet of Brigid giving a father's sword to a poor man to feed his family. People donated money as they went by, and students gave the money to victims of the Gulf War, to bring those young women to the United States. They brought the carpet to the States and gave it to the Merton Center, dedicated to those opposing the Gulf War.

Beth: Molly, what's going on on this Train?

Molly: It takes a while for me to figure it out. I've had a little disappointment over not as much interface with women along the way as I'd hoped. Shirley and I go on our own to find women and men to talk to. In Bucharest, in the workshop on women and work, we had good interaction with young, activist women. The real thing is person to person. Our compartment is a community: Helena is Finnish and lives in Switzerland. Anna comes from a tiny village of Switzerland and knows no English.

Beth: What about justice issues on the Train?

Molly: Justice issues on the Train are not being addressed. It is not environmentally sound. It's a ship of comfort going through seas of poverty and misery. I've talked with some people at our stops. I met a Bulgarian woman with a man fixing the plumbing in the hotel. They were living in hopelessness and despair. I met two Ukrainian men in Voronezh, one who had lost his job as a teacher and is now on the hotel staff. There is so much helplessness in the cities, so much is falling apart. The failure of *Perestroika* and economic distress is everywhere. I met a journalist in Bucharest. She said she feels joy in being united against Ceausescu. There is now food in the market, and the feeling on the street is very different. I'm just looking around, not pretending to be an expert. I enjoy watching the younger and older women together, watching them sewing and singing.

Beth: What about what's going on between the races on the Train?

Molly: The same as in Pittsburgh. With the best intentions, there is such pain, a history of real oppression. We white Westerners don't begin to comprehend what they have experienced and all that is being carried into the smallest conversation. Open sharing helps, but it doesn't bring understanding overnight. We white folks are in power, so there's a need to have them express that openly. Racism is an issue white people need to address.

Beth: Yes, we take so much for granted. We see through a very cloudy lens.

Molly: At home when we join with black folks, there's always a sense of feeling welcome. If it's seen as initiated by whites, it's harder; when blacks initiate actions, whites are generally welcome. At the Merton Center, as Staff Coordinator, I must tread very lightly with blacks on boards and committees. It's very hard. We can't wait 'til it's solved before we get into actions. It gets complicated.

After I talked with Molly, I wrote in my journal, "I am of a gentler, more forgiving spirit because I have been with Molly."

Marijke Meyers-Smals, one of 12 Dutch women on the Train, was blonde, very vocal, and sometimes seemingly unaware of space boundaries. She was energetic and loved singing and sewing. My interview with her seemed a bit jumbled.

Beth: You say you are not a member of WILPF? How did you get connected to this group of people?

Marijke: I met a women's group of Kiev, an NGO of 1,000 members regarding the European Treaty cooperation, with nuclear energy as the focus. As treasurer of an umbrella organization, I go to governments to get money. I'm an intermediary between the government and the NGO. My husband is a doctor, but I take care of all the finances. I'm computer-wise with financial things. In 1970, we celebrated *Acht Maart*, International Women's Day, March 8. In Maastricht in 1989, we received money from the government – $2,500 or 4,000 guilders, to be used for health, justice and women's rights.

In a celebration this year, we had bands, theater and workshops. I gave the opening speech about Beijing and talked about the Train. The Women, Faith and Life Group gave me a piece of a cup they had broken to bring me back home. It's an old Chinese symbol. When I am back home, they will glue back the piece. They also gave signed letters and will light candles to be with me in support. One said, "I hope your dreams will get hands and feet." I work with divorced women who are not allowed to be in church. My NGO tells me I can be.

Beth: What's it like for you on the Peace Train?

Marijke: Like I thought. Delightful things, meeting women at meals, different workshops by different cultures, learning, singing, sewing, conversation.

Beth: Has anything bothered you?

Marijke: That conversation about racism. I've never been in contact with such feelings. I get hurt for the same reasons. There's too much attention to color and race. When a black woman is unkind to me, I have a right to say what I feel and it's not racism. Racism is not always the cause of troubles between people. They have been hurt in the past, but to say that people here are racist is too overdone.

Meals provided the opportunity to share experiences of each other's countries and cultures, and those connections built a sense of "global family," an essential stimulus for the times when the work of peacemaking seems too little too late. At times those "connections" seemed to be more than coincidence. At dinner with Vijia and Simoneel of India and Jane Breeds of Edinburgh, Scotland, I learned that Simoneel had received her doctor's degree from Amherst University in Massachusetts where my uncle was president until he retired. I asked her to talk about her impressions of the USA. "Amherst is a beautiful place," she said, "a very academic atmosphere, not real life, but I had a wonderful time. On student holidays, I traveled in Los Angeles and New Orleans. I loved the music and dance of the Mardi Gras. San Diego is a beautiful city." When I told her I had been to India, she asked me my impressions.

"There were so many people!" I said, "and I had a sense of being very white in that sea of brown skins. I liked the beauty of Bangalore, and the friendliness and helpfulness of the people was amazing. On a trip to Orissa and the tiger reserve, a couple of men on an overnight train chatted with us and shared their potato/egg salad on pieces of newspaper. Where is your home in India?"

"South of Bombay, near Poona. I hate Bombay; it's a dirty city."

"Are you glad to be going home?"

"The people there are making big plans for it; everyone is excited, asking 'did you meet a man, someone to marry?'" Her black eyes lit up. Was it anticipation, or did she have a secret she didn't divulge, I wondered as we left the dining room. We had circled halfway around an azure blue body of water at the foot of purple mountains, camels grazing in open tundra lands. It felt unreal. I was exhilarated, thankful for the chance to build these bridges of friendship and to see this very foreign country.

Mireya Holm was born in Colombia, South America, and has lived in so many countries as to be truly a citizen of the world.

Beth: Mireya, I've been aware that you're one of those late-night revelers on this Train. I think I've been a little jealous of all that energy and youth! Tell me about yourself.

Mireya: I was born in 1933 to free-thinking parents. My father believed one should be free to choose your own religion, which was a radical opinion at that time. I never attended religious classes. I was baptized Roman Catholic at the age of nine, and now I'm sorry I didn't know about other religions. At age 16, I went to McGill University in Montreal; at the time my father's sympathies were not with the United States but with other countries. He was anti-USA and doubted the motives of the Peace Corps. Was it to help or to conquer? My father thought Americans were fanatic people and he didn't want anything to do with that. I live in the US now. I'm married to a Dane. He was in Colombia working for a big Danish firm.

My father had the first currency exchange house in Colombia, so he had contact with foreigners. My husband is Protestant. Society said, "That's not right." I ran the risk of being excommunicated. I made a formal Catholic engagement and a Protestant marriage – avoided saying I'd raise the children Catholic.

I went to Denmark where my husband's roots and family were; had no intention to live there. When we married, we moved to Hamburg where my first child, Erik, was born. I have three sons and a daughter. We moved to Stockholm and started our own coffee business, working with the Colombian government. Moved then to Copenhagen where we lived the longest. And back to Colombia to the family, but it was hard for me to go back to my roots. We couldn't live there because of security. There's a great difference between the rich and the poor and that creates crime. Also, the drug problem created tense situations that were not good for children.

My home is Denmark; I lived 25 years there. Fifteen years ago I divorced and married another Dane, a professor. He retired and we went to Florida selling and promoting art for a Danish artist, Bjorn Wiinblad. I opened an art gallery and worked for a Rosenthal designer. Now I live in Florida half the year, and my children are everywhere. Erik works for the United Nations in Costa Rica. My youngest son is in the coffee business partly in Colombia, partly Europe. Two others live in Copenhagen, one a medical doctor and a girl in philosophy and literature. I have five grandchildren.

Beth: How did you learn about the Peace Train?

Mireya: From WILPF, and also I belong to the NGO, International Federation of Women Lawyers – FIDA. I'm not a lawyer myself, but I'm the sister of Angela Dolmetsch who is.

Beth: What has the Peace Train been like for you?

Mireya: I've enjoyed it very much, especially the physical part, the concerts, the dances, being with women of the 42 countries. Being together for three weeks with women of all ages and races has been an intense and good experience. Oh, some tensions are unavoidable. The Peace Train teaches me that we *can* live together as people of many nations. I see all this Chinese security as protecting us. Angela says she thinks the WILPF information office has created the impression all along that we are going to get into trouble in China. Visa troubles have been talked about a lot and created fear and distrust. There's the expectation that things will not be right in China. I was here earlier and everyone was extremely kind. You know, if things are too democratic, people become anarchic, especially young people.

"Strange comment," I thought. Was she getting at the notion of freedom without responsibility? I think that is no more a danger with young people than with old. Look at the voting records of the people in my own democratic USA.

Vijayalakshmi Balakrishnan's black eyes shone in her brown face. She was 28 years old, beyond her years in breadth of knowledge and depth of commitment.

Beth: Tell me your name again, and how you spell it.

Vijaya: Just call me Viji. My name is too hard to say.

Beth: You were born and raised in India? How did you get on the Peace Train?

Vijaya: Yes, I was born in India. I work for a women's organization in India called the Asian and Local Women in Communications Group. We are a support agency. We facilitate training workshops on women and mass media issues in different Asian countries. We've had workshops in Bangladesh, Nepal, and we just had one in Vietnam. At a later stage, we're working in Burma. We have a publication section where we have a regular newsletter and occasional book. For two years, part of my work was monitoring the preparations for Beijing, just responding to the information flow and reprocessing it for our organization which is specifically Asian women communicators.

We do the Isis International Bulletin which is a Philippine-based network of women's organizations. We brought to the Philippines interesting women from Beijing who represented the group Women and Vision. One of the things we talked about in preparation was the Peace Train, so I wrote and asked if I could be part of that. Application was processed fast, but funding took more time.

Beth: You mean you were funded for this trip?

Vijaya: Yes, completely. Somebody else did that.

Beth: What has it been like for you?

Vijaya: Some of my concern was related to human security issues and there hasn't been much of that. That worries me a little. But I think it's an experience I will always remember. It's a very intense experience, the creation of the team of people which is quite new to me. Usually I come into a more structured environment, then find space. Here we have a lot of space and then you need to create your own structure, which is quite different for someone like me. Living and working with so many women very closely is also a very, very new experience. I love trains, so I enjoy just being able to be on the train. That's been wonderful.

Beth: When you speak of human security, what do you mean?

Vijaya: Human security is a conceptual advance on the term, "development." It concerns six or seven specific components, one of which is gender. The UN 1993-94 report reframes the security of the world in terms of people's needs and desires rather than in terms of national arms selling. It's looking beyond borders and looking at people's lives. In that sense it's a very major conceptual jump, from issues like disarmament and cuts in military expenditure to issues like health and education budget, and changing consumption factors. It talks in terms of redrawing maps of the world, combating drugs, arms trades, prostitution across borders. Also the newer form of prostitution, mail-order brides from Thailand.

Beth: Say more about that.

Vijaya: Buy a bride you find in a catalog. You have books in which you can find a bride. It's a kind of slavery. Human security makes you free to look at all the issues which will lead to the future of the world. It talks in terms of beyond arms. That's what human security is. The UN Human Development Report is specifically on human security. It's in the Journal of Foreign Affairs. There is a lot of stuff going on at Beijing on human security.

Eve Malo of USA led a workshop that focused attention on the idea of an International Women's Party. A woman from Sweden said it is already in place and being implemented in the European Union. Her hope was that they could gather e-mail addresses of grassroots women from all the countries, create a political network and get funding to make women's issues a central concern to governments everywhere. Her very crowded workshop on the Train sparked a lot of ideas as to how to move forward.

Mercedes of Barcelona was Old Spain personified, complete with dignity, sparkle and salt-and-pepper hair. When I asked for an interview, she answered spunkily, "And who are you and why do you want to talk with me?" She agreed immediately.

Beth: Tell me where you were born, Mercedes.

Mercedes: I was born Mercedes Octavia Paniker, February 27, 1920. I'm an old lady.

Beth: I was born in 1922.

Mercedes: Oh well, two years difference. I am more older than you.

Beth: What do you remember from your childhood?

Mercedes: That's a good question. I remember many little things. I had a happy childhood. I remember loving parents, and I had three brothers. The rooms in my home. I discussed with my eldest brother because he wanted to sleep in the same room with my grandmother, and I wanted to. So he got it. Some week he was going and some week was me. But in the end, I was the winner. My mother said, well now, you are too big and you are too old and now Mercedes should sleep in there because then the other two boys were sleeping together.

Beth: Do you have a sister?

Mercedes: None, never. I was so unhappy. Therefore, when my youngest brother married, my sister-in-law became a sister for me. Oh, I was so fond of her. She was many years younger than me, and I discovered that I can have a sister who is a completely different way as I am. She separated and divorced from my brother, and we are still now very good friends. She is always critical to me, says I'm crazy to go to Beijing, I never realize that I am 75 years. She says I have no common sense, I am naive, believe everyone is good and I love everyone. She's the contrary, very rough and bitter and sees what people lack. She has a tremendous insight view to people. She feels that I live the sky. I dream. But she has shown me love, not saying the word but showing it. I broke my hip last year and was two months in wheelchair. Every day she was there. No words. No fuss. But she came. When my husband died very suddenly, 30 years ago, I was only 39 years old. So my house was full of people. It was sudden, he was driving the car and we were going to collect the children who were out for a meeting with the Boy Scouts and he died. So all the people came, was quite a traumatic situation. But in the end, everyone was brave. She stayed. I said, "Why do you not go to your family?" She said, "Go to my family and leave you alone tonight here?" See what I mean?

Beth: A real sister. Talk about what it's like being a widow. I'm a widow, too.

Mercedes: You are a widow, too?

Beth: Yes. My husband died in 1980. My son, my youngest child, was 18. I had four girls and a boy, except I've lost two of my children by death. One by car accident; one as a baby.

Mercedes: That's worse. You lost your husband 15 years ago. I was very young when I lost mine, which is an advantage and disadvantage. The education of my children was special for me and my profession was the first thing, a chemist. I was working my hardest actually when my husband died. The whole family agreed that I should work as a manager, so I didn't feel any economic trouble. We are not very rich family; but I knew how to work and so I educated my children the same way as my husband was. He was psychiatrist, my husband.

Beth: Really? My husband was a psychologist. Our lives are a lot alike, Mercedes.

Mercedes: My brothers used to say only a psychiatrist who knows how to deal with fools can manage Mercedes. Because...well I was very naughty. I used to smoke, wear trousers, work, go to university. People used to say to my mother, "You will never marry Mercedes. She is such a real woman and so independent and doing that and the other. You will never find a man who marries her. They will be afraid of such a woman. So well prepared from university for work, and professional and all that." And I had a man like that! But that was the traditional way of thinking in those times. My mother was worried because I didn't like anyone. "Why not this one?" "Why you don't dance with this one?" But I don't want. I don't know. I didn't meet my husband from my surroundings, not in my studies, not the job. He was older. Seven years.

Beth: Mercedes, how did you happen to come on the Peace Train? How did you learn about it?

Mercedes: By chance. I was in Berlin attending a congress of women in management in 1993. A lady at my breakfast there, a lawyer, sat at my table and started speaking. She said, "You know about Beijing World Conference?" I said "Yes, and I hope to go." "You know there's a train going up the Rhine by Bisberlina," she said. That's an agency we have here. She gave me the announcement of the Berlin agency. I wrote to these and they told me about WILPF.

Beth: Are you a member of WILPF?

Mercedes: No, I'm in business; well, now I am retired from business. But I am the president of an umbrella organization of Business Women's Association in Europe. We have representatives all over Europe and we are now trying to make a survey of how women feel in business that we think is different than men.

Beth: What business were you in?

Mercedes: Chemicals, production factory, metals, a very big metallurgical company selling cables. I was export manager. Stainless steel cable. Then I made my own company, a small business for chemicals for the shoe industry for making glues, adhesives.

Beth: Glues?

Mercedes: To stick on the shoes and to stick on many things. I started when I was over 50. I asked my children, no one wanted to continue it. My first one is a doctor. My second one is an economist working at a very good job with a sugar company. The third one is the girl, who had an accident. The fourth one especially she tried, but she said, "No, I don't like it, Mummy." So I sold it. I sold it to a bigger company. I recovered the money I had invested; that was important. I kept the grounds, and I was renting to the company. Then it burned up.

Beth: It burnt?

Mercedes: It burned, the factory. Fortunately I had put insurance so it was better for me, I received the insurance and I still kept the ground there but there's not very much value. So that is my business life.

Beth: And what is your impression of the Train?

Mercedes: Very positive. In the beginning was little hard.

Beth: What made it hard?

Mercedes: Well, I didn't know anyone. That is the first thing because I need to know people to feel help. Second, my English is very bad to understand the American way of speaking. It's completely different from the English we use in Europe. And third, it was very hard the stopovers, coming down, coming up, coming down, coming up, because I had to move very slowly with a stick for my knee. Actually they want to operate and give me a new knee but I don't want to, so I stay. That means that my movements are slow and painful so I cannot move about, and that going up and down is a lot of fatigue for me. But now I think I go to people I know. People acting very splendid. Every time I speak with someone, they teach me a lesson of something.

Beth: Really?

Mercedes: I learned a lot from the trip. There are many kind people I find. I have a very good roommate. An Indian lady who is very interesting. Very well built up with international things.

Beth: Is that Vijaya?

Mercedes: Krishna. She is from Camara.

Beth: What have you learned from people?

Mercedes: I would say a kind of enthusiasm for lost subjects, for lost items.

Beth: Lost items?

Mercedes: Issues. Yes, because all this kind of thinking against violence, against different economics, low salary, all that which I share completely. But I cannot believe in the forms of simple woman. I've seen too much the power structure to believe we can do anything unless we do something very new, very original, and every woman is different, not all over be the same. And I like to get, how you say, get infected by this enthusiasm.

Beth: But you think that we can't get the power structure changed? Do you think there's no hope for change?

Mercedes: Not at the moment. I will not see that. But it is not the power structure, it is the capitalist system.

Beth: Oh?

Mercedes: This monetary structure is so strong, so powerful, so big, 50 times the value of the whole world trade. It's not the politics. Politics are subjective more or less. But this monetary investment, stockholders buying and selling and maybe stealing the best, this is the great problem in the world. I feel so desperate and weak. I don't worry about other political things. I worry about the monetary system, the economic system.

Beth: Don't you think those two feed each other? The political and the monetary?

Mercedes: They are together, but one under the other. The political is depending on the monetary. We have a socialistic government in Spain and we, the people, are very afraid of what is going to come because the banks are folding. Because the World Bank is folding. Because the people know the control the World Bank and monetary systems impose on them and they can't do anything! And I'm sorry to tell you but the United States has a control problem.

Beth: Say more about that.

Mercedes: United States has the most control of politics. I mean, the imposition, the political imposition comes from the United States to Europe.

Beth: You mean the Cuba situation, that kind of imposition?

Mercedes: Yes, we want to recognize Cuba and send things there, and it is not possible because of the blockade. The United States retaliates. This control is not good. It worries me.

Beth: I'm sorry. I don't agree with what my government is doing in Cuba, Mercedes. In fact, I often disagree and feel ashamed of what my country is doing in the world, and I'm sorry for the worry and suffering it causes you and many other women. Tell me about this Peace Train. Has it been a peace community or has it built walls between people?

Mercedes: That's a good question. Individuality is always strong, in fact separates people. But I think there's a flow of what I call feminine affection going on, and this brings people together in spite of colors and objects. I think there's great love here, but language is still a problem for me. Everybody speaks English. When I speak Spanish with my South American colleagues, I feel relieved. Like more in community. Language is very important. Among Americans I always feel a little foreign.

Beth: Do you feel that now?

Mercedes: No, not with you, because you have this flavor of affection, in your eyes and your attitude, stronger than others. Most of the people, I would say great majority, are very kind. At least to me because they feel I am alone. I have no friend with me; I am old; I manage but it is difficult to walk and talk. The first day this American lady told me I should leave behind the luggage I could not carry.

Beth: An American lady told you that?

Mercedes: She told me, "I have repeatedly told you instructions about the luggage, to take only luggage you can carry yourself." But I didn't pay attention, and many American ladies have come to help me when they see I am going too slowly. I think they want regulations to be kept, but affection breaks the regulations. That's how it worked. I think the reality of woman is to follow their feelings and that is a superiority over man. Men are more restrictive; they think more the logical things. Woman is more spontaneous, in general. But every woman is one woman and you cannot generalize.

Tayba of Egypt came along just then and Mercedes gave her flowing blue scarf a tug.

"Tayba, she's going to take that scarf off you if you stay anywhere near her," I said.

"She's a darling," Tayba answered.

Everybody on the Train seemed to love Mercedes.

Marcia Trawinski of the USA was legally blind. Her ability to maneuver the complex life of the Peace Train journey was a source of amazement to me.

Beth: Tell me about your life as a child and youth, Marcia.

Marcia: I was born in Chicago in 1948 in a section created by the Polish, safe and homey. Everybody knew everybody, and somebody would call your mother if you got out of line. Both my grandfathers were born in Poland. I went to Catholic school, had only nuns as teachers until I was a sophomore in high school. In the 1960s, my dad did shift work in the steel mill. All the dads worked together and were home a lot.

Beth: When did you first know that you had sight impairment?

Marcia: Early. But children think they see what you see. It may have been anoxia, lack of oxygen during birth, or destroyed retina or another substance covered over the retina, probably a congenital dysfunction of the cone of the retina. In second grade, my teacher said I couldn't see the board. My mom didn't like that. They took me to doctors, doctors, doctors to get a good diagnosis. My mom was in denial, so I got to dance ballet, modern, jazz, do gymnastics. I'm in a stable condition now. Can see big things. I have a blind spot in the center of my eye. I have peripheral vision, but no depth perception, all shapes and lines, but I don't know how far away things are, like steps.

Beth: That must be a real problem.

Marcia: I had creative teachers. They'd say, "Let's figure out how we can do this." The diocese provided itinerant teachers and help with large print, exams, tutors.

Beth: Were you able to stay in school as long as you wanted?

Marcia: I got a scholarship to go to St. Xavier College in Chicago and majored in sociology. I didn't get into psychology because I thought I couldn't do the chemistry stuff. In 1970, I graduated from Kent State, the good old days! In 1973, I got a degree in psychology and counseling at Chicago State University and tried to find a job. It was difficult, so I went into part-time teaching. In 1977, I took a permanent position in crisis intervention counseling – chemical, alcohol, divorce, you know. I enjoyed it, but it was exhausting. I got burned out, so I left there in 1985 and went to grad school – seminary, in the sense of training, but not aiming for ordination. There was a cluster of these schools in Hyde Park. I was at Chicago Theological

Union for two years, was working on my thesis, when I had a car accident, very traumatic, physically painful. It took a long time to get energy back. I got involved in feminist things without finishing my degree: women's organizations, NARW (National Assembly of Religious Women), Women for Economic Security.

Beth: You've had quite an illustrious career, Marcia.

Marcia: Yes, I worked to get the American Disability Act passed in 1991. Sixty to 80 percent of the disabled aren't fully employed.

Beth: How do support yourself?

Marcia: I get a Social Security check, and I have a tiny inheritance, enough; to live on. I work as a volunteer helping to train folks who work in shelters, with disabled women, women's reproductive rights, Women's Network of Funding Organizations. I lecture for medical students on disability and HIV/AIDS, give time at Catholic Worker House for homeless and HIV people. Just outside Hyde Park are drugs, violence, guns, gangs, unemployment, you name it. Once a week, I give kids a safe place to play doing crafts.

Beth: Your courage in being on this Train is an inspiration to me. How has that been for you?

Marcia: Really good opportunity to meet different women. Disappointed there are so many US women and so few women of color. It was good to learn to know one another. Now, WILPF is another issue. They put me into a hotel where I had to handle three kinds of public transport. No one met or helped me or called to give hospitality. They put me in a car far away from the dining car. I needed to be nearer instead of climbing up over couplings.

Beth: I used to hold my breath when I saw you doing that.

Marcia: Women on the Train were helpful, but WILPF didn't have a clue about what I needed. It never occurred to them to read some of the stuff to me. The leaders were not collaborative or cooperative. Too few people were doing too many tasks. I signed up to do a workshop on disabled women, but was never given any time.

Beth: I wish I'd known that sooner. I'd have protested it.

Marcia: Well, you can see why my experience with WILPF was not positive. But being with the women was really good. My cabin mates were helpful.

Marta Ixcot has two names. She is "Sonia Cabrera" at home in Guatemala. Right now she lives in Vermont. I liked calling her "Marta." Her shining black hair framed a thoughtful face the color of warm, creamy chocolate; her dark eyes deep, somber, and beautiful.

Beth: Marta, tell me what it was like to be born in Guatemala.

Marta: It was very hard times for me as a child growing up. My parents were activists in our community. Both my parents had very little education, but they believed in learning Spanish, the official language. Guatemala has 22 Mayan languages. I come from the *Mong*-speaking people. Both my parents were catechists, meaning they worked in the church. They didn't take the Bible literally. They took it into a practical aspect, a practical vision. For example, when God cured the blind, the question is who are the blind to-day? The blind today are those who do not read or write. The lame of today are those who cannot stand up to speak their voice to learn about their rights as human individuals. The Mayan make up 80 percent of the population of Guatemala. The other 20 percent are people of Spanish descent, and they are the ones who are running the country. The Mayan people are looked down on. They have no rights. The illiteracy problem is high, like 80 percent. Education for Mayans is not viewed as valuable by the government or the military. During the late '70s and early '80s, there were dictatorships and one military regime after another. People were being killed, kidnapped, tortured, names put on the black list. Because of what my parents were doing, they were automatically viewed as communists, subversives, people who are against the military regime. According to the military and the government, the less people know, the easier it is to control. One way of doing that is not teaching them to read Spanish because then they'll be reading books and newspapers and opening their minds about the realities of the world and questioning your rights in the constitution.

Beth: When were you born, Marta?

Marta: In 1972, and I was just a little kid and not understanding what was going on. I was very young when my father had to leave my town for about three years. So he grabbed me; our house was burned down by the military.

My uncle was burnt out, too. The soldiers came one night into our house and my mother was surrounded by soldiers at gunpoint demanding to know where my father was. I remember this. I was only seven or eight years old. I remember seeing my mother standing in the middle of these men, and I could not understand what was going on. They were asking her, "Where is your husband? We want to know where he is now!" My mother saying, "I don't know where he is. I'm not married to him anymore. He is drunk, womanizer, and if I ever find him, I will deliver him into your hands. I want nothing to do with him." She lied to save the lives of everyone in my house, including her life. So they kind of believed her, but they didn't leave her alone. They were still surrounding her and she still was shaking. Before that, I was sleepimg on the floor and I just remember they ripped cover off me, and I'm looking up and I see four men in military uniform, and I was really scared. The whole house was filled with military men, soldiers everywhere. Lifting this and that, opening this and grabbing things here and there. And then the last words said by the military to my mom was "Next time if we don't find your husband and you don't give our price, we will come and kill the children, everyone." At that point, my mom communicated with my dad and he said, "You have to leave the city."

Beth: Were there other children than you?

Marta: Yes, my uncle's children. This was three months after my uncle was murdered by the military. My mother's brother. So she was already traumatized, my uncle murdered, the house burned, my father had left, fleeing, looking for a better place to live because his life was in danger.

Beth: Where did he go?

Marta: He worked in the coffee plantations trying to make some kind of living. All this time, I thought my father was dead. We were not told where he was because of safety reasons. To speak of military was like you couldn't speak of military. You couldn't speak of oppression, injustices. You were basically putting your life in danger. So my mom didn't even bother to explain to us the political situation.

Beth: Did she know where he was?

Marta: Yes, communications through friends. So it was that during my father's absence instead of me going to school, I became a baby sitter for a family earning $5 a month. I was a child about eight years old taking care of another child, a baby. The money I made I sent home to my mom to help her out.

We left Guatemala near 1983 without telling anyone that we were going. I was very close to my grandmother; she was like a mother to me. I lived with her and spent a lot of time with her. My mom told us we're going for a vacation and coming back in a few days. I was so excited. And the next thing we know, we are in Mexico. My parents had bought working papers for nine months or a year and then we would go back. It was then that my mother told us we were never going to go back. I was so devastated. I hated her for taking me away from my grandmother. I hated them so much for taking me away. And I still don't understand the situation that we had left. I knew that it was going hard, but I just did not understand the roots of the problems and all that was happening, you know.

We lived at the border of Guatemala and Mexico, which is Chiapas, and life was really hard. We worked in the coffee plantations. The soldiers would come into the border and take people away to the other side. We were constantly moving away and afraid of the immigration. Nobody knew my language except my mother. My parents forbid us to speak our native language. I ended up working as a baby sitter for the owner of the coffee plantation family. I was malnourished and sick. It was then that some North American people from the US came in the places where we were living and told us you could make a better living in the States. We migrated toward Mexico City and slowly to the US. My parents learned about the sanctuary movement, the Presbyterian people moving Central American refugees fleeing the atrocities of their countries. At that time, a group of Benedictine monks from the state of Vermont declared their monastery a sanctuary and were looking for a Guatemalan family to live with them. So that's how we came to Vermont.

Beth: What was your life like there?

Marta: Just one challenge after another, learning a new language, trying to fit into a new culture, being the only colored person in the school. I couldn't read or write or do math and I had to learn English. Those challenges were the greatest cross for me. I was only 12 years old and I had never been to school in my life before. It was the worst nightmare. I was constantly humiliated by the other children – "You can't count?" "You can't say the alphabet?" "Where have you been?" "You must be stupid." I had to live with this for a long time. One of my first friends was a boy who came up to me to help me. I graduated with my class in '91 and from college in '95. I had to learn not to give up my identity as a Mayan person, my culture, to find a balance, to have the inner strength to deal with all those pressures. Sometimes it was just like I can't do it. College was the best part because there was so much diversity. I learned to be more independent and build up more strength and appreciate myself more.

Beth: So now you're taking a year off and working for the International Maya League. Then you plan to go back to school and get your Ph.D.?

Marta: My master's. I don't know about Ph.D. I'll work my way up there.

Beth: You were in the Rolling School. Tell me what that experience was like for you.

Marta: The Rolling School was a great experience. To be able to react with other women, hear their struggle. To know I'm not alone in my struggle as a young person to try to find where I can spend my energy, where my ambitions are and how I can do that. Experiences were really different for women in the Rolling School. It was very hard for me to know where they're at and how they got started and why they're doing what they're doing. Other people came in to inform us as young people, and we saw how young people analyze things differently than adults or men.

Beth: How would you describe that difference?

Marta: Young women analyze things more globally instead of by a specific situation. We look at how does that affect others. For example, racism – not only how it affects individual black people but how does it affect the human race, politically or economically. It's more of a global vision and how can I, a young person, do something about it? Young women are more energetic about issues because they are newly exposed to them. They have all this energy that they want to take and be active – let's go out there and do something.

Beth: Change something?

Marta: I'm a young person and it's like I have more like, zest, maybe, because I'm beginning and not bored of it yet.

Beth: Do you think you have more hope?

Marta: Oh yeah, I think we have to. I'm not saying that old people don't have hope. Older people had hope and now they've invested all their energy and are passing on that energy to us to continue, their knowledge. They're showing us the road to continue. These young women are just like "Yes, let's go at it." I like the energy I see in these young women; it gives me more confidence that we can do it, you know? I'm an energetic person, just like you.

Beth: What issues have you talked about that have touched you especially?

Marta: A couple of issues have hit home because I've experienced them myself. One is forced migration. I talked with Tayba from Africa; she personally shared some of her experiences with me. I reached out to her and said, "You know, I've been there, too." She's in the Rolling School. We're doing a project on forced migration with two other young women. We are interviewing women who were forced out of their countries or who are living in another country by choice, talking about the effect of forced migration on your life and how you deal with it.

Beth: There are several women on the Peace Train who have had the experience of forced migration?

Marta: Tayba is one of them, myself, and Krishna, by choice. She's a professor. I want to know how she experiences the same things that I experienced when I lived in the States because of the different languages and what not.

Beth: What are the differences between living in the States and living in Guatemala?

Marta: For one thing, when I was living in Guatemala, I was growing up in political turmoil that just made my life miserable and robbed my childhood away from me. No television. Food was very scarce. Clothing was scarce. Now I'm living in a society where the waste is incredible, where capitalism is the number one thing. I'm surrounded by the media, by technology and electronics. I'm living in a society where we're polluting the earth. And sometimes I get sucked into that society, and then I wake up in the morning and I'm like, "'There has to be a better way for me to deal with this." It's hard.

Beth: It's very hard. Here on this train one of the things that's really bothered me is how much wasted food there's been. I just can hardly bear that. And this Chinese train, the plastic, Styrofoam, think what that's going to be like for three days. I think we share some of the same concerns, Marta.

Marta: Yes. Alternative economics hit home. In Guatemala, I am the victim of private corporations going in and forcing cheap labor on my people. I am the victim of the dictators who borrowed the money and put it in their private accounts in Switzerland or in Germany or in the US and now we have to pay the consequences of this. I am a victim of the International Monetary Fund. My family has been a victim of it. Mayan people and my people have been victims of it. We are the victims of capitalist society. A lady came into the Rolling School to talk about alternative economics. When she gave the history and the system of it, I just wanted to throw up, because it made me realize that I have been the victim of this for so long, and I will continue to be the victim of it unless it changes.

So these are the things that hit home to me. It just hit my heart. It made me angry and it made me frustrated. I've known about the International Monetary Fund, but I just had no idea how it functions, how it was just like being a parasite sucking the life out of my people. I cannot believe I have been living under this system since I was born. I can't believe maybe my children will be the victim of it unless I do something to change it.

Beth: Do you have other things you'd like to say about the Peace Train?

Marta: Yes. I would like other people on this Train to take affirmative action, please. Don't let it be just the conference and the Peace Train and wonderful memories in your diary and something for you to talk about. Take these experiences into your communities and act upon them. If something on the Peace Train really hit you, do something about it. If you are an activist, form a chapter in your community or become connected with one of these organizations. Nothing will change unless we act upon the realities and experiences that we have gone through as a community on this Train.

Beth: One last question. What effect do you think that awful experience of your childhood has on you right now?

Marta: I think it has positive and negative effects on me at this stage of my life. Everything I experienced as a child has made the person that I am today, a person who is ready to take action, ready to speak up against the injustices, willing to give up a good job if it comes along, to work for a non-profit organization, to give my skills and my experiences and my time so that the realities and truth will be known about what's happened in Guatemala.

Beth: Your story is not an isolated story. Haven't many of your people had these awful experiences?

Marta: Oh, yes. Many refugees in Mexico, in the United States and Europe, the atrocities against them, and the genocide against the Mayan people is not something of the past, that happened 500 years ago with the invasion of Spain. It's still going on right now in '95, something that the Mayan people have to endure and live with. Today different corporations come into Guatemala and take the land away from the people.

I am fortunate enough to be living in the United States, to speak English, Spanish, Mayan. To know something about politics, about the world. I feel like it's a noble quest for me to go out into the world and listen to Mayan women, indigenous people, for a change. Give them a chance to speak and hear them out, because they have suffered so much and they are still suffering.

The negative effects that I received, you know, sometimes I'm angry, and also frustrated that it's not going to change. In my own personal life, sometimes I don't want to have any children because I don't want my children to grow up in this society of corruption, this miserable world. To me it would be the greatest mistake to bring another person into this world to suffer, when I could adopt another child that needs help.

Beth: It *is* hard to keep hope when it looks like such a big task. Part of the hope, though, is that we keep working at it. I hear you with that kind of enthusiasm.

Marta: The greatest thing that one can have is hope, to dream, to go out there and believe you can make a difference, to have a lot of confidence and inner strength, be assertive about it and say, "Hey, this is what's happening and I want you to hear me." If you don't have self-esteem and self-respect, you can't give it to someone else.

Beth: You're right. Thanks so much, Marta. I want to let others know what you've said.

There are so many more stories I wish I had space to tell, each one an inspiration. All of them together joined the voices of the thousands who attended the Forum. The world's women were on the move, believing, as Marta said, that we *can* make a difference.

9

The World's Women on the Move

The highest form of goodness is like water.
Water knows how to benefit all things
without striving with them...
In dealing with others,
know how to be gentle and kind.[1]

Water wears away the rock.[2]

In Taoism, water is the symbol for the female.[3]

Multiply a half-time show at an Ivy League football game by thousands, and you have the opening of the Forum, an extravaganza unlike anything I had ever seen in my life. Over 5,000 performers, many of them children, charmed some 60,000 onlookers in Olympic Stadium, and a thousand who could not get in hugged the outside area. As the torch appeared on centerfield, excitement stirred the crowd like an electric probe. We craned our necks to see it being passed from one to another of the conveners and secretaries-general of past conferences. When it reached Khunying Supatra Masdit and Gertrude

Mongella, a multitude of women's voices rose to triple *forte* in a scream that will be heard through history. My heart was doing double time; history was in the making here. The world's women were on the move.

"Seeing you here," Masdit said in her welcoming speech, "makes me know that the women's movement in the world will go forward. The theme of this historic conference is, 'Look at the World Through Women's Eyes,' and that is just what we are here to do."

The next day, I spent almost three hours getting from 21st Century Hotel in downtown Beijing, to Huairou, the site of the Forum. The following day, I decided to move out of my fancy hotel and find lodging in Huairou, where I could get much cheaper quarters and avoid the bone-rattling bus rides. I spent a couple of hours trying to find the Petroleum Building that was handling housing in the makeshift "hotels" in Huairou. Nobody seemed to know where it was. When I finally got there, the man at the desk said, "Are you from the United States?"

"Yes, I am," I said. "I called an hour ago and was told that you have rooms available."

"Sorry. We do not have any rooms left," he said. Was I never to be free of that awful shrug?

"But I was told there are plenty of rooms."

"They were wrong. There are none left." That finality.

"Yuk!" I thought. I took a bus to the next place, where they agreed to give me a room, "starting tomorrow." A friend of mine, housed in the first hotel, told me the next day that the room next to hers was empty.

Back in Beijing, I asked Esther to get me a refund on my advance payment at 21st Century Hotel. I reminded her that I had requested low-cost housing, and now had found it in Huairou. She said she'd see about it. The next morning, she told me that the hotel authorities had refused to release me from my contract. "You can move out to Huairou," she said, "but you will not be refunded any money on the remaining hotel reservation."

I argued; I pleaded; I felt angry and helpless. The irony was that in order to get a visa to come, I had been required to show proof of prepaid hotel reservations. And here I was, caught one more time by my illiteracy. Esther spoke Chinese; I did not, so I couldn't plead my case with the hotel people directly. When I cried the blues to Ellen, she said, "You know, the travel agency is making big profits by keeping us in the Beijing hotels. These rooms are $50 per night. The travel agency is charging us $80." I was fit to be tied! I'd been "had"; I had been too trusting.

I couldn't afford to pay for two hotel rooms, so decided to "redeem" the bus trips by making as many contacts as possible with the women who spent those rattling hours the way I did. One day, I initiated a conversation with a young Chinese woman sitting beside me on the bus. I'll call her "Xiao Hong," not her real name, as she asked me to disguise her identity to protect her from any kind of recrimination.

"Were you born in China?" I asked.

"Yes, in the city of Lanzhou."

"Oh, our Peace Train had a rest stop there the other day on the way to Beijing."

"What did you see there?" her ears perked up.

"Nothing but high blue iron gates and 62 police officers," I answered. "We were not allowed off the fenced-in platform, and even when I looked down through the bars onto the streets, I didn't see a soul. Platforms and streets alike were completely empty of people. I would have liked to have spent some time looking around, meeting some women."

"I'm not surprised to hear that," she had lowered her voice and cupped her hand around her mouth, as if she could have been heard above the rattle and bang. "What kind of train did you say it was?"

"It was a Peace Train," I said, "sponsored by the Women's International League for Peace and Freedom. Two hundred and thirty-two women and a few men visited eight countries between Helsinki, Finland, and Beijing to learn what is going on with women there, and how we can be with them in their struggles. Do you still live in Lanzhou? Where did you learn to speak such fluent English?"

"I was taught English from the time I started to school, but I really learned to speak it from being a student for the past seven years in the United States. What will you do with the experience of the trip when it is over?" Her voice was so low that I could hardly hear her above the grinding wheels.

"I will be writing a book about the whole experience, including my time here at the conferences. I'll put you in the book."

"Oh, I would like to read it! And maybe you would let me translate it into Chinese. I'm sure a lot of Chinese women would like to read it."

I was astounded by her interest and her courage in making such an offer. "I would love to have you translate it, if that could happen. May I stay in touch with you?" I handed her one of my cards.

"The only thing I would ask," her voice was almost a whisper as she wrote her name and address, "is that you never let anyone know my real name."

"I promise," I assured her.

As time-consuming and arthritis-stirring as the bus rides were, they were wonderful opportunities to meet and talk with women I would probably never have met otherwise. I learned later that the same thing was true at the main conference meeting hall. The day that thousands of women could not get in to hear Hillary Rodham Clinton, they had a great time together on the outside.

What I regretted most about spending all that time on the bus was missing out on some of the late-night cultural events on Kuumba Stage. These were put on by women from the different continents. After a couple of days, there was no such thing as a dependable bus schedule to and from Huairou, and in Beijing, a taxi ride was always needed from the bus stop to the hotel. Getting in at midnight or after and getting up at 6:00 a.m. in order not to miss sessions made me feel my age. I felt some urgency to be rested enough to stay well, and that meant giving up some of the fine concerts and dances. I even missed hearing my favorite women's choral ensemble, "Sweet Honey in the Rock," a group of Afro-American women whose lyrics and voices always penetrate my soul. It was a major disappointment to miss hearing them in Huairou.

Resigned to the fact that I had no choice but to go back and forth from Beijing, I meandered around the grounds feeling the immensity of what was going on, dropping in on workshops here and there, Helen Reddy's gutsy song of the 1970s ringing in my mind: "I am woman, hear me roar in numbers too big to ignore."[4] Thousands of women were making sounds too big to be ignored by the world inside China, and hundreds more worked around the clock as journalists, making sure that this women's gathering would not be ignored by the world outside. One thousand NGOs were represented in the Forum; over 5,000 workshops were given.

When it was dry on the Forum grounds, it was dusty dry, and trucks regularly moved around the eating area spraying the sand. When it rained, we all dashed from tent to tent through mudholes that would have made wonderful mudpies, had I been a child with play on my mind. As it was, I was busy avoiding the slipperiness. The possibility of breaking a leg that far from home kept me alert.

Everywhere I looked, Chinese students, young women and men, wore yellow blouses marked "Volunteer." It was obvious they had been trained to be "good hosts," always willing and eager to help with needed directions and information. Dozens of tents that looked like big blown-up, long plastic balloons, sprawled over a wide area, melting into each other in a great interplay of colors, designs, activities and women. Kiosks with food and drinks framed the amphitheater on two sides. I groaned when I saw Ronald McDonald. Here and there huge sheets of plastic in red, white and rusty maroon covered up things and buildings that remained unfinished. Makeshift sidewalks of concrete blocks gave way to a rugged area that was only rubble. All too soon, I was introduced to Asian toilets, holes in the floor, quite a test of my arthritic knees!

Two women draped heavily in black, only their eyes showing, stood at the lesbian tent studying the sign, "Lesbian Rights are Human Rights, International Gay and Lesbian Human Rights Commission." A group of Chinese women met nearby. At the Amnesty International and Oxfam America workshops, the tents were full. In T-58, bright yellow with lace curtains, Japanese women talked about violence against women in Kakogowa, Japan, and prostitution, slavery and trading in women worldwide. In the Displaced Women and Refugees tent, videos were playing. At the "Older Women" tent, the entrance was dangerously high and a group of gray-haired women on their knees were busy building a step out of a big slab of concrete, anchoring it with mud others carried to them in flat, tin pans.

"How typical of the daily lives of women," I thought, "always alert to the possibilities of injury."

A large sign above one tent read, "Ancient Wisdom, New Vision. Asian Indigenous Women's Network." Some tents were full of the culture of far countries and places: Africa, Tibet, Central and South America, Asia, North America, Latin America, India. Others highlighted special needs, such as wheelchair access. The Peace Tent was the meeting place for all sorts of activities and displays; often Peace Train people clustered there in small groups, talking, listening, selling their wares.

In the "Quiet Tent," gentle music invited us to take time for silence, meditation and healing. A handmade tapestry of extraordinary beauty covered one whole wall. It pictured a woman quilting under a tall tree, a child playing with blocks at her feet, another woman kneeling with arms upraised toward a many-colored, beaded sun. Around the sun, streams of gold-embroidered sayings, in several languages: "Women should be revered because it is from woman that the life of man comes." Across the bottom of the tapestry, on black velvet printed in gold, the words:

O sisters
Out of the vessel of justice bathe thine eyes
With the healing waters of truth,
That we may open our eyes to the Reality
Of a new day.

To the side, on white velvet, embroidered in very large gold lettering, the words, ONE HUMAN RACE. It was an inviting, serene place in the midst of the constant hustle and bustle.

I joined a crowd of about 45 people in a tent where the UN report on women was being given. Ten official-looking men gave the statistics. It was discouraging to learn that there has been so little progress in improving the actual lives of women during these 20 years since the first world conference in Mexico City. It's also true that statistics don't tell the whole story.

A workshop on Chinese medicine, given by a team of Chinese women, informed us that the first "medical characters" are centuries old, known as early as 3600 B. C., that 12,100 kinds of books have been written with something over a million volumes. Chinese medicine is non-invasive; there are no untoward side effects; it relies heavily on natural herbs. It functions on the hologram theory, that any part of the body resembles the whole. Palmar creases, the 14 lines in the hand, relate to the internal organs. The ear is a microcosm of the features of the body. Discovering the secret of mystery pathways leads to diagnosis. There were women healers and doctors in ancient China. In the Han Dynasty, around 200 B.C., a female doctor was the first known in the world to practice gynecology.

I was surprised that in most of the tents English was being spoken. In others, interpreters worked hard to make the content available to those of us whose "only English" condition was embarrassing. From platforms here and there, folk singers entertained passersby with politically pointed lyrics or tender folk ballads. I often paused to listen awhile.

In the Cambodian tent, women sewed new banners to the growing Peace Ribbon. On the walls and fences everywhere, all sorts of issues and struggles were portrayed in words, pictures and banners. One stone wall invited the viewer to write "A Message of Peace." Hundreds and more hundreds of such messages revealed lives torn and hungry for a world without war.

An unforgettable experience for me was the silent candlelight vigil of Women in Black protesting violence against women wherever it is happening. My banner read, "No More Landmines. No More Crippling of Children." We dressed in black and walked in silence, hundreds of us. Halfway to our stated goal, we were stopped by security officers who would not allow us to go on, as they had formerly agreed. In response, we simply sat down on the sidewalk in silence, our candles burning. It was a powerful moment of protest and connection.

It is plain to me that, whatever our country of citizenship or lack of it, in the underground of women's lives, all issues, agonies and efforts are linked. In varying forms and degrees of intensity, we experience worldwide distrust and even hatred of the female which expresses itself in dehumanization, abuse, mutilation, objectification, subjugation. At the same time, as we sat in silence on that sidewalk, I knew in my heart that we are sisters worldwide, working to change our societies into places of justice and dignity for all.

Audre Lorde, a great black soul of the United States, said a decade ago, "We need to join our differences and articulate our particular strengths in the service of our mutual survivals."[5] I thought of the millions of women not able to attend this gathering, living in conditions varying from disrespect to abject misery and torture. I thought of the women and girl children whose health and happiness are sacrificed on the altars of men's aggression and sexual needs, on the altars of "religious" rites and customs. The World Health Organization estimates that there are 100 million women alive today who are survivors of FGM, Female Genital Mutilation, and every day 6,000 girl-children between infancy and 14 years old are added to the list.[6] These are some of the sisters who need our strength in the service of their survival. We marched for them, and we stand – or sit – together.

In the area of armed conflict, women and children are always the losers. In a report at the Forum, we learned that 90 percent of the casualties of war are civilians, that women and children make up 75 percent of the 23 million refugees of the world, that rape and war are inseparable. The UN reports that mass rape has occurred recently in Uganda, Somalia, Liberia, Peru, and Cambodia, that in Kigali alone in one year between April 1994 and 1995, 15,700 women and girls between the ages of 13 and 65 were raped, more than 1,100 gave birth, and 5,200 had abortions. It is now believed that the numbers of women who have been raped in Bosnia and Herzegovina may reach 300,000, some having been murdered by the men who raped them, most considered by their families to be dishonorable and responsible for their own victimization.

In Pakistan, rape is considered to be a fringe benefit for law enforcers. It is a weapon commonly used for revenge in family feuds, against political opponents, or even "as a show of raw power" such as when "feudal lords in rural areas use sexual assault publicly to enforce local dictates." "'These kinds of attacks against women are meant to humiliate and demean their menfolk,' says a spokeswoman of War Against Rape, an organization based in Karachi, Pakistan's largest city."[7]

In Bosnia, there were actually "rape hotels" into which women were forced, used, treated as things for men's pleasure and thrown away, sometimes murdered. The trauma and disgrace through which these women now live is reprehensible, unthinkable, not to mention what happens to the babies born scarred and dispossessed. The horror of it is so monstrous that I get sick at my stomach at the picture it conjures up.

One point of hope is that while it has been going on for centuries, now it is being made public and reparations demanded. It is past time for the governments of all the countries that have been involved in these atrocities, including my own, to make public confessions of their heinous wrongdoing and to back up those confessions with money and laws declaring rape a war crime that results in severe punishment. Women want to see governments put these laws into effect, starting now.

Back home in San Diego, I spoke with sprightly 89-year-old Martha Fort about her experience of the Forum. She said she had spent a whole day with the Chinese women who do agricultural work. "They had representatives from every state in China. Each state gave its report, telling what they had accomplished in the way of women's work in agriculture, because it was their way of combating poverty. When the industrial transition came about 30 years ago, the men would leave the farms and go to the nearest town to get work. They might come back home to visit, or they might not. So there were whole villages of females with children or the elderly. It devolved on the women to do what farming they could. So China put in a policy to educate women on being farmers.

"It was fascinating. The Chinese have had a collective farming system for many years. Individuals may farm a bit of land now, but they are largely engaged in combined efforts. There are millions of women in this endeavor. The women learned to do everything from the tilling, fertilizing, planting, cultivating, harvesting and then the marketing and shipping. If they have any of it left over, it's a money income.

"In the afternoon, they took us by bus to one of the collective farms. We heard from a group of six or eight women who were in charge of this enormous farm. Then they served us produce from the farm, and it was wonderful. They had grapes, apples, cooked yams and roasted peanuts. Of course, they grow miles of grains, wheat, corn, some oats and some food for cattle.

"This was a model farm, and they liked to show it off because it had been, in their view, successful. It had its own schools for children from kindergarten up through high school. They did a little dance for us, these wonderful little children, and some of the grade school children put on a drill and song for us. The campus is so big. So many people lived there that they had a clinic of their own where they cared for women in childbirth and the like. Families live in little clusters, in brick houses, many little villages of buildings clustered together."

"You said you were with a special woman that day, a Chinese woman?"

"Yes, she gave me a very pretty pin which I like to wear. There is a generosity that I experienced in the Chinese women."

"I experienced that, too. They are so willing to help, so eager to be friends, even across the barriers of language. What else was important to you?"

"My particular interest is population. I went to the University of Peking where the Population Institute is, a huge campus building. They do research there, and official government planning. The man I spoke with, the associate director, had studied five years for a Ph.D. in the United States, and he spoke English like a Yankee. He showed me their modern computer setup, oh, the latest of everything."

"Did you talk about the one-child policy?"

"He said that when a couple marries, there's no restriction. They can have a baby whenever it happens to come, if they choose. But when that baby is born, the woman is fitted with an IUD.

"Is that mandatory?"

"That's right. That stays in for five years with supervision. Then, if they want another child, they can petition their local area group, and if they get the go-ahead, she can have another child, after which she is sterilized."

"Does she have any choice in that sterilization?"

"No, no choice."

"What about the infanticide of girls?"

"They don't talk about that. We met in a hotel with a group of couples from Canada who were there to get their baby girls for adoption. They were so delighted, because they had been negotiating for so long."

"Were they all girls?"

"Oh, yes. Only girls are placed for adoption."

"Which plenaries of the Forum stick out in your mind?"

"The opening one was a wonderful occasion. We saw a video of a woman from Burma with her picture on the screen talking with us. Her name is Daw Aung San Suu Kyi, and she's a resistance movement leader. She had been under house arrest for six years, had just been released. She didn't want to risk being denied return into her country, so she stayed home and sent this videotape. The place was packed."

"I know. I couldn't get in and was bitterly disappointed. What impressed you most about what she said?"

"Oh, her enthusiasm. Her quiet confidence that the work she was doing will bear fruit, that people do want freedom, want their rights. And that persistence will bring that about. She won the Nobel Peace Prize some years ago."

"Were there other women in that session?"

"Yes, Winona Laduke, a wonderful young Native American who has done so much in the way of organizing for the Native American movement. She gave a beautiful talk on the rights of minority women and the roles they can play when they have access to power.

"Both these women have a great depth of compassion for women, what women need, and the right of women to have that. They are totally convincing and dignified in doing this. They were not radicals, shouting. They were calm and collected and very purposeful."

Every night, in addition to Kuumba Stage presentations, there were opportunities at Yanxi Lake to experience Chinese life and culture – the Peking Opera, dance and acrobatics, the Children's Palace Art Group, sports-dancing, folk singing. China is rich in living arts, and to those were added outstanding cultural presentations from around the world. As someone said, "If you kept going 18 hours a day here, you'd get to only about 2 percent of what is going on."

One evening session is unforgettable for me; it was filled with singing and dancing on the Forum theme, "Looking at the World Through Women's Eyes." What a thrill I felt, singing in the Women's International Choir, learning songs in several languages, pouring them into the open night air on the Kuumba stage: "We are all one people standing in the light, We will join our voices 'til we find the way for the people of the earth today."[8]

"I woke up this mornin' with my mind fixed on women, oh, I woke up this mornin' with my mind fixed on women, oh, I woke up this mornin' with my mind fixed on women, Hallelu, hallelu, hallelujah! Oh, I woke up this morning with my mind fixed on freedom, fixed on justice, fixed on women!"[9]

"'Don't you think it's time? Love will build the bridge between your heart and mind."

One became a theme song that will always ring in my ears:

We're gonna keep on moving forward,
Keep on moving forward,
Keep on moving forward,
Never turning back,
Never turning back.

We're gonna work for women's freedom,
Work for women's freedom,
Work for women's freedom,
Never turning back,
Never turning back.

We're gonna raise our voices boldly,
Raise our voices boldly,
Raise our voices boldly,
Never turning back,
Never turning back![10]

I was a little homesick that night, pulled toward family and a support group meeting I was missing, and the music soothed my soul. The tall, strong black woman leader stopped us at one point and said, "I want to tell you about a letter that I received from a group of women from Nepal. The letter said, 'We are not permitted to come. Our voices have been silenced. But when you sing your songs, we want you to sing loud enough that the sound will vibrate all the way to Nepal.' So as we speak our voices here today, as we sing our songs, we must sing our songs for those women who could not come, those women who wanted to come but dared not cross their husbands for fear, those who wanted their daughters to come and were forbidden, those who were denied visas or access to the conferences, let's sing loud enough for them all to hear! 'We're gonna keep on moving forward, never turning back'." We roared our cheers and applause, and sang our hearts out.

Before the next song, she gave a little pep talk. "We as women are often told what we can't do and who we are not. But I believe that we have to start with loving self, and once you love yourself, you can move out into the world and love everybody else. When we are told that we cannot be whatever it is we want to be, some of us cower down to that. But in strength and unity, we can walk with one another and move forward with our lives, and change the world to make it a better place for all of us. And so this song, I tell you, stands for the resolve of a new message here, that we can change that old message."

> *How can anyone ever tell you you're not valuable?*
> *How could anyone fail to notice that your living is a miracle?*
> *How you are connected to my soul?*
> *How could anyone ever tell you you're anything less than beautiful?*
> *How could anyone ever tell you, you're less than whole?*
> *How could anyone fail to notice that your living is a miracle?*
> *How you are connected to my soul!*"[11]

Marcia Boruta, Director of the San Diego Economic Conversion Council, told me about her impressions of China.

"It was my first trip to Asia," she said. "One of the things that was amazing to me was how much it was like any capitalistic society. When you hear about China, you get the impression that everything is totally oppressive and all that; we would be terrorized; they didn't want us, and all that kind of stuff.

"I call that the politics of distrust," I said. "Governments are experts at it. Too bad that an NGO like WILPF gets into it, too."

Marcia went on: "I was really amazed with the friendship that was extended, signs all over the place, posters everywhere. It felt like, 'they know we're coming and they took some action about it.' If there was a world conference of women in San Diego, I don't know if they would decorate the airport. I also was amazed with how oblivious people were to my presence there. I mean if I walked down the street and went to the department store, I felt like nobody was paying attention; they were too busy running around doing their own thing. Part of their own thing was shopping like you do in just about any other place you know. It was the sense that they're a lot like us. They're not as different as people say. Now if I'd been blonde or gray-haired like you, perhaps I'd have been pulled aside for a picture. Maybe being a brunette, they thought I was Chinese.

"Maybe. I was asked for picture taking, and I was approached by security officers lots of times."

"I did not have that experience. The guards would kind of follow me around a little when I went out to smoke at night, but I felt it was for my protection because I was this woman walking around at night."

"You were in both conferences, Marcia. Did you go back and forth on the bus?"

"I actually spent most of my time at the government conference. I was in Huairou the first day for my workshop. It was in the very first time slot."

"I tried to get there, but couldn't for the crowds and security."

"I had no trouble. This is one of the things I think is really striking. I went with 16 people, and every one of us had a unique experience of what happened in Beijing. All different. China is so old. We go from east to west coasts in the US and think 200 to 300 years is old. I went to one place where they've had this maternal society for 5,000 years. The idea was that possession, ownership was through the women. Children were recognized through the women; you don't even know who the husband was."

"What's the name of the place?"

"Ben Pol Maternal Village or something like that. It's an archeological dig. When we went outside of Beijing, people were really interested in talking to us. At the hotel, there was definitely kind of a stigma attached to us, I think. The elevator operator at the hotel tried to teach me my numbers. That was kind of sweet.

"Shanghai was a whole amazing experience just looking at the high rises and all the development there. We seemed to be right in the middle of some big residential area. On the back side of the hotel, all the laundry poles stuck out and all the back porches, and you could see all the television sets in all the rooms, sort of chaos that you look out to. The other side was very neat and orderly, masses of people. And I loved The Great Wall. Actually I didn't know until I got there about all the people who had died building it. I was really disappointed because we didn't have enough time there. We had spent way too much time shopping at cloisonné factories and this type of thing."

"What do you remember about the Forum?"

"They had incorrectly titled my workshop, 'Economic Conversation,' instead of 'Economic Conversion,' but it did have a little descriptive phrase that said what women are doing to redirect resources from the arms race to sustainable development. It was totally amazing to me that 126 people came; it was just unbelievable. The first woman who came was from Yugoslavia which is where my grandfather was from, my ancestral lands. It was very interesting because she was saying that they felt the war has to end eventually and when it does, how can they start redirecting their resources toward rebuilding their country? What was really astounding to me was the diversity of women from all different parts of the world. That was really neat. Some people who came said their problem is that the US is pushing the sale of our old weapons on their countries and they were all increasing their police forces. It was interesting to see that this issue touched people in all different countries.

"During the workshop we had some young Chinese women interpreters, and I always wondered if they were there to sort of spy, listen to what was going on, or interpret. But they stayed there the whole time and actually participated in the discussion."

Marcia was right that our experiences were all different. One day, I spent six long hours in a plenary sponsored by The International Guild of Women Lawyers. It was called, "Global Tribunal on Accountability for Women's Human Rights." Twenty-two women sat on the podium, each with a story to tell.

Gladys Acosta, moderator of the panel, began the presentation. She told the story of a blind woman in Pakistan who was raped by her employer and his son. In Pakistan, the law requires that there be four male witnesses willing to testify that a woman has been raped! Being blind, this woman could not tell who was present, but she did recognize their voices. That was not acceptable to the courts; she was accused of seduction and sent to jail. Gladys went on to say, "I can go on, but this sort of violation cannot continue. I know from my participation in Copenhagen that the stories you will hear today, the stories of these courageous women who dare to bare before you their lives, their suffering, their scars, will be moving and powerful testimony to the obstacles and violations that millions of women around the world confront every day. But these women here are not simply victims. They are initiators of change. They point to the end of abuse for many other women and the creation of a new world where violence against women will no longer exist, and we can have peace, not just for ourselves but for our children."

The first global tribunal on violations of women's human rights was held in 1993, at the World Conference for Human Rights in Vienna. At that conference, women began to tear down the wall of silence that has surrounded the abuse of the human rights of women for too many centuries.

Charlotte Bunch of The Center for Women's Global Leadership, introduced the panel members. She said, "Today, as in Cairo and Copenhagen, we return to remind the world on the occasion of the 4th World Conference on Women that there are still only a few holes in that wall of silence, that there is still too much abuse that is hidden, that women are still enslaved and tortured, mutilated and killed in every region of the world. Too little has been done to end these abuses. We are here today to challenge the United Nations Conference that claims to defend the human rights of women, and to demand accountability from the governments and the United Nations. We want some questions answered. What are you doing to fulfill the promises made to protect and promote the human rights of women, promises made in Mexico City in 1975, made again in Copenhagen in 1980, and again in Nairobi in the Forward-Looking Strategies document in 1985, promises made in Vienna at the World Conference on Human Rights in 1993? Most of these promises remain unfulfilled.

"The UN is on trial in this time of transition and change in the world. The question is, will it rise to the vision of its initial statement as a defender of human rights or must we go elsewhere to find a way to promote and protect the human rights of women and other marginalized and oppressed peoples of the world?

"We are saying today that we do not need more words; we want action. This tribunal is a testament to the fact that we are a global movement that *will* change the 21st century. Many times in the last few months I have doubted that. Today, I believe it."

Radhika Coomaraswamy, Director of the International Center for Ethnic Studies in Sri Lanka, is the UN Special Rapporteur on Violence Against Women, a position created at the women's human rights movement in Vienna in 1993. She spoke with passion. "We are gathered together," she said, "to hear the voices of women who are not now so much victims of violence as they are empowered women who have reversed their victimhood to make it a source of strength.

"To tell the story of your victimhood requires a lot of courage. It is to break the barriers of silence, shame and privacy, to let the world know the extent and nature of cruelty and the violation of human rights in the whole community of nation states.

"These women remind us of the fundamental fact that women's rights are human rights, and that women should be the beneficiaries of legislation and protection. The flow of information is controlled by men. The world of the written word is completely their domain. These oral testimonies are a dent in this power. They give the other point of view and validate experiences which for all these years have been hidden from the world. That is why the women gathered here are so special. They have become empowered, and in that they are an example to all of us here.

"Perhaps the strength of this tribunal is to let it be known that women can survive, that a grievance becomes a right, and a right leads to a remedy. This ability to get a remedy, to assert one's rights, to demand a remedy, is the process of empowerment.

"Privacy and the concept of the sanctity of the family are causes for violence against women in society. These doctrines require women to be silent when they are battered and wounded. The public/private distinction has been responsible for silencing women. Today there is a new approach. Realizing that violence against women violates a fundamental human right, states are required by standards of due diligence to prevent and punish crimes of violence which take place in the private domain. Even in the public sphere, trafficking in prostitution and sexual assault are seen as private acts of individuals, and therefore treated less seriously. It is only in recent years that people have begun to speak out against this kind of enforced silence in the public sphere. Sex as a private act, man and woman in their relationship as a private contract, these are myths which have allowed for a great deal of abuse. It is timely that these are now being challenged by the brave women who have come forward.

"In the world of armed conflict, rape and sexual assault are treated lightly. It is believed that these are normal acts of war. Only recently have women who have been kept in sexual slavery been able to make their voices heard. New institutions, such as the International Tribunal, and the Hague are working to remedy centuries of injustice in keeping women's voices silent. Countless brave women are resisting the curtain of shame to come forward and speak their minds. Whether they are 'comfort women,' women living under Muslim law, victims of armed conflict in Bosnia-Herzegovina or domestic violence, they shock the conscience.

"The organizers of this tribunal have created a revolutionary movement, both in Vienna and now in Peking. They have given a window of opportunity for the women's movement to unite around shared real life experiences."

Twenty-two courageous, brave women told their stories, or "became" one of the clients whom she had represented in court, telling her story as if it were the speaker's own. Behind each one, we heard echoes of the millions of women whose rights are violated in these and other ways, every day of every year in every country of the world. Documented atrocities committed against women were pictured so vividly that it was almost beyond my endurance. I wanted to run from the meeting, to get away from the horror of violations against women that are so inhumane and cruel that even now, as I remember, tears come, and I feel outrage.

One Bosnian woman's story still haunts me. She had been buying groceries for her family at the market when two soldiers abducted and blindfolded her, and threw her into the back of a pickup truck. They drove far into the countryside where they were joined by five others who raped her viciously, over and over. Bleeding and half dead, she was once again thrown into the truck and driven deep into the mountains, where they dragged her into the bushes, threw her into a ditch and drove away. She did not know where she was, and she wandered for days eating roots and leaves. As the weeks went by, she realized she was pregnant. Now she knew that she could never return home because she would be considered a disgrace to her family, defiled and responsible for what had happened to her. After months of wandering, scrounging for food and water, she found a cave where she gave birth to the child, wondering what would become of them. Finally, one day she came out on a road where she was overcome with terror when a passing truck slowed and invited her to get in. It so happened that the driver was the director of a shelter for women; he knew that women were being abandoned in that area and wanted to help. She was given food, housing and legal counseling, and was able to make a new start. The tribunal had asked her to come to Beijing and tell her story. As heartrending as it was to hear it, along with the others like it, I knew that these women's lives were concrete manifestations of the issues listed as critical areas of concern in the Platform for Action, the agenda of the United Nations World Conference.

In that plenary, it was burned forever into my mind how urgent it is to understand that the violation of women and girls' rights is a violation of the Universal Declaration of Human Rights, the centerpiece of the Charter of the United Nations:

"All human beings are born with equal and inalienable rights and fundamental freedoms... These rights belong to you... Help to promote and defend them for yourself as well as for your fellow human beings."[12]

Later that day, I attended the workshop, "The Rise of Religious Conservatism." What I learned there was no less disturbing. Fundamentalism is not only insidiously taking over the religious institutions in my own country; it is sweeping the world, carrying with it the subjugation of women and supremacy of men, all in the name of God. It is unconscionable, a cause for protest, a travesty of the sacred, made all the more lethal for women and girls by their acceptance of it.

Jan Goodwin speaks of this in *The Price of Honor*, a heartrending picture of the effects on women of the rise of Islamic fundamentalism. "It is ironic," she says, "that the most outstanding contradiction regarding the inequities suffered by Muslim women is that Mohammed, the founder of Islam, was among the world's greatest reformers on behalf of women...Islam, in fact, may be the only religion that formally specified women's rights and sought ways to protect them."[13]

Yet, horror stories like Laili's of Afghanistan persist among Muslim women today. She lived her teen years in New Jersey where her family had been exiled because her grandfather had criticized the monarchy. She married an American man who was also disturbed by what was happening in Pakistan, and they moved to Peshawar to try to bring about change. Both were offered jobs with an American relief agency. Radical Islamists were enraged to see an Afghan woman cohabiting with an American. Early on, Laili began to receive death threats. Even though she wore the chador, completely covered except for her eyes, she has been spat at by Arab extremists, attacked with stones, threatened with machine guns and forced off the highway when she drove a car. Several of her friends have been assassinated, and she is convinced they are trying to kill her. She believes that fundamentalist religion is used to keep men in complete control of women. "We have a proverb," she said. "'When you can't beat the donkey, beat the saddle.' Women are the saddle."[14]

Indeed, I thought as I read, the rising tide of fundamentalism and the push for Muslim domination is actually a worldwide backlash to the worldwide women's movement. Small wonder that men feel threatened; women today know they are "right" and are linked in a global movement that will require changed attitudes and behaviors on the part of the men in their lives. For some men, this is little less than earthshaking, a challenge to their understanding of what it means to be "a man." For some, it is downright terrifying and elicits a fighting response. I would like to think that the world of the patriarchy is shaking at the foundations. For women, it requires the courage to "work out your own salvation with fear and trembling, for God (the Spirit) is at work in you."[15]

Anne Hoiberg of the United Nations Association in San Diego spoke with me about her impressions of the Forum.

"One of the most impressive workshops," she said, "was meeting the women who are involved in an organization called Jerusalem Link. These are Palestinian and Israeli women working together to try to create a peaceful solution in Israel. To see these women sitting next to each other, Palestinians and even women legislators from Israel, was a truly touching moment. The place was packed. They had TV cameras there and everything.

"I was upset when I saw Representative Christopher Smith from New Jersey in the Forum. This man had no business being in Beijing, and there he was, making noises. He's a very strong anti-choice conservative. There were a lot of women from the Moral Majority."

"There was a lot of talk before Beijing that the conference had refused admission to anti-choice people," I replied, remembering a friend's comment to that effect.

"That isn't true. They were allowed a certain number just like other groups. Even our US delegation was very diverse. There were several men on it, which amazed me. I think the US government went out of its way to identify true experts to be there, like Geraldine Ferraro on human rights. We had attorneys who were experts on our Constitution, so that if we signed the Platform for Action, we wouldn't be in violation of our own Constitution. I was quite impressed with our delegation and how hard they worked. The Platform for Action is very pro-family. There was a lot of press saying that it was anti-family and that's misinformation.

"I really enjoyed the speakers at plenary sessions. Both conferences had representatives from each of the five regions. You never had a sense that the United States was the star country, and of course, we weren't. We were one of 189. I liked the democratic sense of that.

"We didn't have our official head of state there, and Boutros Boutros-Ghali wasn't even there. He claimed he was ill."

The official UN Governmental Conference opened on September 5, 1995. Many of us who wanted to be actively working in caucuses and lobbying were kept on the outside, denied that privilege. That was a major disappointment for me, and a lot of women said they felt the same way. Groups are often woefully lacking in the ability to call out the gifts of people who are willing and eager to work. One more time, I thought, "we are being denied access to the places where decisions are being made that will have long-term effects on our lives. Our contributions are not recognized or mobilized. The helplessness we feel results in dull resignation, which in turn creates the debilitation of unexpressed rage, which in some people leads to terrorism; in others, despair."

Surveillance and control officers around the governmental conference area were as thick as The Great Wall, and as impenetrable. At the end of the days, those who were "in the inner circle" reported back what they had seen and heard – a crumb thrown to the outcasts. But it was a pale image of the rising loaf of bread.

In contrast, those few who were given access felt both the satisfaction of working on the segments of the Platform for Action that were important to them, and incredible time pressures rewording it and lobbying governments to take action to remove the "brackets" that blocked consensus.

Marcia Boruta described it this way: "At the Forum, I went to a workshop called 'Alternative Economic Frameworks from a Gender Perspective,' given by The Society for International Development. I figured that this group would tell me how I could get involved in lobbying for these kinds of issues during the governmental conference. They talked about the Women's Linkage Caucus who were going to be doing this lobbying. It was made up of a bunch of little caucuses. I made some really solid contacts there. At the UN Conference, I went to the Economic Justice Caucus meeting and just got sucked up in the process, totally absorbed in this lobbying effort.

"It was so exciting to be engaged like that. That caucus split up into four different groups. I ended up working on the group that was modifying the opening Declaration to the Platform for Action. A woman from India and I worked really closely together. This whole group of ten or so people made their suggestions. We made multiple revisions, running back and forth to get typing done and copies made.

"Part of the work of our lobbying group was to circulate our recommendations to the other caucuses. What does the environmental caucus say about the Declaration? What are the sustainable development or poverty people saying about the Declaration? Do you like what we did? It was this process of constantly getting feedback, trying to incorporate it, collecting the feedback from all the different caucuses, but you know it didn't really end there. We had to get it in the hands of the committee person. It was a madhouse, caucuses running hither and yon, people running hither and yon, trying to reach this person or that person.

Then we took our recommendations to the US delegation and got them into the hands of the woman who was on the Declaration Committee for the US delegation, and pushing and pushing and modifying and seeing what came out of that committee for more recommendations. The Indian woman had to get it to the Indian delegation. And we asked, 'Did it do any good?' I don't know."

"And that was being done in 13 areas?"

"Exactly. Women running ragged everywhere. What was really exciting about it was that you had this common ground with women from all over the world. I mean you all wanted peace, economic justice. You could talk to them more than you can talk to your neighbor at home sometimes. It felt so powerful, women all around the world who believed the same way you did and thought it was a reasonable thing to believe. And you just felt, we're all working together; we can change the world."

One thing that became very clear to me in Beijing is that there are *global* forces affecting the quality of life for women and girls and for the whole human family. Some of these are approaches to governance, including questions of citizenship and political participation; obstacles to peace and human security, the effects of militarization, violence and poverty; challenges posed by globalization of the economy, including the impact of the technological revolution on work, unemployment; the rise of conservatism in various forms, whether it be religious, nationalist, racist, homophobic; challenges and opportunities as a result of media, culture and communication.

These global forces became the framework within which The Platform identified the 12 critical areas of concern for women worldwide: Economy; Governance and Politics; Human and Legal Rights; Peace and Human Security; Education; Health; Environment; Spirituality and Religion; Science and Technology; Media; Arts and Culture; Race and Ethnicity. To these 12 from past conferences, a 13th was added in Beijing – The Girl Child.

The everyday lives of women around the world are shaped by these realities. We are second-class citizens, or with no citizenship at all, outside the mainstream of official governmental systems, refused access to resources and decision making that affect the quality of our lives. We are looked upon as expendable and for the pleasure and service of men.

This gets lived out in the lives of millions of refugees who are denied citizenship and any kind of protection under the law. It's lived out in environmental devastation resulting from nuclear testing, such as the more than 200 tests done by the US alone from 1945 to 1962, not to mention nuclear accidents like Chernobyl.

Poverty plagues women in every country; a high percentage of women and children are homeless. In rich United States, 15.7 million children lived in poverty in 1993. In 1994, 6.5 million were provided nutrition assistance by WIC (Women, Infants and Children), 72 percent of the number who were eligible to receive help. Today that program, along with many others dedicated to human need, is being cut to balance the budget. Every *day* in rich United States, 27 children die from poverty; 2,699 infants are born into poverty; and 100,000 children are homeless.[16] In the developing nations of Asia, democratization and the "free market economy" mean that funds for necessities once provided by the state are no longer there. As a woman in Russia said, "There are more products available and less money to buy them. The privileged get ahead; the poor suffer." This is not to say that democracy is no good. It is to say that capitalism is a cutthroat system that actually drives the widening gap worldwide between rich and poor. Justice and the well-being of the environment require that privileged people use less and share more. Capitalism encourages us all to use more and share less.

Violence against women in the world is on a rampage. Almost everywhere we look there is torture and abuse of women and girls. The girl child is a grave concern. It is reprehensible that to the already known trafficking in women in all parts of the world is now added trafficking in girls. One example: the abduction and disappearance of girl children in Vietnam and neighboring countries to meet the needs of the young men of marriageable age in China. The underside of that is a crime in itself – amniocentesis used to determine the sex of the fetus which, for females, often results in abortion, midwives and doctors instructed to "accidentally break the necks or backs of female infants" or to discard them on doorsteps of orphanages. One Chinese obstetrician spoke of losing her license to practice medicine when she refused to comply with that directive. In Germany, every fourth girl has endured sexual violence; every fourth partnership between a man and a woman is violent.

The US Army's School of the Americas (SOA) in Fort Benning, Georgia, *teaches torture*. Graduates of that school include dictators and some of Latin America's worst human rights violators. Father Roy Bourgeois, a Maryknoll, spent time in jail for demonstrating against funding the school. Recently, Duncan Hunter, my California state representative, in answer to my protest against funding SOA, wrote: "I firmly believe that the closure of the SOA would not only be detrimental to our relationship with Latin America, but could also hinder the progress of human rights efforts in these countries."[17] I thought of the basic policy of the UNESCO Constitution, "Since war begins in the minds of men, it is in the minds of men that the defenses of peace must be constructed,"[18] and wondered, "What would it take to change his mind?"

A major theme of the UN Conference, the Forum and the Platform for Action was "Women's Rights are Human Rights." It is a fact that women are denied all sorts of basic human rights. In Sudan, for example, it is illegal for a woman to own land or to inherit property of any kind. In Saudi Arabia, women are not allowed to drive a car, walk freely on the street, or even allow one hair to escape the heavy veiling prescribed by men. In the United States, women do not have legal protection provided by CEDAW (Commission on the Elimination of Discrimination Against Women), a document signed by over 150 nations of the world, nor do we have an Equal Rights Amendment, which China put into law in 1975! I could go on and on and on.

In the midst of this grim picture, however, The Fourth World Conference on Women showed unmistakable *signs of hope.* Knowledgeable and informed women, clear thinkers and truth tellers, demonstrated the power that comes in being connected by knowledge of the issues, skills, determination and dedication to the struggle for transformation. The telecommunications highway now makes it possible for us to know and give support to each other around the world as we work for change. We are no longer in competition with each other over differences in the ways the issues express themselves or how the work for change must be done. We see the global nature of the forces impinging upon all of us in the same way – deeply entrenched fear of women, ancient disrespect, and an understanding of power as domination and control.

We are no longer willing to accept things "as they are." Together we are saying NO to self-ordained male privilege, injustice, greed, abuse and "power over" ways of viewing the world. We are saying YES to new ways of governing, to new and peaceful nurturing of the earth, and to an end to the nuclear age and war. We are *together* in respect for each other's visions, cultures, struggles, methods, differences. We sing, dance, dream, weep, rage and laugh as sisters on a common journey toward a transformed tomorrow.

We now know, out of a wisdom born of past agonies and struggle, that unity in this world women's movement does not mean a vat of homogenized female conformity. Rather, it means genuine understanding of differences and putting those differences to work as learning tools to enrich and expand our own private worlds.

Unity means understanding that the real enemy of women is not other women of whatever race, creed, sexual orientation or life situation. The real enemy of women is a patriarchal system that labels us "inferior," "subordinate," "expendable," "not of as much value as boys and men," "men-bashers," "anti-Bible," "anti-life." And on and on.

What happened in Beijing goes beyond Beijing into a long future of courageous action, because we know that whoever, wherever we are, we face a common enemy, and the health of the human family and the planet hangs in the balance. After that long week of negotiation and determination, a victory, a major victory for women and girls was achieved! The Platform for Action was adopted by consensus by 189 nations of the world. It was a cause for gratitude and hope.

This is the "Platform" on which we firmly stand as we now take action *beyond Beijing.*

10

Beyond Beijing

What was an inner light becomes
a consuming fire that spreads outward.[1]

And when we have built an altar to the Invisible Light,
we may set thereon the little lights
for which our bodily vision was made.[2]

I left Beijing filled with vigorous energy and a sense of determination, hope and possibility. The Forum motto rang in my ears: Think Globally; Act Locally. I would go back now, along with those thousands of other women, to the lone place, that place where our individual experiences of sexism are painful, sometimes very lonely, where the immensity of the task is overwhelming and our efforts seemingly inconsequential. At the same time, I would never lose that awareness of being connected, linked in a chain of courage and strength with all those women, in a world movement often invisible to the naked eye, germinating and growing like seeds under winter snows. As Lisa Hofman of The Netherlands wrote 18 months later, "I saw in China the enormous strength and diversity at the NGO Forum. In the government part, I saw the power struggle and empty words. Although: there was a spark, there was hope, and it will go on."[3]

I left those strong and dedicated women with a very personal, self-appointed task, to write this book to help link lonely women to each other – the writing itself a lonely task, and always the temptation to belittle its importance. I wanted most of all to put my life on the line to empower women with the courage and strength it takes to challenge oppression against ourselves and all women wherever we find it, in our marriages and relationships with men, in our churches and communities, in our governments, in our work and in our play. I wanted to be a part of making visible that invisible web of *women for women* that eases the loneliness and gives us courage to withstand demands, put-downs, and discounting.

If we are awake, aware, and honest, we know these are a part of all women's daily living. The intensity of the repression varies from one situation to another, that is true. Some of us are wonderfully fortunate. In our privileged places, it is urgent that we remember that there is no place on this globe free of this women's burden. But the UN Forum and 4th World Conference on Women also gave us the assurance that there is no place on earth without *women helping women* to lift that burden off ourselves and the girl children who are living through it now, and those who will come after us. Women of honesty, courage and strength are everywhere, working for change, keeping on, even in the face of discouragement over the slow and painful pace of victories. It was almost *two centuries ago* that Sarah Grimké spoke her immortal words: "All I ask of our brethren is that they take their feet from off our necks and permit us to stand upright on the ground which God designed us to occupy."[4] The women in Beijing raised that noble standard higher: we want action, now, we *will* stand up and join men as full partners in privileges and responsibilities for the world's family and home. We must!

In my mind's eye, I see millions of lights burning in every corner of the earth, being held high by women of privilege and those who are denied privileges, by women in pain and those healed of their pain, by women determined, as Gertrude Mongella said at the opening of the Forum, to move beyond words to action. Now we want to see it happening.

We want our husbands, lovers, and friends to show us genuine respect, to value our perceptions as they do their own. We want them to assume that we know best what is right for us. We want them to encourage us to make our own decisions, trust our own judgment, and take positions of leadership that challenge us to use our gifts. We want men and systems at all levels of life, the personal intertwined with the political, to speak out for women and to take their fair share of responsibility for the abuses, inequities and indignities women endure every day and have endured over centuries of time. We want our governments to make laws, or change them, to ensure that women are protected from domestic violence, that they are given wages equal to men for the same jobs, that they have equal access to education, that their contributions are counted in the Gross National Product tallies of the nations. We want the religions of the world to stop using an "Absolute Father God" to justify men's positions of authority and control over women, to stop relegating women to subservience and to a set of rules that denies their full personhood.

We are not willing to wait until men are ready, for the terror and torture of too many lives of women and girls are at stake. We are women on the move toward justice, dignity and peace, and nothing can stop us now.

I left China with a wild mixture of emotions. I was glad to leave the surveillance which seemed to permeate the very air I breathed and which crept like gooseflesh on my skin, quite unlike my experience in any other foreign country I have visited. And I left with a sense of immense loss.

Three weeks I had spent in that great country, and I felt as if I had seen only a tiny fragment, that I had had such limited access to the people, to the way they live their lives, to their hopes and their fears. I left without seeing some of the wonders I had hoped to see, the ancient clay sculptures in Xian, great art museums and treasures of areas other than Beijing.

I left wondering what happens to the Chinese women now, the ones who spoke out so plainly and forcefully against human rights violations, oppressive governmental restrictions, preferential treatment of boys and devaluing of girls, all the things that they want to have changed in their own country. I had felt suspect in China, only because I was a woman among women who are struggling and working for a better life for women and girls, and, therefore, for everyone in all parts of the world. For it is a fact that when you better the conditions of women, you better the quality of life for families, communities and nations. As a woman of Uganda said, "When you educate a woman, you educate a family."

Because Delta did not fly out of Beijing, I flew to Hong Kong and had 24 hours to explore a city where people on the streets are as thick as flies stuck on the dangling flypaper back on the farm. I checked into my room in a downtown hotel, washed my face and hands, and rushed to make the most of the little time I had to be out on the town. Then frustration took over. The key to my room was nowhere to be found. "Oh, dear," I thought, "now I will have to face the authorities and admit I have lost my key."

The man at the desk took me by surprise. Cheerily, "No problem! Our man must have forgotten to tell you that it is in that little holder on the wall." My mind did a doubletake. "I have left China! I don't need to prove anything or feel guilty about my ignorance." I felt amazingly free as I raced toward a departing tour bus.

Hong Kong blew my mind in several ways. The high-rises rose like solid walls above highways of unending concrete slabs beside an ocean as "blue as mine." Gargantuan advertising placards formed canopies over narrow cobblestone streets bustling with shops and businesses, all vying for attention from hurrying tourists. Tour buses rattled into the countryside to ancient Buddhist temples, tended tenderly by ancient, stooped, gray-haired women who shuffled about as if in prayer.

I felt a chill inside, remembering that Hong Kong would be "returned" to China by Great Britain in less than two years, a decision made by governments without any choice on the part of their millions of citizens. An incredible act of imperialism! By what right did Great Britain *own* Hong Kong in the first place? Indeed, what right has *any* government to own another nation and its peoples? What will Hong Kong lose or gain? What will happen to these pleasant people when they *belong* to China? Will there need to be a war to keep the human rights they now enjoy? I shuddered.[5]

The next day, we had scarcely taken our seats for the flight home on the big Delta bird, when the announcement came from the cockpit, "There will be some delay because of a malfunction in the operational system. Please stay on board, as we are expecting to take off soon." Three hours later, we began the 16-hour trip which would put my feet on "homeland" soil.

Home. When my feet touched the ground in the USA, the lump in my throat welled up in thankful tears. It was as if a blanket had been thrown around me, and I was being held in its warmth. I could read and speak the language. I knew where I was going and how I would get there. I didn't see a security officer anywhere. I felt free. And, in my mind's eye, I saw the burning candles of women's lives inviting me to light my own and keep it burning.

Now I know there are women in Africa, attorneys-at-law, creating and fighting for passage of legislation to outlaw female genital mutilation. I remember the words of Miria Mtembe of Uganda, as she spoke in the workshop, "Approaches to Governance, Citizenship and Political Participation": "Africa was once called 'the dark continent.' It's now called 'the lost continent.' I assure you that Africa is *not* lost. We are committed, determined and ready to face the challenges of the 21st century."

I know there are women in Iraq and Iran, Burma and Bangladesh, protesting wife-beating and repressive restrictions based on the assumption that they are the possessions of men. I know there are women in Germany protesting the sale of arms to Turkey, organizing caravans for peace. I know there are women in Mexico, elected to the highest courts of the land, creating and fighting for passage of laws to punish rapists and anyone guilty of violence against women; women in Surinam, developing parliaments challenging the state to take action on women's crucial agenda; women in Ohio, moving toward Ph.D.s in psychology, demanding respect and support from their husbands and boy children, no longer willing to take more than their share of responsibility for the emotional well-being of marriages and the physical well-being of children, treating husbands as full-grown men responsible for their own needs.

I know there are women in Maine, challenging traditional values and practices of medicine, encouraging their daughters to full self-expression; women in the church, taught to think of God as Father and refusing to live by that, aware of how destructive it is of their relationships with mothers and sisters, insisting on recognition of the Divine Feminine, praying to Sophia, Goddess of Wisdom; women everywhere, training themselves in telecommunication, using it to build networks of support and encouragement with those isolated in the struggle. Worldwide, women are training for and entering the political arena.

Active chapters of the Women's International League for Peace and Freedom are all over the world. WILPF USA is engaged with Colombian women in the war on drugs, has programs of outreach to women in labor unions, is co-sponsoring with the Federation of Cuban Women an International Solidarity Conference in Savannah, Georgia. US member, Felicity Hill, is traveling across the United States, meeting with students on 65 campuses to inform and challenge them to get involved. WILPFers Robin Lloyd of Connecticut and Barbara Anderson of Canada have created films, including *Beyond Beijing*, that capture the excitement of the Peace Train. Robin edits a magazine, *Toward Freedom*, dedicated to human justice and liberty. And I know that these are only a few of the thousands and thousands of women who are making a difference on the homefronts of the world.

I remember with warmth the Chinese farm woman of Ningxia who gave me a smile and a bag of "Fructus Lycii," pointing to my white hair, saying, "Long life, stay well, good liver, no cancer, strong blood, live long." Women helping women in millions of different ways to confront the great wall of injustice and violence against women.

All over the world, albeit too slowly and with innumerable setbacks, The Platform for Action is being addressed by individuals, NGOs and governments in countless ways. In July of 1996, the Economic and Social Council of the United Nations identified four critical areas of concern among the 12 set out in the Platform: education and training of women, women and the economy, women in power and decision making, and women and the environment.

In the area of education alone, there are multiple issues. There are crucial links between population, environment, sustainable development and the education of women. More women are needed in top management positions and in political decision making, and education is essential to achieve that goal. Women's education yields numerous benefits: higher economic productivity, decreased maternal and infant mortality, improved family health and nutrition, delayed marriages and lower birth rates. When women are poorly prepared to enter the job market, they remain in unfavorable positions, at the edge of exploitation. In 1995, 63.8 percent of the world's adult illiterates were women. In sub-Saharan Africa and Central Asia, more than two-thirds of the children who never go to school, or who drop out, are girls. Even where there is access to education for girls, the quality of their education is influenced by stereotyping; biases persist in teaching materials and teachers' attitudes. This kind of discrimination reduces girls' options for future choices by underestimating or downplaying their talents and capabilities.[6]

To deal with this issue, the UN Division for the Advancement of Women sponsored the World Conference on Vocational Training and Lifelong Learning of Women, held at the International Training Centre of the International Labour Organization in Turin, Italy, in December, 1996. There is urgent need for remedial education for adult women who are illiterate. Elderly women need special attention. They are a resource of accumulated knowledge, skills and experiences; they need opportunities for self-expression and continuous training to increase their participation in public life, prevent disease, maintain a healthy lifestyle, and stay active.

It is the responsibility of governments to provide the required funding for such education and to have as public policy the reduction of gender inequalities and the promotion of equality between men and women through incentives, legislation and advocacy. Two immediate goals are targets for action: the eradication of illiteracy and universal primary education.

Dolores Wozniak is Dean of the Department of Human Resources at San Diego State University. In March 1997, I asked her what difference going to Beijing has made to her personally and in her work. She voiced a concern about the attitudes of young women toward higher education in the United States.

"I've been in this business a long time," she said. "I think back to how difficult it was for a woman moving into higher education when few women had degrees, few women had management or leadership positions, and fewer still were in the political arena. The young women today are reaping the benefits of those more difficult times, and they're not even willing to hang on to it because they don't know what it's like if they lose it. They're willing to negotiate it away for this idea that women belong in the home. That's frightening to me."

"I wonder if that's because they seem to have no sense of history," I asked. "They have nothing with which to compare the present, so it's not so urgent to hold on to those hard-won rights. How does this connect with what you experienced in Beijing?"

"I was on both sides, in the Forum and the Governmental Conference. Being at the Forum reminded me of being on the east coast as a young person breaking into the business world, so to speak. I spent many a time standing and fighting issues, and finding that it's pretty hard to be a risk taker, because you are out there alone. Many times you think you're with a group, and all of a sudden you turn around, and you find out that every one of your colleagues, the women, have disappeared into the woodwork, and you are out there by yourself."

"I know that from firsthand experience," I said. "It's a painful place to be."

"When I went to interact with the women at Huairou," Dolores went on, "there was this depth of feeling that they have for women's rights and human rights, and their need to share that, their beliefs and why they continue to fight. It was that rush of feeling of why I did what I did over the years. It was a really good feeling for me, because it brought me back to my very active days, you know, 20 or 30 years ago, when I was engaged in those activities and saying it was all worthwhile. I'm more of a mentor to people now, getting them involved."

"Were there other things that made the Forum worthwhile for you?"

"It was a connection with the women, the passion that they spoke with, you just had to be affected by it. If I was old enough, I could say it felt like I was a suffragette. Those women were risk takers. They did things that people today would not even consider doing; they gave up their lives; they placed their families in jeopardy. They went to jail. They stood for something. And they worked night and day to help the people on the street, and to get women to be heard. In Huairou, it was the camaraderie, that the fight is not finished. I mean we are still in it knee deep. So we have to re-educate women to know what they have, and should not lose. I'm trying to work with younger women, to get them involved.

"In the governmental conference, it was the traditional presentations, the majority of them by men because they sit in those positions in the countries. They gave platitudes, talked about programs, made political statements. You could see the difference; I left there saying, 'This is the political arena. This is what we still have to change'."

"Was there one issue that particularly touched you?"

"It was in Huairou, where women were saying that they had experienced torture, and they sold their rings so they could bring their daughters to this event so they could understand the significance of it. Then, at the government conference, the debate over the Platform for Action, trying to get the language acceptable to all countries, watering down its effectiveness because of religions and cultures. That is just another cloak for maintaining women in the status that they've been in in the past. I just felt like standing up and saying, 'Get with it, folks. This is the 21st century upon us. When are you going to recognize that we exist?'"

"Talk a little bit about what's happened for you since you came back from the conferences. What other impact have they had on your life and work?"

"When I came back, I felt a responsibility to present the Platform for Action to as wide an audience as I could find, especially what the issues are that we are confronted with in this country. I did a number of presentations on campus, some off campus. Some of the male students came, and that gave a chance to talk about the traditional, inbred, negative questions that came up. I'm participating locally in several groups that are working on issues. I select the audiences that I feel I can impact the most. I work with the women students to make them aware. I establish a mentor role with them and guide them in their career decisions.

"Lily, my assistant dean, is of Chinese descent, and she's so glad I made her go to Beijing. It broadened her horizons, and she realizes that she has to do something. She's a lot more political now, and sometimes when she does something, I'll have a chat with her and say, 'Why did you take this position? Where are you on your women's rights on this issue?'"

"How would you describe whatever it is about Lily that's Chinese?"

"Well, she takes a second position to the male. She'll step back and allow the man to take charge when she is indeed capable. Women have done that over the years, so it's not just Chinese.

"I'm always looking for how we can effect the long term change. If you pay attention to women's conversations, they're usually that of a subservient individual. With women, it's 'May I do this?' or 'Can I do that?' Men don't talk that way. We also have to support women in these conversations, so that they have the courage to speak for themselves. I do that best on a one-to-one basis. Sometimes in a general meeting, you make a suggestion which is a substantive one, and it goes around and around and the men don't place any credibility on it. Then after they've digested it, another man suggests exactly the same thing and it becomes a reality. What we need to do, as women in the room, is to say, 'Well, that's what so and so suggested. Why is it now so credible and it wasn't when she suggested it?'"

"I'm excited about what you're saying, Dolores. Millions of these one-to-ones around the world are bound to make a difference. The changes are subtle, but they are happening. I think China got radicalized in ways it doesn't even know yet, especially those 5,000 Chinese women who were allowed to come. And those who weren't allowed to come were radicalized even more. They knew what was happening, and they knew why they weren't allowed to come. And they will go on working behind the scenes to put teeth into what they want to see happen."

In the area of armed conflict, women and children are always the losers. But the rape and torture that come with war are not the only modern horrors for women and girls. When I asked Martha Fort how the conferences had influenced her, she spoke intensely about the use of land mines and their impact on women and children, another hideous aspect of armed conflict.

"I've been so concerned about the land mines in Africa because my family lived in Africa for quite some years, and I know how those people suffer, especially in Angola, where my family lived. The land mines are just blowing people to bits, blowing part of the body away. People can't locomote without feet. It's horrible, just horrible. There was a land mine conference recently in Maputo, Mozambique, for the southern part of Africa, where land mines are most in use. I proposed to my Quaker Meeting that we send money over to that conference and ask for reports back to give us direct information about how we can work to get our government to stop shipping land mines around the world.

"Clinton has come out against [shipping land mines], fortunately, and we have a good chance to get some action on that. But it's one of the world's awful problems. Refugees try to flee someplace, go through a mine field, and are badly damaged, if not destroyed. I know from working in Vietnam how awful it is in a Third World country for a child to miss a piece of the body. Third World countries can't take good care of the disabled. A child has to have a prosthesis re-fitted every six months because the body is growing. In Vietnam, when we'd get children ready to go home from our rehabilitation center, they didn't come back. The family disposed of them or they just died. Who can serve somebody in a wheelchair when you live in a rice paddy? In Third World countries, they don't survive, except maybe in the cities as beggars."

"Martha, what difference did Beijing make in your own life?"

"I feel such an attachment to those women whom I don't even know. There's a sense of the oneness of the human race, and the need for us to learn how to get along together. Cooperation is the only way we're going to survive. This armed conflict is destroying people. Right now two million refugees are sloshing around in the middle of Africa. And children are dying off."

""What about in San Diego?"

"I would guess that San Diego as a whole is not particularly aware that the conferences on women happened. There were some newspaper articles, and some of us have put on conferences on the anniversary date, and have brought up again the 12 critical areas. I worked hard on this last one in Tijuana, Mexico. I serve on the Border Environment Committee of the United Nations Association, and they're concerned about waste water, the sewage system, the lack of drinking water, and the maquillidor workers whose children are neglected. So here are the same issues that we worked on at the Forum."

"What is our government doing about all this, Martha?"

"President Clinton appointed a Women's Interagency Council. So he's trying to get people to communicate with each other on women's issues within the government structure."

"Yes, I know about that council. It was chaired by Donna Shalala, with Hillary Rodham Clinton as honorary chair. It consisted of high-level representatives from a variety of federal agencies such as the Departments of Education, Justice and Commerce. Each agency was to demonstrate its effort to implement agreements made in Beijing. Unfortunately, the Council was funded for only one year with an extension to December 31, 1996.[7] Now it's defunct.

"Also, it's not government action, but Bella Abzug has organized the Women's Environment and Development Organization (WeDo) to keep a finger on the pulse of the international women's movement. There are thousands of members all over the world. They have just put out a video and handbook called *Beyond Beijing*. In the handbook, the UN Department of Public Information Report gives an impressive list of governmental actions by numerous countries around the world. One thing I learned is that there is now what is called 'Global Faxnet' which gives all sorts of information on follow-up to the Beijing conferences. So, lots of good things are happening.

"Is there anything else you want to add, Martha?"

"Yes, millions of women are in poverty and in ignorance. It's right here in San Diego, too. This is what people don't realize. Some are so poor, so malnourished, so mistreated that they can't even think. It's shocking. When you think of it, some women are caught at the very bottom of humanity. Those of us who have had a chance have an obligation to do what we can where we are, to aid them to stand up and speak for themselves. I think these two are the most horrible factors, the poverty and the ignorance."

"You work in all sorts of issues, don't you, Martha? Population growth, environment, poverty, affordable housing, peace. You are a very busy woman."

"Yes, I stay busy. I work on the Peace and Social Action Committee of my Quaker Meeting, too, and with the pastor of Spring Valley's Quaker group on these land mines. He was reared in Burundi, so he knows about that. I believe we've got to all work together on these things."

Martha takes the Forum motto seriously. She thinks globally, acts locally. We're all called to do that, even when we know there's a price to pay – in criticism, loss of jobs, friends, and credibility; but that price is miniscule compared to what women and girls are enduring every day. One of the hardest things for me to deal with is that the religions of the world *contribute* to the abuse and mistreatment of women.

In May, 1997, I preached the baccalaureate sermon for the University of LaVerne in California. I spoke of the ancient queen Vashti, who was demoted when she refused to be "shown off" as the property of King Ahasuerus. I likened her time to ours – filled with racial hatred, women being sold and tortured, girls denied education and forced into marriage too early, millions of refugees roaming the earth, environmental devastation as a result of wars and abuse of the land, widening gaps between rich and poor, starvation, disease and poverty everywhere we look. I said that women who stand up for what they believe, who speak their own truth, are ostracized or punished, even here in our own "enlightened" country.

As if to prove my point, at the end of the service, a man with graying hair came to me, shook his fist in my face, and accused me of "bashing men," and not believing in the Bible. "God's truth is clear to believers," he shouted, his eyes burning with near hate. "A man should be the head of his household! The Bible says so. You are not fit to be standing in a pulpit. Whoever asked you to preach should be fired."

I thought of those millions of women and girls around the world who are caught in the terror of abuse and control by men like this, who claim their "truth" as having *divine* sanction, who rule women by force and threat of disenfranchisement or even death, whose male self-worth depends upon absolute obedience on the part of "their women." It reminded me of Lord Byron's comment about the guerrilla fighters of western Greece in the 1820s: "Their life is a struggle against truth; they are vicious in their defense."[8] I was one of the lucky ones; I was not in bodily danger. Nor was I alone in the weary darkness of the struggle for women's liberation. Standing beside me was Dr. Stephen Morgan, president of the university. What an "amazing grace" it was when he spoke up, disagreeing with the man's accusation of "male bashing," affirming the importance of having people hear what I had said. Candles lit by informed and caring men burn with a unique brilliance of their own. His warmed my heart.

In the United States, the network of organizations and individuals working to implement The Platform for Action is growing in numbers and influence. WILPF peace trains roll. An advisory panel appointed by President Clinton has warned that "the $22 billion global trade in conventional arms threatens to undermine the security of the US and its friends." I'm glad for his action and there it is again – enemies-friends, that damning dualistic thinking that is basic to all forms of social domination in Western society. As feminist analyst Bell Hooks says, "Our emphasis must be on cultural transformation: destroying dualism, eradicating systems of domination."[9] Clinton called on Washington *and its allies* to exercise more restraint in selling such weaponry to other countries, to slow the proliferation of advanced weaponry, and ensure that civilian technologies are not being diverted to military use overseas. In 1996, he signed the nuclear test ban treaty.

That same year in June, 400 women of California met to create CAWA, California Women's Agenda, aimed at implementing The Platform for Action. CAWA is now the working document for 200 organizations with "at least a half million members."[10] Marilyn Fowler, coordinator, asserts: "This CAWA Agenda is a dynamic document, a collection of needs, frustrations, actions, successes and challenges. Use it as a guide to *action*! Create new coalitions in your community! Network with other groups! Share resources! Document your successes! Recruit others! Get on-line and let CAWA know what you are doing! Let's turn California into the *Opportunity State* for girls and women!"[11] Each of 12 task forces identified strategic objectives and specific actions that need to be taken, and are now working actively to implement these. California is not alone in this effort. All 50 states and many cities in the US now have an active "Women's Agenda."

Hundreds of colleges and universities across the nation are providing educational seminars on arms control and disarmament. The International Conference on Peace and Conflict Resolution was held at Juniata College in Pennsylvania, in 1996. Peace Studies Programs focus on alternatives to war and mediation for people and situations in conflict. The University of Missouri sponsors a journal, *Peace Talk*, which recently devoted one whole issue to "Women as Peacemakers."[12] In 1995, UNICEF proposed an Antiwar Agenda urging nations to fight poverty and other underlying causes of violence, and to teach young people to resolve conflicts peacefully, promoting the idea of children as zones of peace. And 187 countries have pledged to protect the human rights of their youngest citizens by ratifying the Convention on the Rights of the Child.[13]

High on the list of issues in the Platform for Action is poverty. More than a billion people today live in extreme poverty, and the overwhelming majority are women. Women are poorer because they have fewer economic opportunities, less autonomy, and limited access to economic resources. Marcia Boruta was particularly interested in these issues. In April, 1997, we talked about her experiences.

"Marcia, are you different because of Beijing? Has it made a difference in your life since you've come back?

"It was an incredible learning experience. I've learned one more way to participate as a citizen of the world. In terms of networking locally, the 16 women who formed a San Diego UN delegation to Beijing now have a continuing relationship which is really good. We had meetings leading up to International Women's Day and a lot of meetings before the two follow-up conferences to report on The Fourth World Conference. Women 2000, a computer network, wants to have a global women's conference on-line in the year 2000 to review the implementation of the Platform for Action.

"Beijing for me was a culmination of following the UN Women's Conferences for 15 years. In 1980, I started tracking the news coverage in our local papers. I was part of a thing called the 'Women's International News Service' which tried to expand the coverage of the 1985 Women's Conference. We did a whole news monitoring activity locally here in San Diego. The idea was that women in Nairobi would write their stories and feed them to us, and we'd get them into our local papers. I was also involved in a project at University of California at San Diego that linked up kids on computer networks in countries all over the world. In 1995, something was in the paper every day of the conferences. It was like a big culmination of a 15-year interest. Also, I learned some skills on how to work a world conference.

"Since then, though, my financial situation has been so tight that I haven't had the luxury to follow up on it in the way I thought I would, other than the work with the local network."

"Lack of money again. Now we're back to talking economics," I said. "It's an analogy of what happens at the world level. When you think about the sheer poverty of women and how much energy it takes just to survive, to feed their children, there's no room for these other issues that we want to be working on."

"Like sustainable development of people, living in peace, having respect and human development. People all around the world recognize these issues are right and are putting their energy into them. Somehow it gives you hope that you'll succeed in your own little corner. I work at redirecting financial resources from the military to development. On one of those bus rides, I told a woman from Lebanon about the work I do. She said, 'Oh, your work is so important. If we can point to the US and say, see they're converting, then we can get our governments to do the same.'

"The US has an incredible global leadership role that it could play, but it's not. I was really disappointed that the US was actually blocking efforts to strengthen the idea in the Platform for Action that we should reduce military spending and redirect resources. Instead of saying that more money should be made available for this, they talked about reprioritizing government spending. The women of Uganda have put through a new constitution that is completely, fully, addressed to affirmative action, and we in the US do not even have an ERA. It's an incredible disparity between what we *think* we are and what we *are*, as other people in the world hear us."

"It certainly is. I was ashamed at the Forum when a lot of different countries actually joined together in a protest march against US imperialism. You'd think we would soon catch on to how we're seen."

"I think that San Diego has an important role to play in keeping things the way they are or in changing them. It's our elected officials who lobbied for more military spending here. That's discouraging."

One of the 12 areas of concern in the Platform is decision making and access to full participation in power structures, governmental bodies and public administration entities – including the judiciary, international and nongovernmental organizations, political parties and trade unions.

Anne Hoiberg, Director of United Nations Association in San Diego, is working actively in the political arena. I asked her for her impressions of the conferences.

"I was quite upset that we were shifted to Huairou," she said. "I thought that was totally unacceptable, and I can't believe we accepted that shift. To me there was no reason for the NGOs to be located away from the governmental conference. That was a strong disappointment to me. We had spent a full year getting our delegation geared up for this trip.

"We put on five workshops at the Forum. Dee Aker and I put on one on political participation, one of the 12 critical areas of concern. We had two women from Uganda on our panel, so we had a developed country's standpoint and a developing country's standpoint on how to get women involved in the political arena. Of course, it's identical. We're all grassroots type people getting into politics and becoming involved.

"It was fun being with our delegation of 16 people. I think we formed some very strong friendships. I for one felt that I was blessed in getting to know Dee and to become a good friend of hers. When it comes to me personally, the experience was rich as far as friendships go.

"I very much enjoyed the sense of sisterhood I felt throughout that whole time in Beijing. Even though all of us thought it was an inconvenience having to go to Huairou, somehow it didn't matter. We formed good relationships on the bus. We tried to sit with different people every day so that we would get to know people. I got to know some fantastic women, parliamentarians from Namibia, college professors from Australia. It was exciting to have that opportunity.

"When the governmental conference started, we shifted gears and spent a lot of time observing parts of it. Both Dee and I had press passes, so we went to press conferences. We also had observer status, so we were able to observe activities in that area too. It was a tremendous learning experience, seeing how delegates operated; how they did their lobbying and working to achieve the goals that delegates had set up. I attended many workshops, both out at Huairou and the governmental side of it. There were some tremendous experts putting on workshops for the governmental delegates. It was wonderful having that opportunity at both ends. I was disappointed that we didn't stay until the end of the conference. We had decided that because part of my delegation did not have access to the governmental part, it wouldn't have been fair to them to stay much beyond the NGO forum."

"What has happened since you got back?"

"I am very much motivated to implement The Platform for Action; it's my all-consuming mission. My goal was to create from the Platform for Action, a San Diego Women's Agenda. We started putting on a series of conferences and presentations throughout San Diego County. Sometimes we had two or three speaking, sometimes just one. At our conferences, we tried to include as many who were part of our little UNA delegation as we could. By the end of 1995, we probably had put on a hundred presentations and two major conferences. We participated in the Bella Abzug Forum at the Hilton Hotel."

"That forum had lots of fire. Bella's experience as an astute congresswoman always shows through in the way she gets at the real issues."

"You're right, Beth. She is totally dedicated to justice for women.

"In March, on International Women's Day," Anne continued, "we did a six month follow-up. At that point, we stopped just speaking out on what the issues are and started to talk about what we were going to do to have an impact. We collected data on what the organizations are doing in these 12 critical areas of concern and when and where. On the basis of that, I started pulling everything together so we could create this San Diego Women's Agenda. At the same time, Marilyn Fowler was working on the California Women's Agenda. She wanted to have those of us from San Diego who were involved in the San Diego Women's Agenda to be a part of that. There is a wealth of activity going on to deal with the problem of violence against women in San Diego County. But you know, what are we doing for poverty, for peace? Do we need all these organizations? What can we do to be more efficient, more united? Where could we be combining forces? That's one of my concerns."

"What is happening here in San Diego about peace, Anne? I know Peace Resource Center is very active. Are there others?"

"San Mateo Economic Conversion. The World Federalists. Of course the United Nations Association, The Buddhist Group, SGI, The Quakers,

Friends. This is so important to women and children. We are the victims in wars. And what irritates me so much is that Bob Dole is creating another monument to soldiers killed during World War II. That's fine, but what about the children who have died since 1986 in wars – 2 million?

"Anyway, there is now a document, The California Women's Agenda. We're beyond the point where we identify what we need to do. Now we absolutely have to start implementing. Several of us sat down and talked about what kind of goals we want to achieve in 1997 and what's the time frame. That's where we're working now.

"We've identified seven different committees that would be oversight committees to ensure that each of these goals is being addressed. Education and Training is one of those. If we want to create peace, we need to get into the schools and help create curriculum that will work on conflict resolution, peace pledges, or what have you. That would be part of Education and Training. We also have a Media Watch."

"Where did you get the women to do this?"

"We have this nucleus that came from the delegation that went to Beijing. Then we picked up more women who were interested. We asked people to sign up. We have people interested in participating in each area. The weakest one is resource development. No one wants to be in fund raising. We're okay for now. Once we take off with these committees, we might need an executive director or more paid people to take on the mission of the Agenda."

"How will you know if you reach the goals?"

"We have a research committee actively collecting data. They have been providing us with a lot of information. We've identified how many teenage pregnancies there are as we go into this year. We can establish from our starting point to the end of this year if we've achieved anything. We know that California has come out with a very strong prevention program. Governor Wilson pumped $52 million into this teenage pregnancy prevention program. I couldn't believe it!

"What's interesting, I have all this information on the number of pregnancies and live births among teenagers throughout San Diego. The downtown area has the highest rate, then spilling over into National City and somewhat in the south of San Diego, so that's the target area. In San Diego county alone, there are 14 births per day, and we're not even the highest county; we're in the middle. It's high among Latinas, high among African Americans. We know what those numbers are. Our goal is to cut teen pregnancies by 50 percent."

"Ambitious."

"Of course. If you don't have an ambitious goal, you don't do anything. This is all-consuming for me. Everything I do is trying to figure out how to implement the actions in Beijing.

"I just came back from the United Nations in New York, where we worked on four critical areas of concern. I was particularly interested in political participation and decision making. Our goal for San Diego County is to get more women to run for political office and elect them. My questions to our US delegation and the ambassador were, 'How are we going to do this? Is there funding available to train women and girls to become leaders?'

"She said, 'Well, the US government isn't going to add new funds for this, but we're certainly going to push to reallocate educational funds, so we can get into our curricula work on self-esteem, so that girls will be able to be leaders.' She also mentioned that the government will be very supportive of organizations like the National Political Women's Caucus in training women. Being a past president of that Caucus, I'll be working very hard recruiting women to run in our next election cycle.

"Political participation is such a strong issue for me. I was interested in hearing how the Nordic countries were able to get quotas and affirmative action enacted into their legislation. They now are at 40 percent women in Sweden and Norway. It was great to hear that. I enjoyed the panels on peace and how we have to get away from militarism because of its impact not only on people, but also on the environment. I hadn't realized how devastating wars are to the ozone layer. They have tremendous impact. Another issue is the 110 million land mines that are waiting out there to kill and maim people – 26,000 civilians every year. We really have to do something about that. The United Nations Association here in San Diego will be adopting a particular land mine in Cambodia or Bosnia to let the government know of the urgent need for action. We're working on that right now.

I met a man in New York who is with a Norwegian organization that goes into mine fields and destroys these mines. We're going to find out how we can help that effort, or if there is a like organization in the US. We did establish a policy last year that we were no longer going to use land mines. We were still manufacturing and stockpiling them, but we weren't going to use them. Then, the Department of Defense said, 'Wait a minute. We have this problem in Korea.' So the policy was rescinded and now we will use land mines 'for humanitarian reasons.' Now is this an oxymoron!? How do you justify saying that you will only use land mines for humanitarian reasons? We're going to be actively working on this. We, China, and Russia are the top producers of land mines."

"You said you learned a lot about how the delegates work and how lobbying gets done."

"There was so much work going on behind the scenes in working committees. Each one was designated to work on a certain area in The Platform for Action, so that brackets could be deleted and agreement reached. To me, the most amazing outcome of the Beijing conference was the fact that to begin with, there were 411 areas on the document where there was not agreement, and by 4:45 the morning of September 15th, all of those brackets were removed and delegates from 189 different countries reached agreement. That's amazing."

"It's an incredible feeling of world solidarity."

"It is. To me a true reflection of women working together for a common goal."

"Anne, for you personally, is there any one influence that this trip has had?"

"Oh, I feel like I'm totally empowered. If something annoys me, like the *Union Tribune*, very often I write a letter. I'm not going to take any more anti-women articles. People are going to know about it. I'm just not going to sit still and accept it. Nobody who knows me makes sexist comments anymore, because I won't stand for it. I just say, 'I'm sorry, but you're way out of line.' I think that's what we have to do. We can no longer be gracious and accepting.

"I really work on encouraging women in whatever they're doing. I've been trying to help different women get jobs. I write letters of reference for jobs that I think are good career moves for them. I think I've become a mentor at the same time, of women in general. It's had a tremendous impact on me. I really feel empowered. We've lost a lot of women prime ministers this last year. At one time we had ten; it's down to four or five now. Having the opportunity to meet these women was incredible. They're role models for me. Like Geraldine Ferraro, hearing her sit with some man from Sudan talking about female genital mutilation and how wrong it is. She turned to this man and put her hand on his hand and said, 'You and I are going to have to sit down and have a conversation about this over coffee.' That's what women can do. It thrills me. That's what Madeleine Albright is doing with Jesse Helms; she's sweet-talking him. Every once in a while I just get so excited about that woman. She sweet-talked the Chinese people, and has a certain dignity about it. It's a woman's approach, not a man's."

"I think women are more personal in their approaches to opponents," I said. "I feel empowered when I am with empowered women. I even got a kick out of walking from one part of the plaza to another with Winnie Mandela."

"Really?"

"Really, just being in her presence was, as you say, an incredible feeling. I was close to Hillary, too."

"So were Dee and I. That was really funny. We had managed to get into the conference site. We're standing there, and the doors open and in walk two or three Secret Service men and then Hillary, and there were a couple behind them, so Dee and I just joined this little group and walked all the way through the conference site."

"That's how I got into the governmental conference," I said. "My roommate, May, was a journalist for the United Nations in Geneva. We had gotten to know each other really well, and I said, 'You know, it breaks my heart not to be able to get into this Conference at all.' And she said, 'I have my pass. Why don't you just walk in with me and see if we can get away with it?' So I walked right through the security guards as though I belonged there. I had to chuckle about outdoing them for a change. Seeing the frenzied activity in the newsroom was an eye-opener! The efforts to get these conferences onto the world newspapers were just amazing!"

Dee Aker is Director of the World Youth Education Program for the World Affairs Council of San Diego. We spoke about a remarkable experience she had with the women of Dalian, China, who "didn't have the right connections to be allowed to come to the Forum."

"Dalian is a very progressive city. The Women's Federation there has put together a $7 million enterprise which includes 700 different little enterprises. They bought land for their own building, built it, and are working with everything from the first legal-aid society for women in that region to production of arts and crafts and day schools. What they are doing is impressive. They have a school in music and dance for children. There was a whole community of women, 3,000 in one town. From what they said, the people who were allowed to come to the Forum were well connected in universities or groups, very much 'approved' people. I visited university women in their homes. They were very astute in terms of their economic enterprising abilities and their commitment to other women. They weren't allowed to come to Beijing because they are way advanced.

"I had a credential to the NGO Forum; I was an observer delegate for the UN conference, and I also had press credentials. You weren't supposed to have all three. Finally one day they took away my press credentials. I was frustrated that we didn't have access to tell the story. The editors back in the States cut off the real information and distorted the picture. But I thought the experience was very positive. When you get that many people together, there's something started that you can't undo – you can't put the genie back in the bottle. Those women in Dalian felt connected even though they weren't allowed to come, and it just added to their sense of purpose, and you can't undo that.

"A year after the Conference, I went to Washington, D.C. for the Association for Women and Development meeting. James D. Wolfensohn, President of the World Bank, has set up this gender group. He said, 'I made commitments in Beijing just like governments and now I can go and say, "You signed this document, and we agreed in principle, so this is the way we have to do it."' It will take a long time for a big organization like that to transform, but it was impressive what they have done to follow up.

"Since Nairobi in '85, African women have emerged as a major force. Three countries have constitutions that have affirmative action written in. I know one of the women who helped write that constitution out of her experience in Nairobi in '85. She said everything in her life changed when she realized that women worldwide have this same struggle to face.

"Women from 24 developing countries came to Washington last September to study US women in politics. I had to laugh, because we have a lot to learn from them. In Uganda, besides their new constitution, they've put together something called the Forum for Women in Democracy. They do research and give women support in writing laws. One of the women said, 'You know what else we do? We play wife to these women. We give them a shoulder to cry on. We go get their kids if that needs to be done. We help them write legislation and understand the ramifications of what they do. It doesn't make any difference what tribe they're from, what party they're from, you know, it's women helping women in the way that women do.'

"They have also established a Ministry of Women in Development. Winnie Byanyima, a member of Parliament said, 'We are children of many cultures who do not accept the divisions of religion and tribe. We don't know ourselves until we are intimate with the whole world around us.'"[14]

I attended a workshop at the Forum on the situation of rural women in China. It was led by Meng Xianfan of the Chinese Academy of Social Sciences. At the close, I gave Meng packets of flower and vegetable seeds I had brought from home. I've wondered since if they're growing somewhere in China. Six months later, I wrote to her, asking for her view of China's participation in the Forum, and what effect it has had there. She answered.

"I have wonderful impressions about the Forum and women attending. They really care about the women's world; they are so enthusiastic, so caring. I still remember an Australian lady who showed us how to deal with sex harassment. I was deeply touched by the effect it had. All these are very different from the negative reports a lot of US media made.

"After the Forum, when I talk to friends about it, they show lots of interest. From this meeting, our country will pay more attention to the status of women. For instance, the government built a beautiful building for the All-China Women's Federation in the best site of Beijing. In 1995, publishers accepted many books about women's study. Each women's organization began to realize how important it is to communicate with the outside world, which makes it possible to know what people think out of China, which is very useful.

"The market economy brings women unemployment, and there are a lot of free training programs for unemployed women, a lot of services available. The government is paying more attention to education of female children in the countryside, also women's health care.

"I'm an editor. I've edited papers about female population from the countryside working in the city. Also, I spent some time in Tibetan nationality living area to study female children's education problems there.

"China is developing very fast. China women have more opportunity than ever, but there are many problems, too. Anyway, I'm positive about the future. The biggest improvement Chinese women have is most of them realize they have to be independent rather than depending on males, fight for their right. From my point of view, it's important for all of us."[15]

Good things are happening for women and girls all over the world, important things. In Santo Domingo, Krishna Ahooja-Patel, originally of India, now president of Women's World Summit Foundation in Geneva, Switzerland, guest-edited the Newsletter for UN/INSTRAW which focused attention on The Platform for Action and strategies to implement it.

In Sweden, the Women's Budget recommends a 10 percent cut in the defense budget this year with a 50 percent cut by the year 2005; a goal of converting military expenditure into programs for health, social security, and environmental concerns.

At the grassroots level, women are creating all sorts of projects to keep the issues alive. Genevieve Vaughan, who funded the Peace Tent in the forum in Nairobi, and called it "the highpoint of my life," founded and directs the activities of Foundation for a Compassionate Society. She told me "Beijing was another big shot in the arm, a deep breath of hope." The foundation put on two major conferences. The theme of the first was "Feminism and Family Values" led by intercultural leaders, Gloria Steinem, Angela Davis, Mililani Trask and Maria Jimenez; 2000 women attended. In 1996 the focus was "Feminism and Fundamentalism" led by Robin Morgan, Mahnaz Afkami of Iran, Yvonne Deutch of Israel, and Marta Benevides of El Salvador. Three significant projects – Sierra Blanca, Philippines, and "Stonehaven Goddess" – are focusing on theology and religion. A fourth is an effort in peacemaking called "The Earth and Sky Women's Peace Caravan to End the Nuclear Age."[16]

In the shadow of each woman and organization mentioned here are thousands of others working to implement The Platform for Action, a worldwide network of *women helping women,* a living source of encouragement and challenge as each one of us "in our little corner" find the niche that is ours and the cause that calls us to become involved. Getting involved may be the only way to resist the temptation to powerlessness and despair in the face of the immensity of the task. Margaret Mead's words of 30 years ago ring like a bell: "Never doubt that a small group of thoughtful, committed citizens can change the world. Indeed, it's the only thing that ever has."[17]

History is in the process of transformation. You and I will never see the "Promised Land" of equality, justice and freedom, but the journey toward it makes every effort worthwhile. As Susan B. Anthony said almost a century ago: *Failure is impossible!* [18]

Remember, no one but you can do what is yours to do in answer to "The Call."

> *Women in black picked up their violins*
> *To play, backs turned to the mirror.*
>
> *The wind died as it does on the best of days*
> *To hear better their dark music.*
>
> *But almost at once, seized by a vast amnesia,*
> *The violins slumped in the women's arms*
>
> *Like naked children fallen asleep*
> *Among the trees.*
>
> *Nothing, it seemed, could ever again stir*
> *The motionless bows, the violins of marble,*
>
> *And it was then that in the depths of sleep*
> *Someone breathed to me:*
> *You alone can do it. Come immediately.'"*[19]

Come, join the throng that is singing the song,

> *We're gonna keep on moving forward,*
> *Keep on moving forward,*
> *Keep on moving forward,*
> *Never turning back,*
> *Never turning back.*[20]

Permissions

Endnotes

Chapter 1: The Trip before the Train

1 Rubem Alves, *The Poet, The Warrior, The Prophet*, quoting Basho (Philadelphia: Trinity Press, 1933), p. 37.
2 Audrey Lorde, *Sister Outsider* (Freedom, CA: The Crossing Press, 1984), p. 170.

Chapter 2: Five Days in Finland

1 First two verses from *This Is My Song*, by G. Harkness and Lloyd Stone, copyright the Lorenz Corporation, used by permission. Sung to the tune of *Finlandia*, by Jean Sibelius.
2 Purd E. Deitz, in *Masterpieces of Religious Verse*, ed. James Dalton Morrison (New York: Harper & Row, 1948), p. 1. Sung to the tune of *Finlandia*, by Jean Sibelius.
3 Traudel Haury and Elke Chakraborty, *Peace Train Song*, Melody of Italian song, *Bella Ciao*, 1955.
4 Marie Cowan and A. B. Paterson, *Waltzing Matilda* (New York: Carl Fischer Music, 1941).

Chapter 3: The Train on the Tracks

1 Watty Piper, *The Little Engine That Could* (New York: Platt & Munk, 1930, 1976).
2 Niccolo Machiavelli, *The Prince*, completed in 1517, dedicated to The Medici, trans. by W. K. Mariott, quoted in *Bartlett's Quotations*, 16th ed. (Boston: Little, Brown & Co., 1992), p. 136.
3 Based on the Holly Near song, *Singing For Our Lives*.
4 Robert D. Kaplan, *Balkan Ghosts* (New York: St. Martin's Press, 1993), p. 89.
5 American chant, Author unknown.

Chapter 4: Making Peace in a War-Weary World

1 Joel 3:9-10, RSV.
2 Isaiah 2:3-4, NRSV.
3 A newpaper, source unknown.
4 Matthew 10:36.
5 Kaplan, *Balkan Ghosts*, p. 33.
6 This little-known revolt was quickly stamped out by the US government's powerful military force.
7 Robert Frost, "Mending Wall," in *North of Boston* (New York: Holt, 1915), p. ll.
8 Joseph Heller, *Catch-22* (New York: Simon and Schuster, 1961), p. 67.
9 Matthew 23:23, KJV.
10 Edward Everett Hale, "Lend a Hand," in *Treasury of Religious Verse*, comp. by Donald T. Kauffman (New Jersey: Fleming H. Revell Co., 1962), p. 236.

Chapter 5: Crossing Borders

1 Lao Tzu, *Tao Teh Ching*, trans. by John C. H. Wu, (Boston and London: Shambhala Publications, Inc., 1990), p. 39.
2 Kathleen Norris, *The Cloister Walk* (New York: Riverhead Books, 1996), p. 214.
3 Mims Butterworth, "Peace Train Nightmare," Richmond, Naima, and Marilyn M. Cuneo, eds., *Seeing the World through Women's Eyes,* Cushing-Malloy, Inc., Arts Committee, Minnesota Metro Branch, Women's International League for Peace and Freedom, 1996 p. 18. Note: Moldavia is also called "Moldova." When I first saw the poem, "Moldavia" was used.
4 Christopher Columbus, *The Log of Christopher Columbus*, trans. Robert Fuson (Camden, ME: International Marine Publishing Co., 1987), p. 149.
5 Note: Unfortunately, she was defeated in the election of 1996 and a man with fundamentalist leanings was elected.
6 "Turkey, Fall in Love With a Country," The Ministry of Tourism, Republic of Turkey, PROMAT Matbaacilik A.S. Istanbul, 1994, p. 1.

Chapter 6: Strange Welcome to China

1 Paul Theroux, *Riding the Iron Rooster through China* (New York: Penguin Books, 1988), p. 1.
2 Ibid., p. 1.
3 *World Book Encyclopedia* (Chicago: Field Enterprises Educational Corporation, 1958), p. 1395.
4 Ibid., p. 1406.
5 Harry Wu and Carolyn Wakeman, *Bitter Winds* (New York: John Wiley & Sons, 1994), cover page.
6 Quoted by Julie Brooke, who read early drafts of this manuscript.
7 Jung Chang, *Wild Swans, Three Daughters of China* (London: HarperCollins Publishers, 1993), p. 31. Subsequent page references are indicated in the text in parentheses.
8 Mark Salzman, *Iron and Silk* (New York: Random House, 1986), p. 76.
9 Ibid., p. 37.

10 Robert Bellah, Richard Madsen, William Sullivan, Ann Swidler and Steven Tipton, *Habits of the Heart* (Berkeley: University of California, 1985) p. 108.

Chapter 7: Governments and NGOs

1 "Declaration of Independence," quoted in *World Book Encyclopedia*, Vol. D (Chicago: Field Enterprises Educational Corporation, 1975), p. 1908.
2 Chuck Colgan, *Explorations*, Vol. 3, Number 4, Spring 1997, University of California, San Diego, p. 22.
3 "Schedule of Activities," NGO Forum on Women, Frontispiece.
4 CornelWest, *The Progressive*, January, 1997.
5 *The Washington Spectator*, Vol. 23, No. 8, April 15, 1997, The Public Concern Foundation, Inc., p. 1.
6 Ibid, p. 3.
7 Vivian Stromberg, Executive Director, MADRE, in newsletter, April 30, 1996, p. l.
8 *San Diego Union Tribune*, March, 1997, p. l.

Chapter 8: Listen to Women – for a Change

1 Morton, Nelle, *The Journey Is Home* (Boston: Beacon Press, 1985), p. 82.
2 Ibid., p. 68.

Chapter 9: The World's Women on the Move

1 Lao Tzu, T*oa Teh Ching*, p. 10.
2 A Chinese proverb.
3 Joan Chittester, *Beyond Beijing* (Kansas City, MO: Sheed and Ward, 1996), p. 166.
4 Helen Reddy and Ray Burton, *I Am Woman*, in *Great Songs of the '70s,* ed. Milton Okun (New York: Times Books, 1978).
5 Audre Lorde, *A Burst of Light* (Ithaca, NY: Firebrand Books, 1988), p. 38.
6 Theresa M. Klingenberg, "The Cultural Practice of Female Genital Mutilation," in *Social Work Perspectives* (San Francisco: San Francisco State University, 1997), p. 10.
7 Jan Goodwin, *Price of Honor, Muslim Women Lift the Veil of Silence on the Islamic World* (New York: The Penguin Group, 1995), pp. 53-54.
8 Anonymous.
9 Pat Humphries, *Never Turning Back*, copyright © 1984, Moving Forward Music. Used by permission.
10 Composer unknown. The publisher welcomes any information from readers leading to the idenfication of the composer and will happily acknowledge the composer in future editions of this work.
11 Anonymous.
12 *Universal Declaration of Human Rights,* United Nations Department of Public Information, 1995, p. 4.
13 Goodwin, *Price of Honor,* p. 29-30.
14 Ibid., p. 101.
15 Philippians 2:12.
16 Children's Defense Fund, 25 E Street, NW, Washington, DC, 1997.
17 Duncan Hunter, personal letter dated June 9, 1997.
18 Kenneth I. Morse, *Preaching in a Tavern* (Elgin, IL: Brethren Press, 1997), p. 36.

Chapter 10: Beyond Beijing

[1] Rubem Alves, *The Poet, The Warrior, The Prophet* (Philadelphia: Trinity Press, 1933), p. 105. (Quoting Karl Marx).

[2] Ibid., p. 123, (Quoting T. S. Eliot).

[3] Lisa Hofman, excerpt from a personal letter dated July 5, 1997.

[4] Sarah Grimké, *Letters on Equality of the Sexes* (Boston: Isaac Knapp, 1838). Reprinted by (New York: Source Book Press, 1970), p. 10.

[5] Note: The transfer of power has now happened. Ominously, two days before the "takeover," 4,000 Chinese troops entered the city. The Legislative Council was dismissed; China appointed a new governing body. Within hours, they passed a law making public protests illegal, the first step in restricting civil liberties.

[6] Unicef 1996 Review of the Year, United Nations, p. 11.

[7] "Toward Freedom," March-April, 1997, Toward Freedom, Inc., Burlington, VT p. 10

[8] Kaplan, *Balkan Ghosts*, p. 243. (Quoting Lord Byron).

[9] Bell Hooks, *Feminist Theory, From Margin to Center* (Boston: South End Press, 1984), p. 163.

[10] Hernandez, Aileen C., CAWA Chair, Women's Intercultural Network (WIN) San Francisco, CA, 1997, p. i.

[11] California Women's Agenda, (CAWA), p. l.

[12] *Peace Talk*, Friends of Peace Studies, University of Missouri-Columbia, Spring, 1996, Vol. 3, No. l.

[13] Unicef 1996 Review of the Year, United Nations, p. 14.

[14] Dee Aker, "Women's Times," June, 1994, p. 9.

[15] Meng Xianfan, personal letter to the author dated June 26, 1997.

[16] Foundation for a Compassionate Society, PO Box 18987, Austin, Texas 78760-8087 (512-447-6222).

[17] Margaret Mead, *American Wome: the Report of the President's Commission on the Status of Women* (New York: Scribner's, 1965).

[18] Susan B. Anthony, quoted in "CAWA, California Women's Agenda," 1997, p. i.

[19] Jules Supervielle, *The Call*, originally published by Editions Gallimard, trans. by Geoffrey Gardner. This translation first appeared in *American Poetry Review*, Vol. 5, No. 2.

[20] Humphries, *Never Turning Back*.